Shortlisted for the Lambda Literary Award in
Lesbian Memoir/Biography
A *New York Times* Editors' Choice
An NPR, *Literary Hub*, and *Texas Observer* Best Book of the Year

Praise for *To Name the Bigger Lie*

"Strange and wonderful . . . A book for our times, when singular truths seem less certain with each passing day."
—*The New York Times Book Review*

"Viren . . . has pulled off a magic trick of fantastic proportion. There are elements here of the classic thriller that function like a flock of seductive doves, released to distract the eye. All the while, her other hand is shuffling multiple shells that conceal a critical reading of Plato, an examination of the mechanics of memory, a study of the anatomy of a lie and an analysis of misinformation's insidious creep. . . . Ever since Dr. Whiles introduced her to Plato's allegory of the cave, the question 'What is the sunlight?' has bedeviled Sarah Viren. In writing *To Name the Bigger Lie*, she practices the answer. It is poetry, such as Yevtushenko's *Babi Yar*, which 'in sharing that suffering' fights 'to keep that truth from being erased or forgotten.' It is art. It is a book like this."
—*The Washington Post*

"The memoir has the page-turning quality of a thriller, but instead of tracking down culprits and solving mysteries, Viren methodically untangles knotty philosophical tensions in pursuit of what is real."
—NPR

"Chances are, a book based on a viral essay is not going to reproduce the same level of tension—more room to spread out isn't always a net good. But Sarah Viren's memoir, based on her 2020 essay for the *New York Times Magazine* about the false Title IX claims made against her wife, is an exception to the rule: I tore through this book greedily, as if I didn't already know how the story ended."

—*Literary Hub*

"An untangling of a web of lies and fake email accounts and false accusations that eventually leaves questions about the value of truth, the malleability of facts, and our responsibility to the truth. . . . Viren's gift [is] making the stakes of philosophical questions pressing, for turning Plato and Socrates and Schopenhauer and Hannah Arendt into characters in her story about how to make sense of this world."

—*Autostraddle*

"Viren takes the opportunity of these braided incidents to interrogate how our memories function, and show how memories that are technically accurate to us may not tell the whole truth."

—*Chicago Tribune*

"*To Name the Bigger Lie* at first reads like an incisive, if familiar, investigation into . . . conspiratorial thinking. . . . But the memoir quickly shifts from a sociological inquiry into something more subtle. Viren . . . uses a narrative collage to capture the emotional texture of a certain place and time. . . . The result is something rich and confounding: an investigation of uncertainty, that unsettling sensation we tend to shrink from before we can make sense of it."

—*The Nation*

"Past and present collide in this propulsive, one-of-a-kind meditation on truth and conspiracy from Viren. . . . Against the social and political instability of the last seven years, Viren seamlessly weaves her parallel narratives into a bigger picture take on the nature of truth. The result is a mesmerizing page-turner pulled tight with psychological tension. This is breathtaking stuff."

—*Publishers Weekly* (starred review)

"Both stories are gripping; they unfurl with a sense of suspenseful foreboding to show how lies can tear apart the fabric of everyday life and our most intimate relationships. But underlying them is a more groping, philosophical inquiry that chases the implications of Plato's Allegory of the Cave to probe our sense of what is real, how we know, and, most importantly, how we come to that knowledge together."

—*Booklist* (starred review)

"Immersive . . . A compelling and propulsive memoir that interrogates the nature of trust and truth."

—*Kirkus Reviews*

"A poignant musing on the changing nature of truth."

—*Library Journal*

"A thrilling, labyrinthine and ultimately illuminating reckoning with what it feels like to be caught up in a vortex of post-truth, conspiracy, and lies, Sarah Viren's *To Name the Bigger Lie* is a fascinating and deeply disturbing account of our contemporary age of weaponized falsehoods. That what most of us experience only through the news came for her life so personally makes for heart-in-throat reading. This is a memoir, yes, but it's also a view into a terrifying aspect of modernity, and Viren's ability to unspool complicated tangles for the reader is unparalleled."

—Alex Marzano-Lesnevich, author of *The Fact of a Body: A Murder and a Memoir*

"I've never read anything like *To Name The Bigger Lie*. A thriller? A philosophy book? A craft book? A perspective like Sarah Viren's is what's been missing from the debates around truths vs. conspiracy. Viren has written a masterpiece."

—Javier Zamora, author of *Solito: A Memoir*

"A work of radical moral philosophy as much as a memoir of one woman's confrontation with the seeming contradictions of certainty and doubt, truth and conspiracy, of the sometimes unbridgeable distance between the truth we know and the one we can prove. This is one of the most astonishing books I've ever read—a beacon in these uncertain times."

—Lacy M. Johnson, author of *The Reckonings: Essays on Justice for the Twenty-First Century*

"*To Name The Bigger Lie* is one of the most dynamic memoirs I've ever read. At the heart of this magnificent book is an incisive exploration of the concept of truth, a subject that, in an age of proliferating fake news, conspiracy theories, and coerced conflicts, couldn't be more urgent."

—Mitchell S. Jackson, winner of the Pulitzer Prize and author of *Survival Math*

"You don't expect a book on the nature of truth to be so darn readable. It's like Schopenhauer meets *Gone Girl*. Viren chases into nightmarish places the rest of us try to avoid—she confronts shadows, emails monsters—and brandishes philosophers along the way to make sense of what's unfolding. A breathless and edifying read. You come out of this book different, and also more connected to who you once were."

—Lulu Miller, cohost of *Radiolab* and author of *Why Fish Don't Exist: A Story of Loss, Love, and the Hidden Order of Life*

"A personal and philosophical deep dive into the world of fake news and conspiracy theories, this book takes on the big questions about truth with in-depth research, empathy, and humor."

—Toni Jensen, author of *Carry: A Memoir of Survival on Stolen Land*

To Name the Bigger Lie

A MEMOIR IN TWO STORIES

SARAH VIREN

SCRIBNER

New York   London   Toronto   Sydney   New Delhi

Scribner
An Imprint of Simon & Schuster, LLC
1230 Avenue of the Americas
New York, NY 10020

First Scribner trade paperback edition September 2024

SCRIBNER and design are trademarks of Simon & Schuster, LLC

Simon & Schuster: Celebrating 100 Years of Publishing in 2024

For information about special discounts for bulk purchases, please contact Simon &
Schuster Special Sales at 1-866-506-1949 or business@simonandschuster.com.

The Simon & Schuster Speakers Bureau can bring authors to your live event. For more
information, or to book an event, contact the Simon & Schuster Speakers Bureau at
1-866-248-3049 or visit our website at www.simonspeakers.com.

Interior design by Jaime Putorti

Manufactured in the United States of America

2 4 6 8 10 9 7 5 3 1

Library of Congress Cataloging-in-Publication Data has been applied for.

ISBN 978-1-9821-6659-5
ISBN 978-1-9821-6660-1 (pbk)
ISBN 978-1-9821-6661-8 (ebook)

To those denied the sky

Conceptually, we may call truth what we cannot change; metaphorically, it is the ground on which we stand and the sky that stretches above us.

HANNAH ARENDT

Thou strok'st me and made much of me, wouldst give me
Water with berries in 't, and teach me how
To name the bigger light.

WILLIAM SHAKESPEARE, *THE TEMPEST*

NOTE FROM THE AUTHOR

In writing this book, I have drawn from my own memories, as well as from interviews, journals, yearbooks, newspaper reports, and other documentation. Many names, including those of all of my high school classmates and teachers, and of my two kids, have been changed, along with occasional identifying details.

To Name
the
Bigger Lie

PROLOGUE

It was the summer of 2016 and I was in our bedroom in West Texas searching through tattered boxes my parents had recently sent me in the mail. Out the window was a dead mesquite tree that always felt beautiful to me, perhaps because of its endurance beside all the towering pecans, perhaps because it looked a little like the sapling on my wrist, a tattoo that had felt like a metaphor when I got it at eighteen: me the young spindly tree soon to sprout leaves and bury roots. Twenty years had passed since I got that tattoo. I was pregnant after having miscarried the year before, and our baby was due in two months. Our country would hold an election soon after that. I was hopeful on both accounts. I looked out at that dead tree in our backyard, then down at my tattooed one, before returning to an open box on the floor at my feet. That's when I found the photo. It was of my high school senior class on a strip of grass near the cafeteria, our bodies forming a roughly hewn triangle, with me at its point—pregnant. Or so I appear. My bright blue tank top swells, but the bump itself was only a sweatshirt I had stuffed there minutes before, an illusion, or a trick, to upset an otherwise innocuous image.

Staring, I was momentarily trapped in the thick heat of that May afternoon, the dishes from third lunch clinking and clunking on the other side of fogged-up awning windows, the thrum of traffic from Sligh

Avenue a distant reminder of the world beyond our Florida high school. It was 1997. Bill Clinton has just been reelected. Fox News had launched only the year before. We were seventeen and eighteen, toppling over the brink of one world into the bowl of another. The photographer looked down from somewhere above and yelled at us to smile. I cradled my sweatshirt belly and gazed knowingly at the lens. As if I were the mother of that family hedged into a triangle. As if the baby I feigned to carry had been dreamed up by all of us.

Click.

Finding that photo felt like a pinch, like the past nudging me awake. The mirroring of my body then and now was uncanny, but what stayed with me longer was the image of the rest of them: the eighty or so other students beside me—down from more than a hundred originally admitted to our magnet program. We had been told we were smart, the smartest, and yet what I kept thinking in the weeks and months after I found that photo, after the birth and then the election, was that—despite all of our supposed intelligence, despite our education and assumed potential—so many of us had still fallen for lies.

That thought was the real start of what would eventually become this book, because embedded within it was a question not only about us but also about our teacher. He was the one who was supposed to teach us how to think, a man we adored but also sometimes feared, a guru, my friend Lara would later say, and our idol. I began to wonder if a story about that teacher—the way his influence over us complicated easy narratives about who can be hoodwinked and who unveils the truth— might be an allegory of sorts, a narrative to help explain the changes that seemed to wash over this country the year I was pregnant and found that photo, the year of that election, and the years that followed. So I started trying to tell that story, but I kept getting mired in research, stuck in the hypothetical and philosophical, in questions of truth and fiction considered at a distance, like an ornithologist observing faraway birds. I reread Plato's Allegory of the Cave, a story that teacher had loved, and then the rest of the *Republic,* and then what other philosophers and thinkers had said about Plato and his dialogues. I planned a class on the literary history of fake news at the university where I taught and started collecting quotes about truth and lies, a Word document that steadily expanded as the years passed, as that baby, our second, learned to walk and talk, as our new president, our forty-fifth, took office and neo-Nazis marched in the streets and a man ran into a Pittsburgh synagogue and killed eleven people.

My work on that imagined book might have continued as such, with me collecting quotes and reading philosophy, researching the past and reading the news and interviewing everyone from high school who would agree to talk, everyone except our teacher himself, but then, in the spring of 2019, my wife, Marta, got a strange email. We had moved from West Texas to Arizona by then. Our girls were three and six. Everything felt ordinary and safe until it didn't. That email, and the events that followed it, sharpened and darkened the questions I'd been researching so diligently over the previous three years. The threat they contained collapsed the distance between me and the birds. Because what I hadn't realized when I found that photo was that the world doesn't stop just because you've decided to traipse into the past to tell a story. One story can easily interrupt another, just as questions build one atop the next. The past may mirror the present but the future also casts its shadow back on us. That teacher from high school was not the only person I needed to worry about.

I am finishing this prologue, and by extension this book, six years after finding that photo in a box in my bedroom beside a dead tree in Texas. We are in the north of Spain for the summer, and all around us the world is burning. In two days, we'll fly back to the United States, where the president elected at the start of this project is temporarily gone, but his influence lingers, where our division, not only on opinions but also on facts, continues to grow, and where the fires, both metaphoric and real, keep getting lit. The world in which I began writing this book no longer exists, and it feels some days like the only proper response is silence or screaming. But I know we also need stories. If only to remind ourselves that this world is not a story: the stakes here are real. This memoir is not the book I thought I would write six years ago. It is still an allegory of sorts, but it is also a story doubled, a mirroring of then and now and now and then. It is my response. My attempt.

PART I

"Strange Prisoners You're Telling Of"

1

His first lesson involved a pencil. We watched as Dr. Whiles threw it at the far wall of our classroom, watched as it tracked an amber arc in the air before, clink, the pencil hit the concrete bricks of the wall and fell to the linoleum below. The air-conditioning hummed. Our teenage bodies shifted in plastic chairs, tucked below scratched wood desks as if they might contain us. It was 1993 in Tampa, Florida. A mile in one direction, you ran into porn shops and dying malls; a couple of miles the other way and you found yourself beside a meandering river lined by grassy estates.

"Did it hit the wall?" Dr. Whiles asked us that day.

We stared at the dead pencil, thinking yes but not daring to say so out loud. Dr. Whiles stared back at us, his dress shirt short sleeved, his mustache white and bushy, his belly more barrel shaped than round. School had just begun—it was still only August—but the dynamic was already established: Dr. Whiles would pose a question we didn't understand. One of us would reach for an answer. And we'd be wrong. Another attempt. Also wrong. Until eventually he'd explain himself—or wouldn't. Sometimes, Dr. Whiles just smirked, flipped the toothpick staked between his teeth, and said, "Who knows?" or "Think about it."

But that day, he explained himself.

"To hit the wall," he said, "the pencil would first have to get halfway to the wall, right?"

We nodded. We nodded again when he asked if the pencil would arrive halfway across that second half of space before it touched the wall. And then halfway across that remaining quarter of space? And halfway across that next eighth of space? And so on, until we were no longer nodding our heads, but shifting our eyes between Dr. Whiles and the wall as if the answer might be pinned to the air somewhere in between.

"So did the pencil hit the wall?" he asked.

We said no.

Dr. Whiles picked up the pencil and threw it again. We watched it sail through the air and then—clink—hit the wall and fall to the ground.

The second lesson arrived sometime after that—though it may have come first. I can no longer be certain about the order of events that year. What I am certain of, and what everyone I've talked to also ascertained, was that Dr. Whiles pointed to the clock on the wall one day and asked another question.

"Does the clock exist?" he asked, his voice grave.

I'd gotten high by accident that morning. Lara and I had smoked a cigarette with the burnouts at the gas station across the street before the bell rang, and somehow in smoking, my high from the night before had returned like a ghost, filling my body with a suddenness that might have scared me if it hadn't numbed me first. I walked to class through the same congregations of students shouting at one another or being shouted at by teachers or administrators to hurry along, remove that hat, pull up those pants; but I hardly noticed their bodies or voices, the reality of our shared existence, or reality at all, until I found myself in Dr. Whiles's class. The clock on the wall looked like the clocks on all our classroom walls, clocks we glanced at without thinking, wondering how much time remained in this or that subject, how much longer the day would stretch before the last bell rang and we were released into a world that felt infinitely more real than the one inside our high school. Though rarely did I count the time in Dr. Whiles's class. I never wanted his class to end. It made sense to me that year in a way that little else did. Me in my Grateful Dead T-shirt and ripped jeans, flannels and polka-dot tights. Lara in her steel-toed boots and dyed-black blond hair. We thought Dr. Whiles understood us in a way no one else did. But I saw the clock that day; we all did. The second hand ticking forward on a circle that never stopped.

"How do we know the clock exists?" Dr. Whiles asked, turning to face us. "We all see it. We could go up and touch it if we wanted. But can we confirm it exists outside of our perceptions of it?"

In that moment, I thought I understood. He wanted us to consider more than just the clock. He wanted us to consider reality itself, and how impossible it is to know if the physical world exists for others as it exists for us—or at all. How we are all trapped within the cages of our own perceptions of not only the clock but of all objects, and people, too, which are objects of a sort.

"What the fuck," I said to Lara on our bus ride home that day. We sat near the back, side by side, sweaty thighs sticking to green pleather seats. Tiny wisps escaped from Lara's ponytail and were whipped by the wind from the opened windows.

"I get it but I don't get it," she said. "It's almost too deep."

"I do," I said. "But I can't explain."

Outside our window, reality passed unperturbed by our awakening. We crossed over the Hillsborough River and drove under live oaks trailing Spanish moss, palmetto bushes staked beside them like props in a movie set version of Florida. We passed a baseball diamond where players threw balls into the air, catching them in gloves that I now recognized as ontologically distinct from the gloves Lara or anyone else on that bus might see. Even the other kids—some of whom we'd known for years—no longer seemed real to me if I thought about them for long enough.

"Do you think he thinks about this all the time?" I asked.

"Yep."

"God."

The third lesson was Plato's Allegory of the Cave. We may have read it—the allegory is relatively short—but what I remember, and what others remember, too, is Dr. Whiles telling us Plato's story and all of us listening, rapt.

"It begins with a scene," he said that day. He asked us to imagine prisoners chained to the floor of a cave, staring at shadows on the wall in front of them cast by a fire behind their backs they cannot see. Those shadows are the only reality the prisoners have ever known, he told us, and thus they give them names and spin stories among themselves to account for their existence.

"Those people in that cave," Dr. Whiles said, "are just like you and me. Picture them in your head."

We did as he said. It wasn't difficult. High school often felt like a cave anyway: all of us trapped behind desks, anchored inside concrete buildings or portable classrooms, staring at chalkboards filled with lessons we were told to accept as true, often without understanding them first. It was a reality that felt inevitable, if disappointing—like being cast in a play comprised of predictable, never-ending acts.

"But then one day," Dr. Whiles said, "a man breaks free from his chains."

Or perhaps he is freed, I no longer remember the specifics of the first time I heard the story of Plato's cave—which errors in my memories come from the passage of time and which might be attributed to Dr. Whiles. What I remember was knowing that this man was exceptional. Chosen even. Rubbing his wrists, he stands up, bewildered but also relieved to have found his freedom. He turns, sees the fire behind him, turns back and sees the other prisoners, staring at the shadows, talking about them as if they were real, and the man realizes that he's been tricked his whole life.

That's me, I thought that day in class. That's us: Lara and me. We were the kids other people called freaks, the ones who got high and mismatched their clothes and wrote their own commandments because the rules from church no longer made sense. The kind of girls enamored of the word "ennui" and then enamored of saying we were "enamored of" things, which is to say we were weird kids but also earnest about our weirdness. And I assumed that meant that I would be the one freed from her chains, that both Lara and I would be, that Dr. Whiles was talking about people like us.

I doubted myself only when Dr. Whiles reached what he said was the end of Plato's allegory—though later I'd realize he may have misled us there, too. The man, now free, he told us, stands beside the fire for a moment before he notices light in the distance. He walks toward that glow until he finds the mouth of the cave and, pushing his way through it, he leaves the darkness behind and enters the sunlight above. When the man reaches the world outside, the sun blinds him with its brightness and at first he can't see a thing. It's painful, this birth or rebirth, but when the man adjusts to so much light, he looks around him and finds that everything is real. The sun is the sun. The stars, the stars. The clock, the clock. It all exists, in its true form. He sees this and everything else around him for what it is. He sees the truth.

"The cave is life for most of us," Dr. Whiles said, looking around the room after he finished the story. "But not everyone."

I blinked back at him, wanting his description of the open sky and sunlight to feel familiar, to again recognize myself in the story of that man muted by wonder. But I couldn't find myself in the ending. What felt familiar was the metaphor of standing by the firelight staring at others you think have it all wrong, not finding yourself in the sun, knowing the world for what it is. I stared at Dr. Whiles anyway, hoping he'd look at me like he sometimes did, like he knew I got it, or he believed that one day I would. But Dr. Whiles looked at the clock instead.

"Are you in the cave?" he asked us. "Or are you in the sunlight?"

2

I have a memory of a lake. Lara and I are in a canoe with a guy who looked like Jesus, who years later I will only be able to call Jesus in my mind, because by then both Lara and I will have forgotten his real name. He was older and good-looking, a tennis pro at the country club, where I was on the swim team and Lara took tennis lessons. His shaggy brown hair hung to his shoulders and his body was long and lanky like it might fold itself into a puzzle box. He must have been at least twenty but he acted like he was closer to our age, like hanging out with fourteen-year-old girls made perfect sense. His wide mouth would open to a smile when he saw us ride up after school and park our bikes beside the pool gates.

"Hey, you two," he'd say in a slow drawl that was either Southern or stoned.

We smoked weed with Jesus sometimes behind the tennis courts, and then one night near the beginning of ninth grade we snuck out of my house and met up with him at a park down the road. It was something Lara and I did a lot back then: sneaking out. She'd spend the night at my house, and we'd wait until my parents fell asleep, then slip from my bedroom to the screened-in porch behind our house, and after that down the steps into the backyard, uncaged. The air always hit me at that moment of release, thick and warm; and, entering it, I felt like everything I did had never been done before, like we were grafting our own existence right then and there, mini-gods or demons. Lara and I would run from the swamp that backed my house down the street to Oak Park, where someone was always waiting for us—usually a boy, sometimes a man, and on that particular night, Jesus in his beat-up Honda Civic, already smoking a joint, which he passed to us, grinning like the Cheshire cat, while Lara and I climbed in, twin Alices.

We got high in Jesus's car and then he drove us out to another neighborhood on the other side of Tampa, a place called Carrollwood, and asked if we wanted to steal a canoe.

"Totally," Lara said, as we idled in the night, staring out at an expansive lake ringed by neat two-story houses.

"Definitely," I agreed.

Lara and I had been friends since seventh grade, a year after my family moved to Florida from Wisconsin, two years after we moved away from Missouri, the state where I had all but grown up. Florida had stunned me with its alligators parked in the middle of sidewalks and Spanish moss spilling like piliferous clouds from stately oak trees, but also with the cacophony of concrete and crowds that comprised its public schools, the hour-long bus ride I took to a massive "sixth-grade center" I attended that first year, where the open-air hallways were always filled with too many kids, grabbing ass and hocking loogies or, one day that fall, rushing into lockdown, after a guy ran onto our campus with a gun. It felt like a place where it was hard to be alone. I spent my first year there, before I met Lara, either in school, on the bus, or in church. The church my mom had found for us in Tampa—a Methodist one to replace the Presbyterian congregation in Wisconsin and the Episcopalian community in Missouri—felt unassuming at first. We met in rented rooms in an office building led by a pastor who looked a little like Bill Clinton but with red hair, a man who would later have his own scandal involving an affair with a parishioner. I joined the youth group, where we played sardines and sang Jesus songs but rarely read the Bible. We were almost all white and upper middle class, mildly interested in God, but mostly looking for something to do in the suburbs besides swimming alone in our individual pools or watching MTV. But then a girl on my swim team invited me to a sleepaway camp for Christian athletes, and I came home more religious than many of my peers. I started singing songs to myself about the Lord preparing me to be a sanctuary and writing to God in my journal, telling him about my bangs and science experiments, about how annoying my sister was and the boys I thought I liked or didn't, but also, timidly, about the doubts I harbored. "I don't believe that homosexuality is wrong," I wrote to God in seventh grade. "I'm sorry. I hope you can still love me."

One day, I showed up for a youth group event and found someone new, a girl from school I'd never noticed or talked to before, standing in the parking lot beside her mom. It was Lara. I've always had a strong instinct for good friends, by which I mean that I know right away when I meet someone with whom I'll fit platonically. There's a sort of shimmering between us, as Joan Didion described the subjects she was drawn to writing about, only with early friendship it feels like slipping on a clean dress or moving furniture to just the right spot in a room. It's a feeling of things settling into place, cosmically perhaps, or interpersonally, and it happened when I met Lara that day. We stood under a canopy of trees by the office complex where we met while the church raised money for its own building. Lara's mom's white Infinity was parked nearby and when it came time to choose rides, I asked to go with her. I had permed blond hair then and neatly pressed jeans. Lara had big brown eyes and a quiet voice. We listened to U2 and Lara repeated her favorite lyrics back to me.

After that day, we hardly spent time apart. We sat together on the bus to and from Buchanan Junior High, a chaotic yellow building where I ran cross-country and Lara drew pictures of long-lashed eyeballs into notebooks we passed back and forth between classes. We spent Saturday nights at each other's houses and went to church on Sunday, praying and standing and sitting and singing and afterward eating little cookies with punch while her parents and my mom talked about God or work or the heat. We rode our bikes back and forth from her house to mine in our housing development, a place called Tampa Palms, passing artificial lakes lined with sandhill cranes and a golf course where wild boars roamed at night. Some days we stopped at the Tampa Palms welcome center, where salespeople explained the development's tiered neighborhood system to new families shopping floor plans for houses that hadn't yet been built, and where Lara and I would watch and rewatch a promotional video about the perfect place in which we lived. It told us that our community had been expertly designed. It boasted that parts of the jungle once covering this land had been preserved before all the houses were built, and, because of that, we should call the swaths of wilderness bordering our homes "the preserve" instead of a swamp. We sat in the air-conditioning of that tiny theater, the two of us, spindly legged and tan—Lara always tanner than I was, and prettier, too—watching the public relations version of our life. Then we walked outside, got on our bikes, and started writing different stories for ourselves.

In the stolen canoe that night, in another suburban neighborhood that wasn't all that different from our own, I watched smoke leave Lara's mouth like a river rising up toward the moon. I could hear the frogs chorusing and the cicadas singing high in the trees. Jesus paddled us farther and farther out until suddenly we were in the middle of the lake, exposed to anyone who wanted to see us, if only they looked out their windows, if only they were awake. I took a hit, and passed the bowl to Jesus, who laughed at us, at the situation, or perhaps at the unknowability of all of it: time, consciousness, the self, this world.

Lara took a hit and looked up at the palm-cupped moon.

"It's beautiful," she said, exhaling another river of smoke.

"It's a moon," Jesus said, not meanly. He watched the bowl move from Lara's hands to mine, watched the way I lit it with a flick of gas from my Zippo.

"It's a canoe in a lake," he added when no one said anything. "We're a canoe. The three of us in this lake. We're a canoe."

You're Jesus, I thought but didn't say. The smoke left my mouth in clouds instead of a stream.

When Lara and I first became friends, we were briefly normal, or what people back then considered normal. We wore bright white Keds and bodysuits. We listened to Power Pig 93.3 and talked about boys and music on the transparent phones we got for our birthdays, nameplate necklaces dangling at our throats. We followed the rules, or if we rebelled, it barely counted—like that time we snuck out of the sanctuary during the pastor's sermon and climbed onto the roof of the office building, reveling in the way you could see everything from up there, acres of identical houses sprouting from flat Florida swamp, while somewhere below us our parents and community prayed.

Then the summer before high school, two months before we started in Dr. Whiles's class, something happened that I still don't quite understand. We went on another youth group trip—a week in the Florida panhandle—and while we spent the days at the beach and evenings at prayer services, at night Lara and I began sneaking out, smoking cigarettes with local kids around bonfires on the beach, savoring the way our bodies felt out there, hot sand on our bare feet and fingers singed with the scent of tobacco. We did that all week, and when we got back, the secret of those nights stayed with us, unspoken. Until, that is, we made it visible: first through our clothes and then with everything else. We layered polka dots with plaid with ripped jeans with steel-toed boots, tie-dyed shirts we'd found at Goodwill, enormous top hats we bought at the mall, a brass ring with a naked lady on it I'd stolen at the Renaissance fair, her legs straddling my finger as I took my first hit the summer before ninth grade, my first tab later that year, and soon after that my first pills. We fell in love with the Pixies and the Violent Femmes; we read *Siddhartha* and *The Electric Kool-Aid Acid Test*; we felt like we knew something that the rest of the world didn't, that we were free in a way that so many other kids our age would never be.

By the time we were out on that canoe with Jesus, getting high and looking up at the moon, Lara and I had all but given up on the original Jesus, the one they kept hammering on about in church and youth group, whenever we went, which was less and less frequently. In place of him,

I had found drugs and the discussions in Dr. Whiles's class and of course Lara. She liked drugs, too, but more than that, Lara found a replacement for God in boys, usually older ones with a friend who I would try to like back, and fail. On the lake that night with Jesus, though, what I loved, and probably why I would remember that moment years later, was that Lara was momentarily single, and yet she didn't seem interested in Jesus either—nor did he seem interested in either of us. We were just some kids paddling a stolen canoe to the center of a lake to see what things looked like from out there. I was on the far bench and Lara in the middle, leaning back, her legs toward mine, her tan belly exposed.

"I love this," she said, watching the moon while I watched her.

3

"What is soma?" Dr. Whiles asked us.

This was a month or so into the school year. August had passed and fall had almost arrived, which meant I sweated less in cross-country practice and the air-conditioning felt less brutal in class, but the heat remained—the swampy feel never went away, no matter the time of year. We had our copies of Aldous Huxley's *Brave New World* out on our desks: some dappled with brightly colored tabs, some stuffed with lists of vocabulary words, mine dog-eared and spine bent. I no longer remember who was in class with me that year, but I imagine that James, if he were there, would have already thrust his hand in the air, ready to speak, his thick glasses slipping down his nose. Marcus would have had his head down, tapping out 2Pac lyrics on his desk, maybe, his mind somewhere else. Gayle would have been double-checking a passage in her book, knowing one answer at least, but still doubting herself. And Eric or Joel, had they been in my class period that day, likely would have made a joke.

Years later, I would remember these people like family, but back then, especially in ninth grade, they were mostly strangers to me—except for Lara. What held us together was our acceptance in a new international magnet program, the fact that we—all hundred or so of us—were the only freshman in a public high school of more than three thousand. It was a program we'd all heard about in eighth grade when Mrs. Morris, our guidance counselor and later administrator, visited our junior high school auditoriums and cafeterias and told us how getting into this program would be like gaining access to an education in Europe. You'll be in a big public high school, she said that day, but the classes will be small, your teachers will be smart and better paid, and you'll study things like art and philosophy and calculus 2. You'll get to choose if you want to focus on math or science or literature your last two years, she said, and at the end of it all, you will take a slate of exams that, if you pass, will allow you to skip several courses in college, maybe even a whole year.

Everyone had different reasons for applying. Some because their parents made them, others to spite a mom or dad who said they likely couldn't get in. Some wanted to get to high school early, while others needed out of their junior high school now. Marcus told me he applied because his junior high, Burns, was 5 percent Black, and he was tired of being such an obvious minority, while Chapin High was majority Black. He would have gone there anyway in tenth grade—he and Naomi and I and a handful of others were zoned for Chapin—but this way he got in a year before his friends. "I read the thing that said three hours of homework a night," he told me later. "I thought if don't have to go to Burns, I don't care."

I applied because I liked the idea of studying like they study in Europe. I'd never been out of the United States; I didn't know what Brie cheese was until a college roommate told me years later, and yet I could picture myself smoking in the cafés of Paris, a book open in one hand, my mind alight with ideas. But I also applied, like Marcus, to get out of junior high. I'd dated a boy named Travis there because he asked me to, and then his ex-girlfriend started telling people she was going to jump me. I dated another boy, Graham, after that—again because he asked—and he called me up each night to describe what parts of my body he liked best. What I likely needed was to stop dating boys, but instead I applied to a competitive, international magnet program, hoping that would do the trick.

Lara applied because I had. When we both got in, we celebrated. I imagined us, that fall, spending even more time together, doing homework late into the night and gossiping about all the people we did or

didn't like. Instead, soon after school started Lara met a guy named
Danny, an older kid at Chapin not in our magnet program, a wiry,
high-strung guy with his own car, with whom she fell madly in love.
I started dating a friend of Danny's named Kevin soon after that, and
the cycle continued. Except now I was in a competitive magnet program in a sprawling public high school where the older kids tried to
sell us elevator passes for a two story building and joked about how
small and nerdy we were. We went to classes on a block system, each
course meeting for two hours every three days—maybe the way they
did in Europe, though that seemed less and less likely. Every third day
I would show up in Dr. Whiles's classroom, where our task was sometimes to dissect utopias and drugs called soma, and other times to determine what was actually true in this world and what we might all be
dreaming up. His class that first year was called Inquiry Skills because
the focus was supposed to be on research and critical thinking, but he
taught it like an introduction to philosophy course, like the questions
he posed to us each period were the most important ones we'd ever
have to answer in our lives.

"What is the soma in our lives?" Dr. Whiles asked that day in September, after our initial silence led to more silence and we'd begun to fidget.

The word "soma" came from a Sanskrit term for the drink of the
gods—Dr. Whiles had told us that already—but I knew he didn't want
etymology. He wanted us to say what soma represented in Huxley's
novel, and by extension in our own world. He wanted us to build a connection between that story and our individual, nonutopian lives.

"Christianity without tears—that's what *soma* is," Mustapha Mond,
the leader of the society in *Brave New World*, says near the end of the
book. But soma sounded to me like the feeling of getting high in that
canoe with Jesus, the brief conviction that I existed as a body alone and
nothing else, a body moored in the present tense. And that would make
soma the opposite of Christianity, with its insistence on the soul as our
real self, its imagination of the body as more impediment than virtue. Dr.
Whiles had also told us that "soma" meant "body" in ancient Greece, and

that etymology felt closer to how I imagined this imagined drug and the power it had in Huxley's utopia.

"Maybe soma is TV?" someone in the back of the room tried. Dr. Whiles had been calling TV the "drug of the masses" recently, and some students in our program had begun parroting that narrative back to him, connecting the images on TV with the shadows on the wall in Plato's cave.

"Why do you think that?" Dr. Whiles asked, but when the kid started to explain, he interrupted. "What's wrong with something making you happy?" He flipped the toothpick in his mouth. "Happiness is what you're supposed to want. Who wouldn't want to be happy?"

"Maybe we need unhappiness to understand happiness," I said, and instead of asking another question, Dr. Whiles just nodded.

"Interesting," he said, and I felt a flush of real happiness. I took out my journal and wrote down what I'd just said, as if it were one clue in the larger mystery Dr. Whiles seemed to be unspooling that year.

Dr. Whiles returned to his desk, kicked up his feet, and started talking about the Epicureans and the rites of Dionysus, how pleasure was king in that world, the aim being to release participants from the constraints of society, to strip them of their egos and superegos, leaving only the id. But after the stripping away of constraints, he asked, what happens to the rest of us? Where do we go if we are only the body and its desire to be pleased?

I had no easy answer to that, and I still don't, thinking back on the person I was then, a teenage girl convinced there was a solvable equation for enlightenment, a fifteen-year-old confident she could figure out what was true by the end of the term. Every time I tried, scribbling away in my journal after Dr. Whiles's class, I ended up quoting song lyrics or inventing bland metaphors to describe how unhappy I was.

"I believe no god put us on this earth with the snap of his fingers," I wrote in my journal that year. "But I cannot even define time. Is it moving, does it exist? I'm so confused. Is everyone?"

My biggest obsession then, besides Plato's cave, was the concept of "conditioning," which I'd picked up from *Brave New World*. At the center of Huxley's book is a planned society, a utopia or dystopia, in which books and philosophy are banned, in which citizens all take a drug called soma that offers a "holiday" from discomfort and pain, but also one in which babies are genetically designed and then behaviorally conditioned to accept their assigned status in life and think as a collective rather than as individuals.

"I want," I wrote in my journal, "to free myself from this societal conditioning that has formed me."

My body had become Plato's cave, and yet the problem of escape felt even more tortured. How could I undo the work this world had done in creating me? I asked myself, convinced I'd find an answer. I borrowed another book by Huxley from Dr. Whiles that year, *The Doors of Perception*, which landed on peyote as the answer. But I kept getting high or tripping—once taking so many Dramamines before math class that I thought I was a listing ship—and my self was always there once I came down again. I borrowed *The Tibetan Book of the Dead* from Dr. Whiles after that and started writing in my journal about bardo, a state between death and rebirth, sure the answer to the cave and thus also the self lay somewhere beyond the life I was currently living. But that provided even less help in my quest to identify what was true and figure out who I actually was, before the school year came to an end.

Standing on the sidelines for all this, Dr. Whiles was relentless with his questions. What is true? What is the self? But also, what is this world, this "brave new world"—a phrase that Dr. Whiles told us came from Shakespeare's *The Tempest*—that shapes the self and either shapes, or perhaps hides, the truth? Some days, it felt like Dr. Whiles knew that students like me were losing themselves within his questions, taking them more seriously than we'd taken any subject in school before, and yet he held out hope that we would eventually find the answer. Other days it seemed like he knew we were struggling, and he was glad to see that struggle—regardless of where we ended up.

"Some of you will eventually discover the answer," Dr. Whiles told us at one point that year. "But only some of you."

4

My mom dropped Lara and me off near the entrance of the library at the university where she worked, idling in our gray Astro van while she handed me a note that said I had permission to check out books using her faculty card. In her ID she looked younger: her hair less tightly permed, the laugh lines on her face less deeply grooved. But you could easily see the resemblance between us: both with light blond hair and angular faces, only my mom was slimmer and taller—prettier, too.

"Thanks, Mom," I said, sliding the door closed behind me.

I had told her we were researching an essay for Dr. Whiles on the ethics of the Human Genome Project.

"Is this a repeat of *Brave New World?*" he'd asked us in class the week before. "Or will this help humanity? Think about it."

I told my mom we were going to research those questions, like the grown-up college students we would eventually become, searching for books and articles in the boxy computers on the library's first floor, then riding the elevator up to the stacks, poking around, photocopying, figuring out in the span of two hours the ethics of mapping our biological code so that one day we could replicate it—or "fix" it.

As soon as my mom drove away, though, Kevin pulled up in his VW Bug with Danny in the back seat. Lara and I laughed and climbed in, the Violent Femmes loud inside and the windows down as Kevin steered us back toward his house, where Lara would slip into the back bedroom with Danny and Kevin would lead me to the scratchy plaid couch in his living room—his mom, a nurse, still at work. He was a skinny kid with frizzy chestnut hair, a couple of years older like Danny. They smoked Marlboro Reds and went to school about as often as they skipped, getting high by the river, listening to grunge bands or metal while they waited for Lara and me to get out of class. I'd agreed to date Kevin after he walked up to me at lunch one day, his T-shirt tugged aloft, puffy-paint words written across his pale belly: "Will you go out with me, Sarah?"

I liked that he'd read *Siddhartha*, and that the week before we'd talked on the phone for more than an hour about heroes' quests and enlightenment and whether we should both give up traditional learning and go find ourselves on the road somewhere. But on that couch that afternoon, he wasn't interested in nirvana. He was interested in lifting up my shirt and unhooking my bra. He wanted to pull down my shorts and push aside my underwear, to snag my pubic hair with his fingers while he poked inside me, asking again and again if it felt good.

"Do you like it?" he breathed in my ear, hot and a little wet, and when I said yes, I didn't recognize that I was lying.

"I want you to touch me," he said, and when I didn't respond, he turned my hand palm up, spit on it, and showed me how to jack him off, how to hold tight but not too tight, how to pull and stroke.

"That's good," he said again and again, as if he had discovered its true form.

"Did you see Kevin and Danny at the library?" my mom asked after she'd picked us back up later that day, after we'd dropped Lara off at her house, and it was just the two of us in a Florida evening turning into night. I watched how tightly she gripped the steering wheel, the clenched muscle in her jaw.

"No," I lied.

"Sarah," she said. "I was early to pick you up. I saw Kevin's car driving away."

My mom used to tell this story I loved. When she was in high school, she and her mom lived in a small apartment in Chicago. Her father, a French professor turned university president, a man from Georgia who smoked Lucky Strikes and drank bourbon out of thick glasses, had died of a heart attack when she was thirteen, and her older brothers had gone off to college soon after that, which meant by the time she was a teenager, my mom was alone with her mom in a quiet apartment, still trying to be the perfect daughter she'd been before. Her mom had worshipped her father and struggled to find her place in the world after he was gone. My mom would comfort her when she broke into tears at dinner. Sometimes she tucked her own mom in at night. I suspect she never had a chance to mourn her father's death, much less rebel, which is likely why she secretly took up smoking in high school. When her mom was out of the house, my mom would smoke a cigarette alone, relishing that small rebellion, I imagine—maybe on the balcony, the bitter winds biting her face, or maybe in the living room, like the adult she longed to be—until afterward, when she was left with the butts, evidence of her transgression. She could have thrown them away. A better liar would have done that. Instead, she stashed them one by one on the top shelf of their linen closet, until eventually they formed a neat row: organized evidence of her quiet lies.

My grandmother Margaret never said anything about the cigarette butts, and the first time my mom told me that story, she said she assumed her mom never knew. I accepted that version when I was younger, but over the years, I realized how improbable that was. Cigarette butts smell. And she'd put them in the linen closet. Behind the towels, I imagined, stinking up everything. A more probable explanation was that my grandmother had noticed and decided to ignore it. Maybe she wanted my mom to nurture one small rebellion. Maybe she didn't care. But I did. I thought about those cigarette butts all the time.

"I'm not lying," I said as my mom pulled into the garage and we both heard the familiar barking of our dog, Ubu, then the voices of my brother and sister yelling about something, as I opened my door, grabbed my backpack, and ran into my bedroom. My mom followed but stayed in the kitchen. I heard her sigh while she started dinner.

Growing up, I used to thrill at the unconventional ethics of our family. We could swear all we wanted as long as we never swore at anyone. I could say "shit" or "fuck" when I stubbed my toe or dropped a glass of milk, but if I said "fuck you" to someone, my dad's fury would rise to the surface. "'Fuck you' is like telling someone you want them to die," he told me once, and I hung on to that definition for years. I didn't want anyone to die, I decided, so I never said "fuck you" again. We never talked about sinning at home, or any Christian conception of right and wrong—probably because my dad was an atheist and my mom went to church more out of habit than any deep faith. But lying was something both my parents abhorred.

My dad was the son of Swedish immigrants, Lutherans who eventually gave up on God but retained the severity of their church's teachings. He grew up poor and severely nearsighted in the shadow of a petrochemical plant in Southern California and became an adult who had the utmost faith in capitalism and yet was unforgiving of anyone who would cheat to get ahead. He'd been an academic, twice, but he hated bureaucracy enough he eventually quit. He became an economist for the state government, until he was fired for speaking out against ethical lapses of his elected bosses. He believed in following the rules if he could see the reason for them, but he didn't give a damn about stupid ones like color-code requirements for houses in our subdivision or, years before that, the Vietnam draft.

When I was in eighth grade, Lara and I stole bowling alley shoes once because we thought they were cool, leaving behind the shitty sneakers we'd worn bowling on purpose. The next day, we slid into our new stolen shoes before school, and Lara's parents laughed at the audacity and oddness of their kid, but when my dad found out that afternoon, he put me in his Toyota Camry and drove me back to the bowling alley, where he waited, drumming his hands on the steering wheel, while I returned mine.

"That's stealing," he said, though theft itself wasn't the problem— I knew that—it was the deceit inherent in theft.

My mom hated lying for other reasons. She had a job as a social worker when she and my dad got together—around the time my dad left his first wife and my mom was getting ready to divorce her husband—and when I was a kid, she enrolled in a PhD program in psychology. I remember watching her draft mnemonic devices to memorize mental illnesses in the *DSM IV*—trichotillomania and Tourette's syndrome, pica and malingering. I remember her telling us about Freud and the superego, ego, and id—the same concepts that Dr. Whiles would later tell us were essential terms that all thinking people needed to know. Honesty, for my mom, was important because she equated it with psychological wellness. If you lie, you might be rebelling, but you also might be crazy. If you tell the truth, you're mentally sound.

More than doing drugs or skipping school or jacking off boys or lusting after my best friend that first year of high school, what felt rebellious to me was when I started to lie. Lying separates you from another person, briefly, temporarily, by creating one reality they believe and another you know is true—and I felt that acutely that year, even as I tried to ignore that guilt. I lied in tacit ways when I snuck out or skipped school, but I also began to lie directly to my parents' faces, like when I told my mom I hadn't seen Danny and Kevin at the library. Or later that night, after I came out of my room and told my mom I was ready to tell the truth.

"You were right, we did see Danny and Kevin at the library," I said. "They came to help us study, but they'd only stayed a little while."

I started crying without meaning to and I knew my mom saw that as evidence that I was telling the truth. But I was crying because I wasn't, but also because something else had happened that afternoon at Kevin's that I didn't want to share. At one point after separating we all came back together again and Danny had said it'd be hot if Lara and I would kiss, so we had. I'd noticed her teeth first, how they clinked against mine in a way that had never happened before with boys, but also how much softer her lips felt. There was air in the middle of our kiss, like space had opened up between us within the movement. But then before I wanted it to end, it was gone. Kevin and Danny were there again, too close, saying how hot we were, how hot that was, how much it had turned them on.

5

"What is the answer to the Ultimate Question of Life, the Universe, and Everything?" Dr. Whiles asked one day after he had turned off the squat TV in the corner of the room and flipped on the lights. I blinked and remembered where I was: in school, fifteen years old, near the middle of our ninth-grade year.

"Forty-two," we responded in unison, happy to have a concrete answer, even if we knew it was a joke.

Dr. Whiles smiled—a rarity—and I wondered if it pleased him, too, the prospect of an easy answer to all the questions we faced.

"But what is the question?" he asked.

The TV series we'd watched on VHS, based on the books I'm still not sure we ever read, was about a man named Arthur Dent who is rescued from the earth just before it is destroyed. The earth, we learn, was never a real planet but instead a complex computer, created by another complex computer named Deep Thought that was itself created by aliens intent on figuring out the answer to the Ultimate Question of Life, the Universe, and Everything. Deep Thought determines the answer is forty-two, but then says that the question itself needs further development for the answer to make sense. Because the earth no longer exists, Arthur Dent becomes the aliens' only hope for excavating that central question so that they can ultimately understand the answer they've been given.

"Isn't the question," I said, "what is the answer to life, the universe, and everything?"

Dr. Whiles looked tired. He shrugged and, instead of answering me, he walked over to his desk and tapped on a stack of books he called his library, books like Huxley's *The Doors of Perception* and Will Durant's *The Story of Philosophy*, but also John M. Allegro's *The Sacred Mushroom and the Cross*, and Erich von Däniken's *Chariots of the Gods? Unsolved Mysteries of the Past*, which wasn't on the stack that day because I had borrowed it the week before. In that book, von Däniken argues that aliens built the pyramids and other natural wonders of the world, an idea that felt ridiculous at first and yet seemed more and more plausible the further I read. I was intrigued by von Däniken's analysis of Egyptian hieroglyphs that looked like spaceships and helicopters. I was intrigued by a vision of history that ran counter to the one I'd been taught.

"The question is where the answer lies," Dr. Whiles said, thumping harder on the books this time. "Think about it, folks."

By that point, some kids in our program had started to say that Dr. Whiles was a little nuts. We were all required to take his class, but not everyone reacted the way Lara and I and a handful of others had. Hope, the child of religious Filipino parents, was so worried about him being an atheist that she used one of her papers in his class to try to convince him of the existence of God. Jamie, a girl from church I'd known since seventh grade, complained that he was the first teacher for whom she couldn't figure out how to get an A. Bobbie, who immigrated to the States from Hungary as a kid—would softly mock Dr. Whiles when she wrote in my yearbook at the end of that year: "I had fun 'manifesting adolescent behavior' with you," she wrote, quoting the accusation he often hurled at us—that "manifesting adolescent behavior" was preventing us from being able to think. Students like that didn't understand why Dr. Whiles harped on about TV and how it was brainwashing all of us, or why he kept asking so many questions—first philosophical questions, but as the year progressed, also ones about the material world: Why is there an eye on the dollar bill? Who invented LSD? What is the New World Order?

He posed those questions almost like a joke, like the question at the center of *The Hitchhiker's Guide to the Galaxy*. But those of us who took his class seriously, who had been rapt when he told us about Plato's cave and spent hours writing essays for him on the difference between wisdom, knowledge, and beliefs, had a hard time brushing off anything he said, even if we thought he must be joking, even if that was the only explanation that made sense.

"Some say the eye on the dollar bill is a symbol of the Illuminati," he told us one day. "Look into it."

We stared at him, unsure what to do or say, but before we could respond, Dr. Whiles switched topics. The toothpick flipped. His feet were up on his desk, and he was back on the subject of *Oedipus Rex* or Plato's theory of Forms. But later one of us would always research what he'd said and report back to the rest. The Illuminati, we learned, was a secret society that some believe has ruled our world as a shadow government for years. The government invented LSD. And the New World Order was like the United Nations, only scarier.

Our final project for Dr. Whiles's class that year was an essay on a topic of our choosing. Lara planned to write about Jim Morrison's Oedipal lyrics, and I was focusing on Pink Floyd, a band I never liked until Dr. Whiles suggested I find their early albums, when Syd Barrett sang lead and wrote most of their songs—before he went insane and dropped out of the band and of life in general. I'd been listening to his album *The Piper at the Gates of Dawn* on repeat in my room at night, trying to make sense of lyrics that made little sense, even as there was something eerily familiar to them, as if they'd been written in a code I might crack. I still didn't know what to say about the band or their music, so one day I stayed after class to ask for Dr. Whiles's advice. He looked at me for a long time before he spoke.

"Look into the figure of the piper at the gates of dawn," he said at last. "I think you'll find something interesting."

I nodded, turning to leave. Outside there was shouting in the hallway and the resonant slamming of lockers.

"Sarah," Dr. Whiles said, and I stopped, turned back toward his desk. "You need to push yourself harder. You're a good writer. But you have to push yourself. Keep asking questions."

"Okay," I said, but I had no idea how to do that.

The Piper at the Gates of Dawn, I eventually learned was another name for the god Pan, who shows up briefly in the children's book *The Wind in the Willows* in a chapter of that name. There is a missing otter boy and two of the characters, Mole and Rat, go out on a boat looking for him in the moonlight. Then at some point, they find the boy and Pan appears, bewildering Mole and Rat with his presence before sending in a spring breeze to help them forget him after he is gone, a spell that in the book is called "the gift of forgetfulness."

The paper I eventually wrote on Pink Floyd included none of those details, mostly because I couldn't figure out what any of it meant or how one story connected to the next. But the figure of the Piper at the Gates of Dawn, and that tale of discovery and then forgetfulness, stayed with me in the years that followed, like clues that nettle the reader of a mystery. Only in this case the mystery was a middle-aged teacher in a semi-urban high school in the 1990s, an ordinary man who nonetheless occupied so many of my thoughts, in large part because I was convinced that he, too, knew magic. And I wanted to know what he knew.

6

As a kid, a feeling would sometimes sweep over me that I used to call "the big picture." I'd be in the creek beside our house in Missouri, a creek my neighborhood friends had named Pompeii for reasons I still don't understand, and I'd be building a fort or collecting rocks, and I would recognize the simple fact that I existed. In doing so, I would then become aware of the life blinking within everyone else in the world, as if I were a camera lens panning out, moving from a close-up on my own hand or forearm to my body and then to the spinning globe. Only at the moment of that wide pan, I would become aware of every other living person, as if I were God, their lives and mine palpable to me like fruit or cotton or rain. It was euphoric, and still is, in the rare moments it happens now. It was as close to ecstasy as I've ever come.

Akin to that feeling was a much scarier sensation I also had growing up, one that had no name. It was auditory and, like the "big picture," would come on with a ferocity I could never predict. All the tiny noises in my surroundings—my pencil writing, a clock ticking, shoes shuffling—would suddenly sound as if they were screaming, yelling at me, irate. The change was frightening when it happened, and I worried that the roaring would never stop. But eventually it would, like a light dimming, the sounds of my every day settling back into their regular configurations, as if nothing had ever been upset. For years, patience was how I dealt with the sounds, reminding myself that eventually the intensity would dissipate. As I grew older, I realized that I could banish the noises more quickly if I started talking to myself out loud. Doing so yanked the voice in my head into the external world, making it into something concrete, but not angry, and that concreteness of self helped me disarm the choleric hallucinations.

I rarely talked with anyone about the big picture or the angry noises. The times I had tried to explain, I knew I sounded either crazy or tedious, so I stopped sharing. They were secrets I kept to myself, along with so much else in high school. And yet every time Dr. Whiles started in about the clock or Plato's cave or the Vedas or the *Tibetan Book of the Dead*, I felt sure that he would understand—if I told him. Some days his class made me feel like I was back in Pompeii again, bowled over once more by the enormity of the big picture coming on. As if by proxy, I also began to trust, or at least feel a kinship toward, the other students in our program who seemed as swept up by Dr. Whiles's teachings as I was. Lara was one of those people, obviously, but I was seeing less of her lately; Kevin had broken up with me and she was spending more and more time with Danny. In her place, I tried to find others with whom to talk about Dr. Whiles, and one of them was James, a kid many of us considered the smartest in our class. He and I never became friends that year, but there was a short period of time in which we talked on the phone almost every night, mostly about Dr. Whiles's class and Eastern religions. Then, one night, James told me he could leave his body if he meditated long enough.

"Really?" I said, turning over on my back to look at my bedroom ceiling.

I slept in my dad's old T-shirts back then, and I likely was in one of those, under the covers in my bed that faced the swamp, a painting of a lightning storm that Lara had made and given me hanging over my head, the cicadas singing from the tops of trees and a sliver of light from the kitchen visible beneath the crack between my door and the carpet. I closed my eyes and imagined what it would feel like. The relief of leaving the physical confines of the body, if only briefly. The big picture never gave me that escape. And the noises brought on the opposite effect. I felt imprisoned in my physical form.

"You have to concentrate," James said, but his voice sounded farther away than before, and I hoped it might be working.

"And if you can do it," he said, "you'll suddenly be up there looking down on your body."

I imagined James at that moment, also lying in his bed, his dirty-blond hair neatly parted in the middle and his thick glasses on the table beside him, while his real self looked down at his inert body. On the surface, we were opposites: James played in the band, always did all his work, always knew the answers in class, and had rarely rebelled in any way I could see. I took acid before class and had started going to Wiccan circles at the Unitarian Temple. I skipped school and had friends who believed they were vampires. But we came together in our obsession with Dr. Whiles's class and with our questions about the unreliability of reality and the possibility of one day discovering the truth of things.

"I feel like he woke us up," was how James put it when we talked years later. "We'd all been hypnotized by things, by TV, and he came in and shook everything up."

I felt that way, too. Like a door had opened somewhere that I could not shut. What felt infinitely more important than grades or almost anything else that year was figuring out what that self was, and how the body related to that self, or soul, and if the soul even existed—a question that likely led James and me to the subject of astral projection in the first place. I imagine we had been talking about where the self resides.

"What I do," James said in the conversation as I remember it, "is close my eyes and then I concentrate on moving out of my body and up toward the ceiling. I really focus, like putting all my energy into one ball that can then slip through the skin. I couldn't do it the first time, or even the second, but now I can do it easily."

I closed my eyes again and concentrated on separating my self from my body. I could almost feel the split in the darkness of my room that

night. I felt my physical self and I thought I sensed something else inside, something pushing for release. I pictured Dr. Whiles there, smiling
slightly, encouraging me to take one more step, to leave the self behind.
The sensation was both sacred and frightening, like I might lose myself
and the parameters of my body beneath the sheets and comforter, the
pillows at my head, the stuffed dog I always slept with grazing my arm.
I imagined that if I could do this one thing, if I could leave my body, I
would slip from the singularity of my perspective. I would know the real
clock outside of any perceptions of it. I would be objective, like a god, or
a philosopher king, freed from the cave.

But then I heard James breathing on the other end or my dad yelling
something at my mom in the other room, or I felt the phone sweating in
my hand, and I opened my eyes. Glow stars shone dull in the sky above
and James began talking about Phil Collins or the Who, and the potential
was gone. I was myself, trapped anew.

7

"How should we start?" I asked that night.

"Let's just kiss," Lara said.

We did.

It was like what had happened before, but also different. This time, we'd taken off our clothes. This time, we were in a tent in Lara's backyard. This time it was just us. It was almost summer. School might have been over, I'm no longer sure. What I know is that there was no audience. No Danny or Kevin saying we were hot. When we pulled apart, I could see our shadows on the tent wall, the way Lara's body made a landscape of small ridges and peaks, how mine curved and sloped more, but at some point, we joined.

We were camping in her backyard because we thought it would be fun, and we'd promised her parents we'd come running if anything happened. But what could happen? Her closest neighbors were just over the lawn line. Her house was on a corner lot with windows lit up in every direction. Nothing bad ever happened in the suburbs—except perhaps what we were doing in that tent.

Lara had been the one to suggest more than kissing. She wanted to tell Danny about it, and I said I wanted to tell Shawn, another friend of Danny's who I was now dating. He was a high school dropout who sold weed out of his bedroom window and grew out his pinky nail to use as a pick on his electric guitar. He thought it was sexy that I sometimes kissed girls.

We kissed for longer the second time, then I moved on top of Lara, our naked bodies like logs piled one atop the next, a tarp covering their closeness.

"Do you think he'll think this is hot?" Lara asked.

Instead of responding, I kissed her like I'd seen Danny do, moving from her lips to her neck. Lara made none of the sounds I'd heard her make with Danny during all those days of being on the other side of a wall listening to her.

"Try my tits," she said, when I pulled up from her neck. I saw the pale triangled tan lines across her chest from her bikini. I saw the hole where she had pierced her nipple herself in eighth grade. Lara's eyes were closed. Her legs were thin and tan, her belly managed to be both soft and slim. People said she looked like a model. I tried her tits.

"Should I go down on you?" I asked after time had passed and nothing seemed to be happening.

Lara opened her eyes, then closed them. She nodded.

We had a flashlight with us and our sleeping bags and cigarettes. Our clothes were in a bundle in the corner. I wondered briefly what we would do if her dad's shadow appeared outside the tent wall. How could we explain any of this?

I moved between Lara's legs and touched her with my tongue.

"What does it taste like?" she asked, sitting up.

"I don't know," I stopped, not wanting to stop. "Weird."

But it wasn't weird.

"Try putting a finger inside," she said.

"Okay."

I had touched myself before, inside, and it always felt both cavernous and ridged, like running your finger along the edges of a brain. But when I put a finger in Lara, it was like the mouth of a baby—a sensation I would know well years later.

"Does that feel okay?" My breath hit her body when I spoke.

"Yeah," she said, but she sounded unconvinced.

"You sure?" I said.

Lara opened her eyes, propped herself up on her elbows.

"Let me try you now," she said.

I pulled my fingers out, and immediately regretted it. But Lara was already sitting up, and I found myself taking her place, my back on the sleeping bag, my eyes staring up at the nylon walls. I could hear cicadas and the frogs crying to one another across stretches of St. Augustine grass. I could feel Lara's weight on me. I closed my eyes.

"Do you like it?" Lara asked each time she repeated what I'd done. I said yes. But I was lying. Or I was telling the truth, while also lying. It felt better than anything I had done with Kevin or Shawn, but also not completely real. It felt like we were acting in a dramatization of reality, one that I wanted to be real but Lara still saw as performance. Because by that point, I'd realized that we had an audience after all. We weren't doing this for ourselves.

I'd break up with Shawn soon after that night in the tent, and in the months that followed Lara would grow closer to Danny. We'd move into our sophomore year seeing less and less of each other and I'd slowly find new friends, in particular one named Lucy, who I'd meet while I was tripping at a party, and who would talk to me for hours about how one could see the universe in the foil seal of a gum wrapper, even though she wasn't tripping, or likely even high. As ninth grade ended and tenth grade began, Lucy would slowly start to take Lara's place. She and I would smoke cigarettes in empty parking lots and dissect song lyrics; we'd drink coffee late at night at Village Inn and obsess over many of same questions that had underpinned Dr. Whiles's class the year before: Who are we? Why are we here? What's the point of any of this? I'd eventually decide that I'd fallen in love with Lucy, too, but she'd be patient with me, with my desire to sort through my sexuality via those who felt safest: my best friends, the women I trusted. Which meant that by the time Lara told me she was moving away at the end of my sophomore year, I'd mostly feel relief, because by then she'd be a reminder of a version of myself I no longer recognized, someone about whom I felt slightly ashamed: for her desperation, her self-delusion, her hope.

That night in the tent, though, Lara and I finished practicing—playing, as we called it—and then we snuck out for a cigarette beside a half-built house down the road. When we turned off the flashlight, we climbed back into our individual sleeping bags, back in our clothes. I said good night, but Lara was already asleep. Or she was somewhere else in her mind, because she never responded. And what happened that night never happened again. We never talked about it, either, and for a long time it was as if I had dreamed it all up. Until I started thinking about high school again, and the teenage girl I once was. Some days I can almost see her. A girl somewhere in the past trying to fall asleep next to her best friend in a tent in the suburbs of a city and a state that probably won't exist one hundred years from now. A girl who has no idea I'll one day be here, at my desk, trying to bring her back to life. That the audience she felt that night was not only Danny or Shawn, but me, staring at her across the distance of so much time, trying to connect this to that, her to me to him.

8

My little sister, Jessie, asked me if I was gay halfway into my sophomore year. We were walking the dog, in my memory of the conversation, and she said some kids at church were whispering that I was. She needed to know if it was true. Jessie had thick red hair and an inability to keep her thoughts to herself. That year, eighth grade for her, she'd started watching her favorite movies alone on tape over and over again in a small space we called the TV room. She'd memorized *The Sound of Music* and *The Princess Bride* and *The Fugitive*. Sometimes at dinner she'd recite stretches of them out loud—"'We can do it without help, Father!'"—while my dad clinked the ice in his Jack Daniels—"'Inconceivable!'"—as my mom prodded us to talk about our days. My brother, Andy, would interject with Jim Carrey quotes. Our dog, Ubu, would lick herself furiously in the corner until she suddenly leaped with the joy of what we had by then realized was an orgasm. The sliding glass doors to one side held us in their reflection and beyond that lay a pool inside a screened-in porch, which everyone in Florida called a birdcage. As if we were songbirds caged by that house and that neighborhood and that period in time.

We were never all that close, Jessie and I. Growing up in Missouri, I usually played outside with two older neighborhood girls, pretending that Communists were chasing us or building forts in Pompeii, while she and Andy stayed home, closer to my mom or the babysitter, playing with the crutches Jessie had requested for Christmas or spinning around in the wok on the kitchen floor or sliding down the carpeted stairs on cushions from the couch. When we moved to Florida, Jessie tried to tag along with the new neighborhood kids I'd met in Tampa Palms, but by then the gap between us had widened, and I told her to leave me alone. She persisted for weeks before she gave up, and I only briefly felt guilty. That we had decided to walk the dog together that night, though, implies one or both of us wanted to close the distance between us. I know I wanted to do that—even if I kept messing it up.

"I'm totally not," I said. "I'd tell you if I were."

Jessie looked over at me. Towering streetlights lit the pavement in sprawling triangles and we walked between their light and the darkness.

"Oh good," she said. "I didn't think you were."

My sophomore year was the year we read Sartre's *No Exit* in English class. At one point, our teacher asked us to take turns reading out loud scenes from that play. Lara was still in Tampa then, and we were chosen for the same scene: she, assigned Estelle, a rich, vain woman; and I, given the part of Inez, the sadistic lesbian. I no longer remember what scene we read out loud in class that day, but I know the scene in *No Exit* that most unsettled me when I read it alone the night before. It starts with the question of a mirror. There isn't one in the room in which the characters in the play are trapped and Estelle wants to see herself, so Inez tries to lure her closer by offering her eyes as Estelle's looking glass. Inez is desperate in her desire, made pathetic by it, and eventually Estelle rejects her, turning to talk to the only other person in the room: a man named Joseph. Reading that rejection alone that night, I felt a queasiness that returned when Lara and I acted out our scene in class the next day. It was a discomfort I'd eventually recognize as shame, the same feeling I had when I told my sister I wasn't gay and she said she was relieved. Shame is a shadow, Carl Jung once said, that falls on a part of your brain where memories stick. "Everyone carries a shadow," he wrote, "and the less it is embodied in the individual's conscious life, the blacker and denser it is."

But I also have to remind myself that shame was not the only emotion that defined me then. Not even close. I was out to most of my friends by my second year of high school, and some of my classmates, too. I know because I found proof in my yearbook: Eric, a friend of mine, who along with our friend Joel was one of the tallest guys in our class, wrote, "Of all the bisexual, liberal, pro-choice femi-nazis I know, you're the best. I don't agree with what you think, but I respect it. Too bad you're going to hell." When I reminded Eric of that quote years later, he apologized and said something he'd later repeat about Dr. Whiles. "I have a bad habit of forgetting things that are difficult." Joel would later tell me he remembered seeing Lara and me get on the bus that first year of high school and thinking we looked like two of the 4 Non Blondes—but we were both blond. But he and Eric always treated me more like a buddy than a girl. They called me "Viren," and I loved that—hearing their voices down the hall as they hollered out my name, their heads bobbing among the multitude.

Gayle told me she remembers me being out before she'd even admitted to herself that she was queer. She was a bigger kid with frizzy hair who had emigrated from Latvia when she was eight, part of the last large wave of Jewish emigrants from the Soviet Union to the United States in the late 1980s. She was one of those kids who physically sticks out, and even though most of that awkwardness sloughed off once she started at Chapin—she'd win Best Personality our senior year—she still worried about coming across as a freak. She didn't want to add one more item to the list of reasons she might be ostracized. Though later she, like me, would be drawn to the teachers we knew or thought were also gay, always looking for an example somewhere from someone older that it was going to be all right.

Coming out is a question of self-knowledge, but it also is a means of speaking a self into existence. It requires honesty, and yet it's one of the few instances in which we rarely blame the speaker if he or she lies. We say we understand if you lie, but what we mean is that we understand why you would. Perhaps because of those stakes, I felt a certain degree of pride by the end of my sophomore year in my limited honesty with people in high school—even if I still lied to my sister and my parents and anyone from church, and even if I'd still never had a real girlfriend. Part of that pride was the conviction that I'd grown, intellectually or emotionally. I knew something about myself that was true, and I remember looking forward to showing Dr. Whiles how much more self-aware I was, more knowledgeable even, once we had class with him again the following year.

9

When we returned to school our junior year, Lara was gone and all our classes had moved to what our new psychology teacher Ms. Ritter called "portable city," a landscape of double-wide trailers wheeled in and planted in the dead space behind the football stadium and the ag buildings on a corner of the high school campus. It was open land that, years later, we'd learn hid a forgotten graveyard for hundreds of indigent Black residents from the turn of the century. But we didn't know that then. We knew that Kurt Cobain was dead and that O. J. Simpson was on trial for killing his wife. We knew how to do the macarena and quote the best lines from *Pulp Fiction*. We may have known that a company named Amazon had recently sold its first book, though I doubt that. We had other things to worry about.

We were sixteen and seventeen by then, and already there had been two shootings on our campus. In the first, the January before, a boy Lucy knew from junior high had been walking with a friend through the courtyard, and the gun he'd hidden in his pocket went off by accident. The bullet hit the kid Lucy knew first and then his friend. Ambulances blared as they rushed into the school's front parking lot, carrying away both boys, who would be all right, we'd learn later, though both would be suspended.

The next shooting came that September, soon after classes started, at a bus stop across the street. A fight broke out among a dozen kids, one of whom had been a student at Chapin until he was expelled the year before. He was shot in the mouth and gut. In his panic, he ran back to the school that had ejected him—across four lanes of traffic. The school resource officer found him, likely the same man who had gotten him expelled, and I imagine that he held him while calling for help. A helicopter ambulance flew in, and afterward our principal, Mrs. Axton, stayed late to talk to parents and the press. "The main thing is that the kids really do feel safe here," she told them.

She might have been right that we felt safe at school, but that was only because the rest of the world seemed comparably scarier. The spring before, a man had bombed the Oklahoma City Federal Building, killing 168 people, including nineteen children. He was inspired—we later learned—by a novel called *The Turner Diaries* that imagined a race war followed by a white supremacist world order. Elsewhere in the South, Black churches were being burned to the ground, works of arson that an assistant attorney general at the time would call "an epidemic of terror." Elsewhere in the country, abortion clinics kept getting bombed, their doctors and staff shot.

We typecast the 1990s as tame, even juvenile, when compared with the world after September 11, but what gets overlooked when we gloss history like that is how much that decade foreshadowed what would later come. It was the first time that right-wing extremist groups became a bigger threat, in the eyes of the FBI, than left-wing groups like the Animal Liberation Front. The most powerful of those was the National Alliance, a white supremacist group founded by William Pierce, author of *The Turner Diaries*, with chapters across Europe but also a significant stronghold in Florida. Pierce advocated for a Nazi state that would follow the "temporary unpleasantness" of a race war, and his members were connected to plans for at least a dozen violent crimes, including a plot in the late 1990s to bomb Disney World. Meanwhile, on our local public access TV, there was a guy dressed like Groucho Marx shooting watermelons while Nazi and Confederate flags flew behind him. Meanwhile, in a hotel down the road, the Holocaust denier David Irving would later

that year give a talk to skinheads and neo-Nazis about how persecuted
he claimed he had been for just telling "the truth."

After the bombing in Oklahoma City in 1995, an investigative journalist named Jean Heller published a long article in one of Tampa's two
local papers, the *St. Petersburg Times*, about the rise of hate groups in
the mid-1990s, a resurgence she traced to the standoff at Ruby Ridge in
1992, when federal agents killed a fourteen-year-old boy and his mother,
and the siege at Waco the following year, where seventy-six members of
the Branch Davidian sect had died. But an even earlier instigator, Heller
wrote, was the first Gulf War, specifically that moment in 1991 when
then President George H. W. Bush characterized the offense as a protec-
tion of a "New World Order."

"Some conservatives interpreted the phrase to mean the United
States one day would forfeit its identity in favor of a nationless world
under the control of the United Nations, a notion that was anathema to
paramilitarists," Heller wrote. "Their rallying cry became 'Death to the
New World Order.'"

Reading that years later, I winced, remembering Dr. Whiles going on
and on about the new world order our first year and again, but with more
intensity, when we had him in eleventh grade. He got angry at one point
because someone had laughed like it was a joke.

"This is happening, folks," he yelled that day. "Wake up!"

10

D r. Whiles's classroom moved to Portable City that year, too; the first
portable in the lot, Portable A. His taught a new course that year,
Theory of Knowledge, but he stood before us just as he had two years
earlier. Only something about him seemed different.

I felt different, too. I knew I looked less like a freak—I no longer
dressed quite as wildly, nor was I getting high quite so often—but the
real difference was psychological or perhaps philosophical. In addition
to knowing myself better than two years before, I'd also thought a lot
about the questions Dr. Whiles had asked us in ninth grade, and I was
convinced that I'd be better prepared to answer them now that we were
in eleventh grade. I felt like I understood so much more. I hoped he
would notice the difference.

"I've been reading Thomas Aquinas," he said once the bell had rung
and we were all in our seats.

We looked at him, waiting to understand.

"Have you heard of him?"

Some of us shook our heads. A couple of kids raised their hands. The
rest stayed quiet.

"He said that reason resides in God, not in us," Dr. Whiles said.

He looked cleaner, I realized, more closely groomed, happier even,
than in our first year, but more intense, too, if that was possible. He'd

eventually tell us that the difference we all noticed was real, that something *had* happened to him the summer before. He'd been born again, he'd say, as a Catholic. He wouldn't explain more than that at first, and we'd wonder if the conversion story was another test, another way of seeing how gullible we were. But then in another class period—not mine but the class Eric had with Dr. Whiles—a student would finally ask him how and why he'd converted, and to everyone's surprise Dr. Whiles explained himself.

"It was as simple as this," Eric remembers Dr. Whiles saying that day. "I was on my porch in my apartment looking out on the Hillsborough River, the sun hit the river, there was an image of the *Pietà*, and that was it."

Eric thought the story sounded peculiar at the time. Here was a guy committed to reason and knowledge, he said, and he converts because of a vision? It seemed uncharacteristic. For me, Dr. Whiles's conversion—once I realized it was real—felt like a betrayal. Our first year, he had identified as an existentialist. He'd told us he didn't believe in God, and his surety had factored into my own slow disavowal of God. His conviction that we alone could figure out the world had been one of the reasons I loved his class so much. And suddenly it felt like he was changing the rules of the game.

In those early weeks of the semester, though, Dr. Whiles mostly acted like the teacher we'd had before. He taught us Dante's *Inferno* and Sophocles's *Oedipus Rex*; he talked to us about Kant and Kierkegaard. Then one day, he pulled out a copy of T. S. Eliot's *The Waste Land* and told us we were about to read one of the greatest poems in the history of humankind.

"'April is the cruelest month,'" he recited as we read the poem together for the first time. "April. The cruelest month. Why would he say that?"

He paced before our rows of desks, and we followed him with our eyes. I knew he wanted us to imagine April not like someone in Florida—where April marks the end of the temperate winter and the beginning of a long period of damp heat—but like those at the center of the world, people in New York or England, where April sits at the end of a longer winter and, in a non–waste land, signals the renewal of spring. He wanted us to talk about irony, and I almost raised my hand to say as much, but he interrupted with another question.

"It's the cruelest month, 'breeding / Lilacs out of the dead land, mixing / Memory and desire, stirring / Dull roots with spring rain'—what does he mean by that?" He stopped, staring hard at us. "Why lilacs? Come on. Think!"

At some point that day or maybe the next, Dr. Whiles got tired of asking us questions we couldn't answer, and he started deciphering the poem for us himself. The first time he did it, we were baffled. Dr. Whiles had told us what he thought before, or what others thought, but he almost never told us how to interpret a text, what one thing meant or another symbolized. When he first started explaining *The Waste Land*, it felt like a slip, an accidental gift, and we scribbled down every word he said.

"Realistic situation," I wrote at the top of my copy of Eliot's poem, which I still have, "a man walking through the streets."

Those streets were the streets of London, I clarified, but the poem could be set anywhere. It had something to do with the Holy Grail, the Fisher King, and also Jesus.

"The man in this poem," Dr. Whiles told us, "he is walking around and he is thinking about myths and Dante's *Inferno* and trying to fit Christianity into the whole thing."

"'For you know only / A heap of broken images.'" He read a passage out loud, looking at us to see how we'd respond. When we stared back without answering, he added, "We can't explain what's happening because it's all we've ever known, or seen. This is our world, folks."

I read *The Waste Land* probably ten times that year, obsessing over it like I had Plato's cave two years before: as if it were a secret code that might reveal an answer to a question I hadn't yet articulated, or a quest whose path I would follow if I could only figure out where it led. And yet, when Dr. Whiles started to decipher Eliot's poem for us, when he gave us the answers instead of asking us to figure them out ourselves, I experienced none of the relief I thought I might. In fact, for the first time in his class, what I felt was doubt.

What I loved in that poem, and in poetry in general, was not finding the answer buried within its lines, but experiencing the mystery within the layers of meaning. I reveled in the language Eliot used, the sense of dread that crept up at moments, the thrill of reading it. I loved when Dr. Whiles repeated lines out loud, his voice lowering ominously to say, "'I will show you fear in a handful of dust.'" Or "'Those are pearls that were his eyes'" and then, more loudly, "'Look!'" I heard lines like that one in my head some nights before falling asleep, as if both Dr. Whiles and T. S. Eliot were beside me, trying to spook me into seeing a truth about this world.

"Look!" Dr. Whiles repeated in class, and then he looked at each of us. "Are you looking?" he asked.

We nodded, but we had no idea what we were looking at. I looked at the desk next to me, half expecting to find Lara, doodling in her notebook, drawing another eye rimmed by long lashes that reminded me of her own. But she was gone. Next to me, instead, was James, or maybe Gayle, frantically taking notes.

"What does he mean?" Dr. Whiles asked one day. "About the pearls being eyes?"

The air-conditioning unit hummed behind him. We stared at the fake-wood-paneled walls and Dr. Whiles stared at us, silhouetted by the sun from the windows without blinds. He complained about the lack of blinds all the time that year, asking us if the state of Florida really cared about us if they wouldn't even give us blinds, why our parents wouldn't complain that we were studying in such conditions. We wondered if the blinds stood for something else. Or if his anger was actually about the sun.

"Isn't it Shakespeare?" someone asked.

"*The Tempest*, in fact," Dr. Whiles said, and he looked happy for a moment. "Same play that gave us 'Brave new world that has such people in't.' Only this is a different sort of world, isn't it?"

The line about "pearls that were his eyes" is sung by the spirit Ariel in *The Tempest*, we eventually learned. It's a song about a death at sea, and the line about eyes that became pearls implies a metamorphosis that comes with the end of life, how a living body is replaced by the organic things of this world: pearls and coral and currents of sea. I loved that notion of metamorphosis in water until I realized where Dr. Whiles thought that reference should lead us. Ariel's song, he said, connects the reader to the moment of transformation in *The Waste Land*'s final section "What the Thunder Said."

"We see here," he said, "the absence of water. There is a dry cracked earth, 'only rock / Rock and no water and the sandy road.' This is a world very much like our own, isn't it folks? And look! The chapel is empty, religion has been lost. But what happens next?"

He stared at us, waiting for us to say out loud what we could see clearly in the poem, how after the cock cries (representing Judas denying Jesus, he'd said), and there is "a flash of lighting"—as there is so often in Florida—"Then a damp gust / Bringing rain."

"Water," Dr. Whiles said—and I wrote down his words even as I doubted them—"means hope. At the end of the poem, Jesus reappears, and then rain comes and there is hope again."

11

I fell into my seat beside Lucy in journalism class—one of the few electives I could take outside of the required courses for our magnet program. It was on the second story of the main building at Chapin, and the setting and mood always felt distinct from the rest of my required classes. There was more light in that room, and fewer familiar faces, but also less intensity and pressure. Lucy, and most of the others in that class were "traditional students," as we called them, and being among them, tucked within the larger population of our high school, felt less conspicuous.

I was about to tell Lucy something I'd heard in my English class, when I noticed a new student sitting behind us. She was Asian American and grunge, reading a big book.

"What's that?" I asked, and the girl looked up.

"You don't know Bukowski?" Her voice was friendly but with an edge. "He's like the best poet that ever lived."

Her name was June, we learned, and she was there, in our class, even though school had started a month before, because she had just gotten kicked out of her mom's house. She was living in an apartment with three friends—all older and already out of high school—in a new school district, so she'd had to transfer to Chapin. She was Lucy's age, one grade older than me, a traditional student as well.

"I'm living in a house full of lesbians so the drama is kinda high," June said, and I glanced at Lucy to see if she'd heard, but she was already flipping through the Bukowski book as if a house full of lesbians was the most ordinary of things. I caught my breath.

"That's cool," I said.

June looked at my pants, at the holes in the knees and dirt smears over the front thighs. They were the jeans my mom groaned about when I put them on, the ones I wore that day with my Bob Dylan T-shirt and Vans.

"Cool jeans," June said.

The bell rang before I could say thanks. Miss Snyder stepped out from behind her desk, her bleached blond hair perfectly coiffed. She smiled at Lucy and Becky, her favorites, passed right over me, and landed on June.

"We have a new student joining our class," she said before asking June to introduce herself, which June did with a nonchalance I wanted for myself. It was like she was there with us, at that moment, but she might not stick around that much longer, and it wouldn't matter to her either way.

We were working on the October issue of the newspaper that week, and Miss Snyder told June she'd be assigned a brief article about Republican candidates for the presidential election the following year: Bob Dole, Pat Buchanan, and someone named Steve Forbes.

"The idea is to figure out which one of them could beat Clinton," she explained.

A girl named Sally planned to write about the sales tax vote and Jimmy would cover homecoming, which I already knew I wouldn't attend. Lucy said she wanted to write a review of Mumia Abu-Jamal's memoir, and Miss Snyder said that sounded fabulous, but it was clear she had no idea who Mumia Abu-Jamal was. I said I'd be writing an editorial about the evils of watching TV. Miss Snyder sighed.

"Did you know," I said, "that by the time the average kid finishes high school, she will have witnessed eight thousand murders on TV?"

"That is unfortunate," Miss Snyder said before turning to the next student. I knew she found me unnecessarily earnest, but I thought she lacked curiosity, which seemed like a bigger sin. I loved journalism, though—writing as a form of service, investigating issues and problems and reporting back on what you'd discovered—and for that alone, I looked forward to Miss Snyder's class. That and the fact that I got meet some people outside of our magnet program, people like Lucy, but also June.

After the bell rang, I turned back to look at her.

"You should hang out with us," I said.

June stared at me before answering. I'd eventually learn that she was Korean- and Cuban-American, but also that she was straight.

"Cool," she said.

Two weeks later, we found ourselves at the Salvador Dalí Museum in St. Pete. Lucy and I brought our friends Amy and Chad. June brought two of her roommates, Kris and Gina. They were both thin with skater haircuts, attractive in an androgynous way that made me dizzy, but it was Gina I kept staring at when we were introduced, at her shaved head and tiny tuft of bangs, at her thin stretch of torso and the bloom of pants hanging from her hips.

Inside the museum, we drifted as a group past Dalí's drawings and toward his larger paintings, pointing out the symbols and the round curve of so many muses' asses, laughing at the jacket lined with bottles of trapped flies. I could feel Gina whenever she was close, and I found it hard to concentrate. At some point I fell behind the group, telling myself I needed more time to look at a particular image. Gina lingered, too.

"I'm looking for more ants," I said, when she moved closer, the two of us standing alone before a barren landscape with ants squirreled away in a corner.

Gina said she was searching for keyholes.

"I like how they show up sometimes," she said, "like a secret."

She stepped closer, and I could smell Calvin Klein and something else—what I'd later realize was the Mexican restaurant where she worked as a line cook. I looked down at her Doc Martens and then at my own Birkenstocks. My hair was still long back then and I kept it loose most of the time, a hemp chain braided into it that ran down my back.

I knew I looked like a hippie next to her, and I felt our differences—but also something else. She touched my arm.

"Look, more ants," she said. She moved her hand to point out another cluster of ants in a landscape that was also a portrait.

We stared at the ants, which represented death, we read, but also— I realized years later, looking them up again online—sexual desire.

"I like the ants better than the clocks," she whispered like it was a secret.

"I like the clocks better than the eggs," I whispered back.

The rest of that afternoon went something like that. We searched for clocks and ants, and then we looked for crutches, pianos, eggs, grass-hoppers, and anything melting: clocks and bodies, stern women lording over men and nannies without faces. We talked about what the symbols might represent, but never in a serious way—not like when Lara and I had once listened to songs backward for Dr. Whiles's class, convinced that we'd find hidden messages, or when Lucy and I talked about mean-ing we'd resurrected from the novels we were reading: *Invisible Man* and *One Flew Over the Cuckoo's Nest*, *A Clockwork Orange* and *Beloved*.

"Do you think it's about time?" Gina asked when we found ourselves in front of a painting of three faces—an old man, a middle-aged man, and a baby—that was also a landscape, as if the stages of life had been written into the world around us, each stage happening simultaneously without us realizing it.

"I think it's about connection," I said. "Or a continuum. Something like that."

"The baby's kind of creepy," she said.

I looked at the baby and saw what she meant. Its teeth were nestled into a beach scene and also seemed to grow out of the back of a woman sitting in the wind. It reminded me of reading, or dreaming, how images layer one upon the next, how a person can be your mother and then change into someone else: your teachers or your lover. But also, how the baby or child or teenager you once were stays with you as you age, digging their teeth into your back while you go about your days, deluded into thinking you have left that earlier self behind.

12

A box of books occupied the back corner of Dr. Whiles's portable that year. Inside were copies of the textbook for his class that we should have read, the book required by whoever determined the reading list for our international program: *Man Is the Measure: A Cordial Invitation to the Central Problems of Philosophy* by Reuben Abel. But we never read that book. We never even held copies in our hands. Some days, Dr. Whiles would point to the boxes that held them, as if we had forgotten their existence.

"Folks," he'd say, "you're supposed to be reading that book. But you're not going to."

Some days he explained why: something about the secular humanistic perspective, or moral relativism, something that would make sense years later but that we accepted without protest, just like we accepted the pile of papers Dr. Whiles had stacked on his desk in place of the books that had been there our freshman year. Some days, he'd pluck one of the printouts from the pile and read from whatever theory it contained: about shadow sovereigns of a new world order meeting on an island somewhere near Italy, about the oil magnet Armand Hammer using his connection to the Bush family to profit off World War II, or about the CIA's MKUltra experiments aimed at developing a truth drug via torture, psychedelic drugs, and brainwashing during the Cold War.

"This stuff is happening, folks," Dr. Whiles would say some days. "This stuff is out there."

We would later learn that some of those theories were true—the MKUltra experiments, for instance—but the rest were either half true or total invention, and yet we accepted all of them, not as truth, necessarily, but as stories that we should take seriously because Dr. Whiles had told us to. Just like we also accepted it when he talked about God in class that year, when instead of questions of the self, he started to refer to the soul. When he rattled on about the perfection of the *Pietà*, how beauty like that is analogous to truth. Some days Dr. Whiles would look over at someone we all knew was religious, like Eric, and he'd nod, as if to say "You get it." Other days it might be Jordan—short and misogynistic— or Hope—sweet and evangelical—or Dale, who just like Eric would grow up to be the pastor of a church. The list of his disciples, as Marcus would later call them, seemed only to grow that year. They were mostly students who had either been religious before or those, like James, who had started going to church because of Dr. Whiles's influence, who I later learned had enrolled in the same adult catechism classes that Dr. Whiles had taken before he became a Catholic the year before.

"I was at a point when I was searching for something. I felt like I was having an early midlife crisis," James told me. "And the way he presented Catholicism, what I liked about it was that there was a way to do it. You took the classes and it was all very ordered. I thought I will just go through these steps and I'll have this worldview and everything will be okay."

I thought I'd given up on God by then, but as I listened to Dr. Whiles talk about beauty and Christ, as I watched more students taken in by what he was saying about religion, I started to question my beliefs in a way that would have seemed impossible only a year before. I found evidence of that shift in the essays I wrote for Dr. Whiles's class that year. The early ones incorporate many of the same theories and ideas that underpinned our discussions in ninth grade: Aristotle and *Oedipus Rex*, Platonic Forms and Kant's distinction between phenomena and noumena. At one point, I argue that "knowledge appears to us after a search, a search in ourselves." But as the semester wore on, I also began quoting Saint Augustine and writing about ontological proofs. Reading those essays years later, I sometimes couldn't recognize myself. "I can see that I cannot be God, or the creator of thoughts because I know myself to be finite, limited," I wrote in one. "I know that it is possible to know everything: past, present, and future, yet I also know that I will always be lacking knowledge that exists somewhere. Because of this, I know that a God exists."

Dr. Whiles put a check by that paragraph: the closest he came in my papers to praise. But on the next essay for his class, about truth and beauty, he corrected me when I lauded the cityscape, the ordinary filth of our daily lives. I had my driver's license by then; and some days Lucy and our friends and I would drive directionless through Tampa, like suburban flaneurs, surveying the strip malls and blinking gas stations, the women walking Nebraska Avenue, the panhandlers and Hare Krishnas in Ybor City. Afterward we'd talk about how beautiful it all was: the dirt and drift of our Southern city, the racket and sprawl amid the swamp. The roar of it all felt like poetry to me; and in that essay, I wrote, "When viewing a smoggy city or an old beer bottle, or a corporate skyscraper, one sees humanity, for these are its products." In the margins, Dr. Whiles scribbled "an aspect of / a part of," reminding me, or perhaps instructing me, that real beauty lay outside the material world, that it could not be man-made.

"I find myself agreeing with Dr. Whiles's opinions," I wrote in my journal at one point, "because I have nothing substantial with which to disagree with them."

Our freshman year, Dr. Whiles had given us a list of one hundred words he said we needed to know if we wanted to understand the world, if we wanted to be philosophers or scholars one day. Words like "epistemology" and "ontology"; "epicureanism," "sophism," "skepticism," "existentialism," and "nihilism"; "a priori" and "a posteriori" knowledge; "simulacrum" and "dialectic"; but also "cognitive dissonance." "Cognitive dissonance" is a term, he said, used to describe a mental civil war. We feel cognitive dissonance when holding two conflicting ideas in our head, which is exactly how I started to feel our eleventh grade year, as Dr. Whiles kept reading to us from that pile of theories on his desk, as he kept talking about God and the soul and the afterlife, and as more and more of our class seemed to be falling in line behind everything he said.

13

I had stopped paying attention to the documentary, and when I looked up, I saw gay pride flags waving on the screen. It was a symbol I had only recently come to recognize—on cars or trucks while driving with my mom, or alone, or with friends. Seeing those tiny rainbows had become a secret game, like Gina and me looking for symbols at the Salvador Dalí museum: each pride flag a brief confirmation that my desires weren't aberrant or immoral, but part of a continuum of experience placing me within a larger community of people with its own history and norms and flags to fly.

In the documentary, though, the pride flags read differently almost from the start. I spotted a couple at first, and then a small parade of them borne aloft by people marching down a residential street somewhere where the sun shone brightly but the music sounded ominous. The documentary we were watching that day was called *The Christian History of America*, and it followed the thirteen-part *Civilisation* series with Kenneth Clark that Dr. Whiles had shown us over several weeks earlier that year.

"Civilization is our greatest potential, our greatest achievement," he had said before we started the Kenneth Clark series. "And then there is culture—everything you see around you now."

He had been talking a lot lately about the stages of art or truth, how we were once in an idealistic stage or integrated one, but now seemed to be slipping into a sensate world or—worse yet—a postsensate one. He said he wanted us to understand what we risked losing, or perhaps had already lost, a warning the *Civilisation* series reinforced. Clark opens by telling viewers that European civilizations had collapsed before and could again. Each video in the series documents Western history, starting with the fall of Rome through the Renaissance and Enlightenment, focusing mostly on artistic achievements but also on religion, literature, music, and philosophy. The final installment begins with images of World War II, then moves to the atom bomb and concludes with a view of New York City, which—unlike European cities, with their cathedrals built to glorify God, Clark says—was a metropolis built in the name of money alone.

"This next video takes us up to the present day," Dr. Whiles told us that morning before pressing Start on the *Christian History of America* documentary.

When he'd rolled the TV to the front of the portable classroom, there had been some quiet groans, but most of us took out our notebooks without complaint, prepared to write or nap or daydream. Only briefly did it seem odd that Dr. Whiles wanted to show us something on TV yet again, as if his long monologues two years earlier about the dangers of television had never happened, as if the very TV in our classroom that year no longer had the bumper sticker he'd put there in ninth grade: "Kill Your Television."

The documentary started, and soon my mind was elsewhere—back to the Saturday night before, when Gina had followed me home after we'd met up at a coffee shop with friends. Not long after that trip to the Dalí Museum, she and I had hung out, just the two of us, and though I no longer remember what we did, I can still see, and almost feel, the moment I dropped her off that night. I was driving my dad's Toyota Camry, idling in a parking spot outside the three-story balconied apartment complex where Gina lived with June. I said something about hanging out again, but before I could finish Gina kissed me. It happened slowly, and I remember realizing: this is why people kiss. It was soft and then intense and it built and expanded, lasting so long we fogged up the car windows—just like they do in the movies. Gina stepped out of the car, saying goodbye one more time, and I sat in our leftover heat with a vibration in my body so frenzied I thought I might be evaporating.

A few days after that, she left a note under my car's windshield wiper at school. "It would be great to have a whole day with you," she wrote. Beside that she laid a wreath made of flowers. I wrote back that I wanted that, too, and tucked that note under her car's windshield wiper outside the Mexican restaurant where she worked. A week after that, late on a Saturday night, we were sneaking into my bedroom without talking, closing the door behind us, and I was turning to face Gina in the dark. She had dark, straight lashes that always seemed wet, that shaved head I loved to touch, and the slightest peppering of zits on her face, endearing instead of unattractive. We kissed again, still standing, until my legs began to shake, and I moved to my bed. Gina kissed my neck and collarbone. She kissed my shoulder and pulled my tank top up and over my head. She was still dressed, taller than me and slighter, too, and I loved her boy-like shape, her breasts so small she never wore a bra. She leaned down and kissed the underside of my breasts, the side of my stomach. When she reached my hip bone, I felt the muscle spasm, as if that part of my body belonged to itself, "like the signal of something right, or me finally right for it," I wrote in my journal the next day.

Two days later, I was pulled from that memory by the parade of gay pride flags on the TV screen. The marchers' cheers were turning to shouts as they left the street and arrived at a church. The camera angle shifted and suddenly, still wrapped in rainbow colors, the marchers ran toward the chapel with crowbars and baseball bats that seemed to have appeared out of nowhere, breaking stained glass windows, their screams reaching a scary pitch. They were zombies, they were a mass of bodies rather than individuals, animals, no longer human. The camera shook; I saw blood somewhere. A voice-over said: "Sodomy was institutionalized to kill our civilization and take God from the state."

The credits began to roll, and Dr. Whiles flicked on the lights. Looking around the room, I noticed that no one returned my gaze. No one even seemed upset. Years later, no one I talked to remembered that video. They would remember *Civilisation*, some would talk about watching productions of *Doctor Faustus* and *Antigone*, but no one would remember the church and the mobs of gay people breaking into it, or the silence that followed their assault. And though I tried, I could never find a copy of the documentary online. The only proof I have it existed at all are the notes I wrote in my journal after the fact. Some were measured, apparently ideas I'd jotted down regarding the biases of history making— a topic for an upcoming essay in Dr. Whiles's class. But near the end, my penmanship reduces to a scrawl.

"I hate myself for hating them for making the video," I scribbled. "I hate the video for attacking me and the class for not caring, but I fucking hate him."

14

When we got back from winter break that year, they told us our teacher for Spanish and French, Mr. Garza, had died. "Of AIDS," Gayle said later. "We all knew that, but nobody said it. It was fucking tragic."

Gayle had gone to see Mr. Garza in the hospital as soon as she heard he was there. Gina had broken up with me the week before, so I won't be sure, years later, if I even realized he was dying. I spent most of winter break driving around Tampa, screaming Tori Amos lyrics into the void and crying. I cut off all my hair. I went to a punk show with Lucy and Amy and, when they wouldn't let us in, I kicked at the metal doors of the alley entrance and hollered obscenities into the cool wet night. The anger exhilarated me, but under that rage hovered a sharp sadness. With Lara, we'd agreed we were pretending, playacting, so when that experiment ended, I could tell myself that it hadn't existed in the first place, a self-delusion that diluted the intensity of what I'd felt. But with Gina, I knew it was real. I loved that it was real. And I hated that she could end it without my permission.

While I was parsing that loss, Gayle was processing something arguably more complicated. Years later she would realize that she'd taken Mr. Garza's death more personally than the rest of us because he represented something—being gay? being closeted? suffering?—that she wanted desperately to figure out back then, but couldn't.

"It was completely inappropriate, I know," she said about visiting him in the hospital. "My mom took me. He was all wrapped up in tubes and completely zonked out and dying. His parents were there, so I talked to them instead of looking at him. I told them about him. How our French class is super small. I said we all love him, and that was more or less true."

What she meant by "more or less true" was that some kids in our program joked about Mr. Garza being gay. After they learned the French word for a bundle of sticks, *fagot*, they tried to work that word into every class conversation. In my Spanish class, kids would imitate the way he walked and talked behind his back. But Mr. Garza never let on that any of it got to him. He always joked right back.

"He was sassy even to the people who made jokes about him," Gayle said.

"He was witty, caring, and a friend," our other Spanish teacher, Mrs. Perez, told a reporter from the school newspaper. "I will miss most of all his sense of humor."

The article on Mr. Garza's death, when it ran a month later in our school newspaper, stated that he had "been battling a long-term illness." But we all knew it was AIDS. I don't know how we knew, but we did. AIDS was everywhere back then. In school, they told us that one in four of us would contract HIV in our lifetime; on the news, they reported that half a million people in the country were infected. A new drug had been developed to treat HIV, but few of us knew about that. We were told that if you got HIV, you would die. At the same time, we were told that only certain people died from AIDS. Gay men. Intravenous drug users. Blacks and Latinos. No one was talking then about the white men bringing it home to their wives in the suburbs. No one mentioned Ricky Ray, a kid in nearby Arcadia who contracted HIV from a blood transfusion and was kicked out of his public school eight years earlier. When he sued to get back in, neighbors burned down his family's home. He died in 1992.

At the funeral that January, Mr. Garza was remembered for how much he loved teaching. He was described as a world traveler who spoke three languages in addition to English—French, Spanish, and Latin. But his biggest pride was the work he did in the classroom. I'm sure that's what most of us wanted to hear: his students and colleagues. Maybe that's what his parents wanted to hear as well. But what did we elide in remembering him as a teacher and traveler only? What about the men he may have loved over the years? What about the disease that killed him? The Reagan administration had ignored the AIDS epidemic for years, pretending it didn't exist and that the people it was killing weren't real: and because of that, the disease was allowed to spread and more people died.

I remembered my tenth-grade year, how Mr. Garza would yell at me to put on my shoes as I approached his classroom. I had turned into a hippie that year, and for months I'd walked around our large, open-air public high school barefoot.

"Sarita," he'd say, scrunching his face into a tortured knot of disgust. "*Por favor.*"

"*Lo siento,*" I always responded, pulling my sandals out of my backpack and slipping them on.

"*No, lo siento yo.*" He'd wave his hands in front of his nose.

I loved Mr. Garza because he was funny and because he made me feel a little less lonely in school. For Gayle and me and anyone else who was gay in high school then, at least in a place like Tampa, teachers like Mr. Garza provided a brief respite in our days, simply by existing, by showing us that eventually we would grow up and be, maybe not okay, but at least here, on this planet, as adults. He reminded me of a bird or a willow tree. He wore huge square glasses and kept his hair cut short. He had dimples even when he wasn't smiling. He was handsome, though none of us would have characterized him as such. There was something permanently resigned about him, a quiet defeat wavering below the surface of his jokes. I wondered if that was also what linked him to Gayle. And me.

After Mr. Garza died, Gayle needlepointed one of Shakespeare's sonnets as a gift for his parents; and one of our English teachers, Mr. Barker—who was also gay, though I didn't know that then—took her to his partner's frame shop to get it properly framed. At the funeral, Gayle gave Mr. Garza's parents what she had made and his mom cried. His dad just stood there. The sonnet was number 18: "But thy eternal summer shall not fade / Nor lose possession of that fair thou ow'st / Nor shall Death brag thou wand'rest in his shade / When in eternal lines to time thou grow'st. / So long as men can breathe or eyes can see, / So long lives this, and this gives life to thee."

It was a poem we'd read in Dr. Whiles's class. I know because I quoted it in one of my essays that year. But Gayle wouldn't remember that connection. She remembered that she wanted to give Mr. Garza's parents something that would help them to remember him, but also maybe her, and that sonnet felt perfect.

After the funeral, something Dr. Whiles said once about AIDS kept coming back to me.

"Some people say AIDS was invented by the government on purpose," he said, "to kill off undesirable people.

"Look into it," he added, as if it were a challenge, instead of an alternative truth we could now no longer forget.

I volunteered that year, every weekend, with an AIDS organization in town, driving kids whose parents were HIV positive to Saturday events: paintballing, bowling, the movies. I gave them stickers each time they piled into my car, and they covered the passenger windows with them, so many sticky animals that we eventually nicknamed my car "the Zoo." I dressed up in a huge Barney costume at a picnic for them once, sweating and then crying beneath the heat of my disguise while they hugged me with abandon. A few were HIV positive as well. At least one of them, like Mr. Garza, would later die. The reality of those deaths was what incensed me when Dr. Whiles mentioned the theory about the origin of AIDS. I couldn't articulate it then, but I knew there was something noxious about feeling glee over a conspiracy theory when the reality itself was still being erased or ignored.

Some time after Mr. Garza's funeral, after the burn of the breakup with Gina had lessened, I began working on what would eventually become my first short story: about a girl who contracts HIV, realizes she is going to die, but then, despite her new knowledge, sleeps with a man with whom she has fallen in love. I wanted the story to capture the fear one might have if a virus had invaded your body, overtaken your cells, and told those cells to start killing themselves. But I also wanted it to show the regret you'd likely feel if you had kept that knowledge a secret, if you had lied about yourself and that lie threatened some else's life as a result.

That story won a local contest, the first time I was ever paid for writing; but more important now, it was the first time I realized that storytelling might be another way of thinking through all the questions Dr. Whiles posed to us our first year, but also the contradictions inherent to everything he was teaching us now.

15

It was spring, and Dr. Whiles again lowered the lights and wheeled out the TV before flipping it on. The air-conditioning rattled in the corner of the portable, the windows letting in morning sunlight.

"Pay close attention," he said before starting the latest video. "You might learn something."

On the screen, we saw a man in front of a podium. He was clean-cut, in a suit and tie. His square-framed glasses retained a slight tint, perhaps because the room was brightly lit. Behind him hung a gilt-framed painting of what looked like an abandoned raft on a shore beside a blue wood-paneled house.

The man cleared his throat and began to talk. He said he appreciated those who had driven out from Southern California for the debate, but also those who would watch this recording of it in the months and even years to come.

"We're speaking about a very important issue," he told the audience, "The Holocaust story."

The portable was dark, the only light from the windows, so it was difficult to see the faces of those around me, but I looked anyway. No one raised their hand. No one protested that word: "story." Years from now, when I asked those I interviewed, most wouldn't even remember this day.

"Just about everyone has heard that the Nazis killed some six million Jews during the Second World War," the man continued, and then he listed all the ways in which the U.S. government supported what he called again the "Holocaust story," including, he said, the Holocaust Memorial Museum in D.C.

"But what is not so well known is that for several years a growing number of what are known as revisionist historians has been challenging the widely accepted extermination story."

As he spoke, a hand appeared in the left side of the screen and lowered the microphone toward the man's mouth. He was short, and up until this moment, the microphone had towered above him. The adjustment prevented distraction.

"For many people, including perhaps some of those of you here today, the revisionist view that there was no systematic extermination of six million Jews seems incredible and possibly even socially dangerous," he said. "When they first hear about Holocaust revisionism, many people immediately react by saying something like, what about Nuremberg? All the evidence? What about all those terrible photographs of bodies in camps?"

At this point, the man indicated something off-screen, perhaps the photos he was talking about, and as we watched him gesture toward a wall we couldn't see, I pictured those photos, the ones we've all seen before: People like human skeletons. Bodies stacked one on top of the next like bricks. A man holding the emaciated corpse of a baby.

"Well, ladies and gentlemen, this reaction is of course very understandable." The man turned his attention back to us. "After all, the Holocaust story of the systematic eradication of some six million European Jews is presented as a fact of history in standard encyclopedias and reference books and even by the United States government. How could anyone dispute the indisputable?"

He took off his glasses and looked up from his notes at the audience before him. Watching him from our desks, we couldn't see that audience, but I imagined what they might look like. They were mostly men. They were older and mostly white. But some were younger, almost as young as we were then. They were sitting, all of them, in uncomfortable hotel conference room chairs. Nicely dressed. Some were taking notes, just like some of us in the portable that day. Some were leaning in, as if what the man was saying were important. In the back, there was a woman who looked like she didn't quite belong. She was blinking too much. As if she didn't understand how she'd ended up there, in that room, listening to this man explain how so much of what she thought she knew was wrong.

"Revisionists do not, as our critics complain, deny the Holocaust," the man said from his podium. "There is no dispute that the Jews were treated horribly."

Then he listed the ways in which they were treated horribly. He said that hundreds of thousands of Jews died, "often under horrendous circumstances" and he added that "many were killed."

"At the same time," he said, "there is impressive evidence to show three things, one, there was no policy to exterminate Germany's Jews; two, the stories of mass killings and gas chambers are mythical; and three, the estimate of six million Jewish wartime deaths is an irresponsible exaggeration."

Again, I looked around. No one moved. No one got up or complained. Some people were already sleeping on their notes. Some were finishing other work. I thought to say something then. But I remembered that Dr. Whiles had told us this was a debate. We would hear the other side after this man spoke. I stayed in my seat.

Everyone else stayed in their seats as well. We sat quietly as the short man behind that podium in front of a painting of an abandoned raft told us that many of the facts we'd believed about the Holocaust had been disproved. He told us how, during the Nuremberg Trials, it was thought that Jews were exterminated in German concentration camps, but now historians say that gassing only took place in Polish camps. He showed us an aerial map of Auschwitz taken during the height of the war, at a time when hundreds of thousands of Jews were being gassed there. He pulled up the picture on the screen, and we all looked at it. It showed a landscape of buildings and no bodies. "You can't see a soul in the picture," the man said. "There should be piles of bodies, and lines of people waiting to be exterminated, at least if you believe the 'story' of Auschwitz that we've been told."

He was warmed up. He spoke more fluidly, with confidence and focus. His opportunity was a rare one, and he knew it. Usually, historians refuse to debate Holocaust deniers, because to do so would give their racist theories legitimacy. The deniers argue that no one will debate them because they are scared of the truth. And yet, watching the video that day, and again years later when I found it online, it's easy to see how just by allowing the debate to happen, that man at the podium, and all the lies and distortions of history he shared, were given a new authority. Perhaps just by writing about him so many years later, I am doing the same. But I don't know how else to tell this story.

The man at the podium said that the Germans didn't plan to kill any Jews, that their "Final Solution" was one of "immigration and deportation, not extermination," and Hitler never ordered any deaths. The murders were all committed by rogue units under pressure during the war, he said, or, much more likely, they came as a result of disease and starvation—tragedies that struck all classes of people during the war.

"I would like to close by simply stressing that as time goes on, the Holocaust story, although more and more propaganda is devoted to it, more and more people around the world have increasing doubts about this story as more facts come to light," he said.

There was applause from the audience in the video as the man stepped down, but none in the portable. Maybe some of us were applauding inside; maybe one or two or more of us were convinced, or at least confused in a way that might make us doubt some or all of the history we'd previously accepted as true.

The man stepped down from the podium and another man, the one who had announced the debate at the beginning, tall and affable with gray hair, bowed into the microphone to introduce the person who would argue the other side. The tall man explained that he wouldn't lift the microphone back up, because the next presenter was short, too, and he was just about to give that man's biography when Dr. Whiles flipped on the lights.

"Interesting stuff," he said.

He turned off the TV and the screen before us went dark.

16

In the days before our next class with Dr. Whiles, I waited for the other side of the debate. I went to precalculus and psychology and Spanish and study hall. I ate lunch with Lucy and my friends on the steps by the gym. I worked on a school newspaper story about the homeless problem in Tampa. I went to bed beside the swamp and ate cereal before sunrise. I drove to school each morning, listening to PJ Harvey and Morrissey, to Bob Dylan and the Indigo Girls. And I thought about the debate.

When Theory of Knowledge came around again, three days later, we all filed into the portable and sat in our tiny wooden desks and looked to Dr. Whiles to begin the class. The TV remained covered in the corner. The bell rang but Dr. Whiles didn't move toward it. Instead, he took one of those papers off his desk and began talking to us about something else—I won't remember what, so many years later. What I remember is a buzzing in my head. It was a feeling I would have again, eventually, when I was much older: the sense that it's not just the individual facts that are wrong, it's the whole premise. Yet no one else seems to be screaming, so I feel crazy for wanting to.

Dr. Whiles kept talking. I looked around to see if anyone else was surprised or angry or even listening, and no one was. But I no longer cared.

I raised my hand. Dr. Whiles stopped talking.

"Yes, Sarah."

"Are we going to watch the rest of the debate?"

For the briefest of moments, he looked surprised. Like I had, for once, done something he hadn't expected. Then his face fell back into a familiar mien—somewhere between knowing and mocking.

"Unfortunately"—he paused—"there isn't time."

I stood up, the anger suddenly so close it must have been there all along.

"You can't do that," I said.

I was crying, though I didn't yet understand why.

"Sarah, please sit down."

I was already packing up. As if we were lovers on a break. As if I were a kid running away. I pulled my backpack onto my shoulder, but Dr. Whiles didn't do or say anything else. Neither did anyone in that room. I walked to the door, fixed on my need to escape that portable, and him. I paused for a second and then I opened the door.

Outside there was sunlight. In Florida, there almost always is, but this time it astonished me. I let the door swing shut and, when no one followed, I descended the wooden steps of the portable and stood for a moment in the sun by a fence lining the edge of our tiny city. No one else was outside. Just me and rows of blanched double-wide trailers parked amid withered grass and a maze of sidewalks, an unending sky above me. I briefly imagined what was taking place inside the classroom. Dr. Whiles would make a joke about me, most likely. Some kids in our class would laugh: his disciples, or, as Gayle would later call them, his bros. After that, Dr. Whiles would go back to whatever he had been saying, or explaining, and it would be as if I had never existed.

I stood in the sun for a long time before I began to walk and, then walking, I found myself outside Ms. Ritter's portable—our psychology teacher, the only other teacher I knew, or thought I knew, was gay, now that Mr. Garza was gone. Ms. Ritter had study hall then, and I knew somehow that I could talk to her. Other students came to her with their problems, about life, dating, their parents, and I hoped I could, too. I opened the door to Ms. Ritter's portable, and inside, it seemed lighter than it had in Dr. Whiles's classroom. Ms. Ritter looked up like she was going to tell a joke, saw my face, and said, "Let's talk outside."

We sat on the stairs outside her portable. The late morning sun wore at the edges of my frame of vision. A group of band kids walked the open-air hallway in the main school building, and somewhere behind us a cow in the ag barn stuttered out a loud moo, quickly interrupted by car honking across the street. Ms. Ritter had lost her normal smirk.

"You want to talk?" she asked. "Or just listen to the barn animals?"

"Dr. Whiles," I said.

She nodded and I told her what had happened. About the first half of the debate and then the second half I thought we would watch today. As I talked, I could tell she was surprised. She lost that teacher face of knowing what to do.

I'd stopped crying by then. I felt calmer, but still not in control. Because what I didn't tell Ms. Ritter was this: I had believed the man at that podium, at least briefly. What he said had made sense to me, or enough sense that there were moments I doubted the Holocaust that day and in the days that followed. That's the reason I started crying when Dr. Whiles refused to show us the rest of the video. I needed to hear the other side of the debate to dispel the doubt I felt. And he wouldn't give me that.

"Sarah," Ms. Ritter eventually said. "Remember you never have to sit and watch or listen to anything that you feel is wrong. You always have the right to get up and leave."

I nodded, but I also knew that in three days, I would have to return to Dr. Whiles's class and pretend like nothing had happened. I would be polite, even nice. I would do my work. I would have to figure my own way out of this cognitive dissonance. What I didn't know then was that after we talked, Ms. Ritter would go to the administration, and to the other teachers. She would say, "Come on. We have to protect these kids." She would try, but nothing would change. Dr. Whiles would keep teaching, and a lot of us would keep struggling to make sense of what he taught. In the years to come, James would become an even more committed

Catholic, sure that his faith would dispel his doubts, until one day he'd realize that the emptiness was still there. He gave up on much of his faith after that, but he would still feel like Dr. Whiles's class, and Dr. Whiles's teaching, had been the most significant part of his high school career.

"I think I was probably depressed in high school," he'd tell me when we talked. "I was looking for something to give me meaning and I think everything seemed so meaningless. The only place in my life where that kind of conversation was happening was in Dr. Whiles's class. And so I think that's why it spoke to me. But looking back, I would never do that. As a teacher, I would never do that in a million years."

Marcus would be one of the few who also remembered the Holocaust video. He'd say he felt bad that he never said anything about it, but then he would tell me something that he remembered from Dr. Whiles's class and I'd forgotten, and it would be my turn to feel ashamed.

"One day he tried to say they interviewed slaves after slavery and they said they enjoyed it," he said. "I was like, okay. But I made a mental note: I don't want to ever be in this position again where someone says something I can't contradict with research."

Gayle would arguably be the most hurt by Dr. Whiles. She would work with him the following year on her final project for our program, something called the extended essay, and eventually she'd get sucked so deeply into Dr. Whiles's teaching that she'd start to believe that parts or all of the Holocaust were a lie. Even though Gayle's family had survived the Holocaust. Even though her mom, Alise, grew up in Latvia going with her father on trips each year to the closest concentration camp, Salaspils, to pay their respects, and in the spring, traveling to a dense thicket of woods called Bikernieki in eastern Riga to hold a collective ceremony for the more than thirty thousand Jews killed at that spot after the Nazis occupied Latvia. They went to Bikernieki in secret, Alise told me, because their trips were not allowed, and when they arrived, they stood in the woods in silence, praying and remembering, hoping their presence on that day might take the place of a historical record that didn't exist. Alise had assumed that denying history was an act she'd left

behind in the Soviet Union. She said she remembered clearly the day she
realized she'd been wrong.

She was in the kitchen, making dinner, while Gayle was studying at
the bar nearby. With her back to her daughter, Alise asked, innocently,
what she was studying, and Gayle said it was an assignment for Dr.
Whiles.

"I said, 'What is this about?'" Alise recalled. "I thought his class was
social studies, and I didn't know anything about it."

Gayle told her Dr. Whiles had been questioning the accuracy of the
Holocaust. Hearing that, Alise remembered dropping whatever she was
holding in her hand—a wooden spoon, a colander, a saucepan, and the
thunk it made when it hit the floor.

"I want to understand what that means," Alise said, and immediately
Gayle started arguing with her—at least in Alise's memory.

"How do you know it was six million Jews that died?" Gayle asked.
"How do you know it wasn't three million or five million?"

"What difference does the number make?" Alise countered, suddenly
angry. "The bottom line is that people were exterminated and were
gassed alive in the concentration camps. Look at the documentaries."

"But what if they were staged?" Gayle asked, and Alise suddenly felt
that nothing made sense. She took a gulp of water and looked hard at
her daughter.

"What is going on?" she asked. "Tell me about this."

That's when Gayle told her everything Dr. Whiles had been teaching her. How he'd directed her to an organization online, and from that
source she'd found more sources, until at some point, she started to believe that the Holocaust was quite possibly a sham. It would take years
for her to process everything she'd read and, for a while, believed. Just
like it has taken me years to try to put in order the memories I've carried
with me ever since high school, never sure until now what to do with
them or where they belong, or even if they were real—until I reached
out to others, like Gayle, and realized that all of it was true.

PART II

"Would His Eyes Hurt and Would He Flee?"

1

It's so hard to believe," the woman was saying, another academic, a writer. Her face was kind but also confused. "Can you say more about him, and about the book?"

We were at a conference table in a basement classroom at the University of Michigan. I was dressed in gray slacks and a blouse I'd bought on sale at Express. The temperatures had been in the low eighties in Phoenix when I flew out the day before, while in Ann Arbor, snow fell in layers covering everything. Slogging through the white landscape on the way to my interview an hour earlier, I'd thought about how settled the snow cover felt—permanent, just as the buildings around me felt permanent, and old, their bricks enclosing offices and conference rooms, some of which had existed for nearly a century. The people in that room with me, academics who were considering me for a position at their university, felt permanent as well. Most of them had taught there for decades. It was one of those places, the kind that invites thoughts of longevity.

"The book is trying to figure Dr. Whiles out," I said. "I see his story as an allegory for what's happening today."

"That's fascinating," the woman said, but she still looked concerned, or confused, perhaps because "happening today" could refer to so many distinct but seemingly interrelated changes: the mainstreaming of phrases like "fake news" and "alternative facts," the multiplying conspiracy theories, the fact that neo-Nazis and white supremacists now marched openly in our streets.

"Where is he now?" someone else on the committee asked, a younger man with light freckles. "Is he alive?"

I told them the scant facts I'd been able to collect about Dr. Whiles over the previous years. He'd retired, I knew that, and was living in a small town in Texas. He'd gotten into nature photography and had a website where he sold prints of his photos of blue herons. He had an Amazon page where he'd reviewed a book arguing that Francis Bacon had been Shakespeare, but also Cervantes. And then there was his dissertation: the whole reason he was able to request that we call him "doctor" in the first place. I'd found it online my first year in Arizona and ordered a copy through interlibrary loan. It focused on the potential benefits but also dangers of teaching philosophy to high school students.

"Does seriously discussing philosophy and religion with adolescents benefit or merely confuse them?" Dr. Whiles asks in the dissertation. "This study resulted from a curiosity about the effects an intellectually demanding high school philosophy course might have on high ability adolescents." The specific inspiration, he added, came from years of having teenagers tell him that his classes "changed the way I look at things."

More intriguing than any of that, though, had been the Rate My Teachers page I'd found the year before. It was filled with comments from students who Dr. Whiles had taught over the years, most of whom lauded him, calling him, as one of them put it, a "great being like Socrates."

"He seeded the youth before the formal operational stages of consciousness consolidated the ego with harmful conditioning patterns," wrote one student, who particularly creeped me out. "HE WAS A HERO TO MY ENTIRE COMMUNITY WE RESPECT HIM AS THE HIGHEST WISE MAN WE HAVE COME TO EXCHANGE WITH. GOD BLESS HIM."

Only a couple of posts showed any misgivings—usually about the conspiracy theories—but that elision was in keeping with the interviews

I'd done up until that point. I'd started by talking to Gayle, calling her up soon after Manuela was born. Once she told me her story, I slowly moved my way through anyone from that high school photo who would answer my emails. Many of them never responded, and those who did often remembered little beyond vague impressions of people we'd known and things we'd learned. Lara told me she remembered almost nothing from high school beyond the feeling that Dr. Whiles had been like a guru, or a sage. Bobbie, who'd joked about Dr. Whiles in my high school yearbook, asked me to remind her of the storyline for Plato's cave. Others remembered tiny details that helped in my reimagining of the past, if not my understanding of it. Eric recalled several of Dr. Whiles's specific mannerisms, including that toothpick he always had in his mouth, and Joel remembered specific conspiracy theories I'd forgotten. But even those who remembered more seemed less perturbed by what Dr. Whiles had taught us than I was. The vast majority of former classmates I talked to, in fact, told me that Dr. Whiles remained among the most influential teachers they'd ever had—even as some acknowledged that he could be strange, and at times mean. But I didn't say any of that during my interview in Michigan, in part because I hadn't yet figured out how to square those perspectives with what I remembered about Dr. Whiles. I was still in the research phase then, so a lot of what would later make sense—once I talked to more people, once I started writing, once future experiences put the past into context—had not yet come to pass.

Later that day, after an interview with a department chair but before a dinner with some faculty, I gave a presentation on creative nonfiction as an act of translation to a group of academics in a small auditorium on campus. I talked about the commonalities between literary translation and creative nonfiction, and what translation studies might teach those of us who want to write true stories. "A famous Italian phrase for the translator is *traduttore traditore*, or 'translator traitor,'" I said, "in part because of the belief that the translator is in some ways always betraying the original text. Something will always be lost, we are told, when a translation takes place, whether it's the sound of a word or the shape of a sentence or the meaning of a phrase that just has no equivalent in the other language." In a similar way, I explained, those of us who write creative nonfiction know that we will never produce writing that is an exact replica of our original text, which is to say reality. We know we are always betraying the truth in one way or another. So what do we do?

I proposed two possible solutions. The first was to try and replicate reality on the page in a way that makes the reader forget the impossibility of our task. Memoirists often do this. They write nonfiction that reads like fiction and we become so wrapped up that we forget about the reality the text replicates. It is what I had planned to do when I wrote about Dr. Whiles. To tell the past like a story, without too much interruption from the present-tense voice, without too many reminders about all that is lost or changed in the sweep of memory making. There is a second option, however, and that is to write in a way that reminds the reader of the impossibility of your task. Translators do this by reminding the reader that they exist, often by making decisions that don't feel fluid or natural in the target language but that represent something essential carried over from the original. In creative nonfiction, I said, we can also remind the reader that we are here, but that requires different moves. A reader of this very book, for instance, might protest, "Of course you exist! This whole book so far has been about you." My response would be that this book has mostly been about my self twenty-five years ago. But who is the person here right now, writing, then rewriting, revising this sentence, cutting that one, adding yet another phrase, writing this very word, and now this one, while her dog snores beside her on the rug in her office in Arizona, where winter never really begins?

Virginia Woolf used to talk about those selves as "I now" and "I then." In her first attempt at a memoir, she wrote: "I think that I have discovered a possible form for these notes. That is, to make them include the present—at least enough of the present to serve as a platform to stand upon. It would be interesting to make the two people, I now and I then, come out in contrast." When you write about yourself, she argues, you are always present, and yet you must be present in double. If the "I now" is the author—or as close to her as we can get—then the "I then" is the person that author remembers being, a version of her in childhood, falling in love for the first time, coming out of the closet, getting married, having kids, landing a job, or losing one. Traditional memoir often works because it allows the reader to feel the younger self's moments of pain or confusion or ecstasy without trapping us in that world, because the older self, the "I now," is always there to make meaning out of the unvarnished and unprocessed perspective of who we once were.

As with most binaries, however, there is something inaccurate, or perhaps dishonest, about Woolf's neat bifurcation of the self within memoir: it assumes the "I now" remains static, that nothing ever happens to us while we are writing an essay or a book. We are all meant to be Michel de Montaigne in his tower, cut off from the world, reflecting on the knowledge and experiences we've gathered within ourselves up until that point. But how often does that happen in real life? I have friends who've gone through divorces while writing books. Others who lost jobs, who gave birth to a child or buried a parent. Do these events not change us? Do they not foist action upon the thinking self? And in foisting action on our "I now," do they not force that present-tense self into the past, into her own "I then" situation?

The short answer is yes, they do. The longer, more complicated answer is that action only exists if we let it into the story. That friend who went through a divorce while writing a book? She let it into the narrative, but she reorganized her "I now," characterizing herself as a divorcée from the start, instead of a married woman, putting her husband always in the past tense, in the "ex" position, and writing about the past through that lens. But my friend who had a baby? She just kept writing, never letting that experience on-screen, never acknowledging the pause in her storytelling that came with birth and the pitched emotions of postpartum. The friend who lost a parent did the same. They wrote while their "I now" changed and never acknowledged that shift. Even if they couldn't stop thinking about her: that person they'd been at the beginning of their books or essays. Just like I will keep thinking about that version of me at that job interview in Michigan. She thought she was writing a book about her high school teacher. She wanted that job so badly. She had no idea what would soon come to pass, and how it would again upset everything.

2

When I told people, back then, the origin story for the book I thought I was going to write, I simplified the narrative. I said the story had started with the man we had recently elected as president and how, after his election, I kept reading or hearing the same explanation for his popularity: how the uneducated and poor in our country had fallen for a politician who thrived on hate, lies, and conspiracy theories. I heard that and I remembered Dr. Whiles but also his disciples. I remembered how smart everyone told us we were in high school, and yet how many of us had believed, or at least failed to dispute, the worldview that I remember Dr. Whiles presenting our junior year: one in which civilization had been lost, a sensate culture loomed in the future, and those to blame were a shadowy government hidden somewhere in the wings. Those memories became the impetus for the book I had decided I would write.

The truth, however, is that there were several origin stories for that imagined book. The first was finding that high school photo when I was seven months pregnant. Like Proust's madeleine, that image returned me to those years with an abruptness that felt a little like drowning. The election that came three months later was another of the book's origins. But sandwiched between those two was a more subtle impetus: the birth of the baby who now is a little girl we call Manuela.

I was thirty-seven at the time. Marta had just turned forty. We had one daughter already, Lucia, who Marta had given birth to via an emergency C-section three years before. This was to be our second daughter, but it was my first pregnancy carried to term after having miscarried the year before, and there was a newness to everything overlaid with a sameness that felt some days like déjà vu. Two months after I had found the picture from high school, and two weeks before the election, my contractions started. Marta and I drove to a university hospital near a highway in Lubbock, where I labored through the night, hypnotizing myself so that I wouldn't feel pain. The method I used had seemed far-fetched, so woo-woo, I almost didn't try it, but I feared pain enough that I would have done anything. Every night in the months leading up to that birth, I had listened to a recording of a woman teaching me how to count backward and lure myself into a trance, to imagine that I'd discovered a beach or a forest, somewhere quiet and gorgeous that wasn't my body as it birthed a seven-pound baby. I had listened for months without feeling like a change had been planted inside me, but then my labor began, and I listened again and the woman's voice restructured time as well as my ability to feel. I experienced pain as if a buffer had been erected between the person I was and the wrenching my body might have theoretically felt elsewhere, in another iteration of that same moment. It felt exhilarating. Like the astral projection I'd wanted in high school, only instead of hovering above myself, it was as if I had disappeared.

Until it came time to push, that is, and the trick stopped working—a magician frozen mid-act, a miracle reversed. With the pressure of pushing—and "pressure" is the wrong word, I mean "violence"—I could no longer find the trance that had restructured me and time and sensation. Instead, I was fixed within my body, and the pain became a body itself. I felt how real it was then, and I told them, the crowd of people who had suddenly appeared around me in that birthing room to help the baby arrive, that I no longer wanted to push out whatever was inside me. What I meant was that I wanted to stop everything and return to where I had been before, a body birthing a baby without feeling the birth herself.

My doctor must have anticipated this fear, because she quickly offered a solution: a rope pulled from somewhere below, I have no idea
where—her black bag, her white coat, somewhere I couldn't see in the
space below my stirruped legs. She handed me one end and took the
other, telling me to pull while I pushed and she would pull, too: like a
childhood game of tug-of-war. I could see us then, kids in a sun-washed
Missouri field beside the blacktop, tiny voices shouting as the rope splin-
tered our hands, and then me shouting over them in the labor room as I
pulled and pushed at the same time, muscles I could not see constricting
around a baby I had forgotten existed.

"Good," the OB said. "Good."

She told me to try again. And I did. Pulling and pushing. Screams of
children mixed with my own. Blacktop and fluorescent lights. Muscles
somewhere doing their work. That red line you can't cross because that
means you've lost. Again and again and again until I lost faith in my doctor's trick and could only focus on the pain.

She must have anticipated that, too, however, because soon the rope
disappeared and she replaced it with a mirror. "Look at it," she told me.
"It'll help."

I shook my head. I didn't want to see the baby I'd forgotten existed
within the pain. I didn't want to see anything. I wanted the opposite of
seeing, an experience that felt embodied in a way I no longer trusted.
But the OB promised it would help, and after some more hesitation,
I agreed to try. I held the mirror up to see between my legs and when
the next flood rushed me, I was still submerged in pain, but this time I
saw the head of our daughter, appearing at the beginning, the opening,
and then disappearing when the pain passed. That sight gave shape to
sensation, a story and a space for me within it. Marta stood somewhere
in the distance holding my hand; our doula beside her rubbing laven-
der oils into my forehead in tiny dabs; and when I pushed again, the
pain haloed, and for a moment everything was what it was. The thing
in itself. Sunlight outside the cave. God. I knew everything in this tiny
universe and everything knew me. I saw her in the mirror arrive and

disappear. Then I pushed again, and the mirror dropped to the floor, and she was born.

Afterward, that feeling, that brief knowledge of everything, stuck with me, nettled at me, and would eventually undergird everything I came to write, and rewrite, and revise in this book. It was a hope of sorts, or an antidote to what had happened, what was happening, and what would soon come to pass.

3

After I flew back from Michigan that year, I flew out three more times to three different interviews for jobs at universities in places besides Arizona. I had just turned forty, the age at which Dr. Whiles once (wrongly I later realized) claimed that Plato had said you were old enough to study philosophy. I thought about that as I flew to Chicago and then Boston and Philadelphia: I should be studying philosophy instead of studying the inane notes I'd written to remind myself of my own teaching practices and research interests. For one interview, I had to take a red-eye, leaving Phoenix at 11 p.m. and arriving at 5 a.m. in Boston with barely enough time to check into the hotel, shower, and run to meet a dean for coffee a few blocks down the snow-blown street. For another, I was so tired I forgot how to pronounce "mimesis."

We were living that year near the university where we taught in Tempe, in a house with arched doorways and wooden floors, a place I loved but that by February looked shipwrecked, everything settling into different spaces and places, rooms covered in crayons, which Manuela or the dog had gnawed to bits, and clothes Lucia had tried on and tossed off, sippy cups and yogurt containers, toys and books and art projects I would feign trying to clean up before heading back out again on another trip with my suitcase full of professional clothes and handouts and flash drives. Most times, when I got home, Marta went straight to bed. One night, after I'd been back for only a couple of days, Manuela woke up sick and I took her to the futon with me in the office, where she threw up all night, and I kept changing the sheets until we ran out of sheets and we both just slept in the wet residue of puke.

"Yucky," Manuela cried each time she threw up, looking down at the vomit on her hands or the pillowcase like it had come from somewhere else.

"I'm sorry," I told her, because she was sick, because I had to leave again the next day.

"I'm sorry," I told Marta when I left.

"I won't divorce you yet," she said in Spanish and kissed me before turning to clean up a bowl of overturned milk.

We'd been married six years at that point, together for almost ten. The daughter of a taxi driver and union worker, Marta was originally from Madrid but had decided after college that she wanted to travel the world: first London, then Paris, then Santiago de Chile, then Beijing, and then, in her early thirties, Iowa City, Iowa. Her brother lived there—a scientist on a postdoc, married with two kids—and she'd moved to be close to him but also to go back to school. She told me she hated Iowa City at first: the quiet politeness, the way everyone ate dinner at 6 p.m. But over the years it took her to finish a master's degree and then a doctorate, she fell in love with the town and the idiosyncrasies of the Midwest. She liked the walkability, the farmers market, the snow. By the time we met, she'd been there for several years. She had a large group of mostly Spanish-speaking friends; went to the same coffee shop almost every day; and had a quick, sharp laugh. I was new in town, recently having left my job as a newspaper reporter in Houston to get a degree in creative writing, a little doe-eyed and perhaps overenthusiastic about the Midwest, about graduate school, about change. We were introduced by our roommates in the winter, but the first time we realized we might like each other was that spring at a rally to celebrate the legalization of same-sex marriage in Iowa. This was years before the country would follow suit, and the ruling had felt like magic. Marta was wearing a leather jacket, and I was handing out cookies I'd made that morning. I gave her one, and my hand briefly touched hers. On the stage, people were giving ebullient speeches: one, and then another, and another. Marta leaned toward me as if to whisper a secret.

"When we passed gay marriage in my country," she said, "we actually celebrated."

What I liked about her was how different she was from me, or anyone else I knew. She once told me that she'd lied to an ex, that she'd told that ex she was a birder when in fact Marta couldn't tell a barn swallow from an oriole, and when I asked why, she just laughed and said, "Why not?" That felt almost sacrilegious to me, but I liked the way it challenged me, she challenged me, to think more deeply about what I believed and why. I started relearning Spanish when I met her, remembering verb conjugations and grammar rules that Mr. Garza had taught us so many years before. I took a class. I went to an immersion program. I read and then slowly began to translate books. And as I did that, it felt some days like I was growing a second self, this new person who could talk and joke and eventually think but also argue in another language.

After we married in Iowa City, after Lucia was born, Marta was offered a job at a university in West Texas, and we moved there because we had to. Marta needed to work if she was going to stay in the country, because at that point being married to me couldn't give her citizenship. But West Texas had been harder than both of us thought it would be and when Marta was offered a job in Arizona, and the university there offered me one, too, we moved west with renewed hope. But Marta still pined for the Midwest: a place she'd hated at first but grew to love the longer we lived in the desert. Of all the jobs I was interviewing for that winter, the one she most wanted—and me, too—was at the University of Michigan.

"Please get the Michigan job," she said more than once after I was back from my interviews, and all we had to do was wait.

For me, the draw was more the job itself than the place. At Michigan, I would be allowed to teach classes that dug into some of the questions about reality and representation that had haunted me for years. But I

loved the Midwest as well. Not just because of Iowa City but also Columbia, Missouri, where I'd grown up. After we moved away when I was
ten, my mom in particular had seemed to mourn the people and landscape we'd left behind. I didn't want that for us, or our kids. I wanted us
to live in a place that felt sane.

I was reading a book about the reign of Genghis Khan during those
weeks of waiting to hear about jobs, and sometimes I'd tell Marta about
it at night when we were in bed and the girls asleep.

"Did you know he didn't torture anyone?" I said from my side of the
bed. "He realized the best way to terrorize people was let the scribes live
and instruct them to write horrible things about all he could do if he
came to conquer you."

Marta nodded from her phone, the news in Spain scrolling before her.

"Everything the scribes wrote spread into Europe and people lived in
fear of what he might do to them, even though much of it was exagger-
ated or made up."

It was that fear, that anticipation of what the Mongols might do if they
arrived, that inspired some instances of blood libel in thirteenth-century
Europe. Local priests and town leaders got it in their heads that Jewish
people were related to the Mongols, and they began attacking Jewish citizens to assuage their fears—even though, in the end, the Mongols never
made it past Hungary.

Marta had turned off her light by then.

"I love you," I said into the dark.

A week later, I flew to my friend Lina's university to give a Valen-
tine's Day reading—my final trip that year, I promised Marta—and the
next day, while I was waiting for my flight back home, she called to say
she couldn't take it anymore. The kids were sick again and she'd barely
had time to work, much less sleep. Our dog wouldn't stop whining and
there'd been a baby cockroach infestation in the bathtub drain.

"I'm so sorry, Marta," I said, telling her I'd be home soon.

But when we hung up, I got an email that my flight had been canceled and couldn't be rescheduled until the following day. I felt guilt that

quickly turned to panic, and suddenly I couldn't calm down. I paced in Lina's kitchen as a tightness clenched my chest and then I called Marta back to apologize for the canceled flight, for being gone so long, for not finding more time for her, for still not landing a job despite all these trips, and mid-apology, I started crying and couldn't stop.

"Sarah," she said, her voice softening. "It's okay."

She told me she loved me and to try to rest. We hung up, and I tried to do as she said, to breathe, to calm down. Lina was teaching, so I was alone in her apartment. I looked out the window at a departing storm. Then I noticed that someone has left me a voice message—one that must have come in while I was talking to Marta. I listened to it and I heard the voice of one of the department chairs from Michigan asking me to call him back. He sounded like he was smiling.

"You were our top choice," he said when he answered the phone. "We'd like to offer you the job."

After we hung up with him, I texted Marta.

"JOB OFFER FROM MICHIGAN."

I flew back the following day, a Sunday, and that night, after Lucia and Manuela were asleep, Marta and I began looking at houses in Ann Arbor. It was presumptuous, we knew that: I was still waiting for Michigan to send me their official offer, and we also had to see if the university could offer Marta a job there, just as Arizona had offered me one when Marta was hired two years before. But we were too excited not to look. There were so many trees in Ann Arbor. So many wide porches and clapboard houses with shiny wooden floors and downy Midwestern sunlight. Marta remembered Iowa City, and the narrow second-story apartment where we'd lived together when Lucia was born. We had a small balcony off the kitchen that looked out over an unruly green backyard. I thought about Iowa, but also Missouri and the two-story house on a corner where we'd lived, the tulips my mom planted each winter just outside the front door that sprung up from the ground in the spring, and just beyond that, the wooded creek we called Pompeii.

4

My parents came for a visit in mid-March and we took them to the desert botanical gardens, one of my favorite places in Phoenix. Manuela wore a blue Brooklyn T-shirt that Lara had given Lucia three years earlier when Marta and I, in New York to visit my uncle and aunt, went for lunch with her. She was a media archivist in the city then, married to a public defender. She looked the same, but she seemed surer of herself, maybe even a bit kinder—not that she was ever mean.

That day at the botanical gardens, Manuela also had on an old straw hat of Lucia's and her blond hair seemed extra bright in the sunlight, especially in contrast with that blue shirt. I took a picture of her sitting by herself on a bench, smiling, and afterward I sent it to Lara. We'd been back in touch after I called her up the summer before to talk about Dr. Whiles.

"We've got the second child wearing that shirt you gave Lucia," I texted.

She wrote back that Manuela looked cute and she loved the photo. I said thanks and told her my parents were in town, that we'd gone to the botanical gardens.

"Haven't told you how much I love your book," she wrote back. "I plowed through a bunch of stories in an afternoon."

She was talking about my first book, a collection of essays that mostly take place after college—during my time as a journalist and then in Iowa and West Texas with Marta—but there are occasional mentions of high school. In one essay, I write briefly about having awkward sex with my best friend in a tent when I was fifteen. At the very end of the book, I write about a scene I will always remember: one day when Lara and I skipped school with Danny and Kevin and went fishing on the Hillsborough River. The image I describe is of our tanned legs dangling in the river's brown water. I wondered if Lara had recognized herself in either scene and what she thought about seeing her past reflected in my book.

"Ah. Thanks!" I texted.

"How's the new one coming along?"

"It's coming along," I wrote. "So weird to be remembering all these things I had forgotten. But it will still probably be a while until I have a full draft. I'll send you part to read once I have it more in some sort of working order."

"I'd love to," she wrote. "Good luck!"

Walking around the desert gardens with my parents that day, the feeling of the past layering with the present briefly allowed me to forget the future, and the fact that I still hadn't received the official offer from the University of Michigan, nor did we know anything more about a possible job for Marta. Manuela had pasted a sticker on her stomach that day and she ambled around with her shirt pulled up saying "belly, belly, belly" in a way that reminded me of my sister, Jessie: Her goofiness, her desire to be the ham. Lucia pulled my mom's hand to look at the crested saguaros and the giant agaves, and her seriousness felt familiar, too. I had been that kind of child: the one intent on watching the world, who always had something pressing to say.

"Have you heard anything?" my mom asked later that day as I was making a quiche for dinner and Manuela was down for her nap. My dad was fixing one of our kitchen chairs, and Lucia and Marta had gone shopping. My mom was talking about Michigan, of course. She always knew when I was upset.

"They say it will be a little longer," I said, trying not to make eye contact. "But it's already been a month."

I remembered the academic job my mom had once been offered and then lost. This was while we were living in Missouri when I was nine or ten. She'd finished her doctorate in psychology and had gone on the job market, just as I would years later, and one day she told us she'd accepted a job in Boston. She even brought back T-shirts and ball caps from the university where she said she'd soon teach. We put our house on the market, began packing up our things, and saying goodbye to friends.

But then she got a call. Her application had gone to the university's provost for approval, she learned—the final sign-off, something that was usually pro forma—except the provost this time decided that her résumé wasn't sufficiently prestigious. The university rescinded her offer. Our house had already sold. My dad had put in notice at his job. I never knew why exactly—maybe all that momentum was hard to reverse— but my parents decided to move anyway. Instead of Boston, though, we moved to Madison, Wisconsin, where my dad found a job. The following year, that job transferred him to Florida, where my mom eventually found a university teaching job as well. But the disappointment of losing that Boston job must have been sharp. I realized I'd never asked her about it, not as an adult. I'd never told her how sorry I was that she'd lost something she clearly wanted—and that losing it had rerouted her life.

"That must be hard," she said back in my Arizona kitchen, referring to the wait.

It was a therapy tic she'd relied on ever since we were kids: using open-ended questions to get us to talk. It had irritated me as a teenager, but as an adult, I knew she meant well, even if I still didn't want to talk.

"It's fine," I said, putting the quiche in the oven. "I'm sure they'll call soon."

5

Near the end of March, we went to a friend's doctoral graduation party. Daniela had defended her dissertation and she and her husband, Ander, wanted to celebrate. We'd met them a year before at a frozen yogurt shop near the Spanish consulate in Phoenix, where we'd gone to get the girls Spanish passports, and Daniela and Ander were doing the same with their newborn baby girl. Ander was also from Spain, but the Basque region, and Daniela was from Colombia, where I'd lived for a year after graduate school on an English teaching Fulbright. We chatted while Daniela breastfed and our girls devoured their frozen yogurt, and when it was time to go, we exchanged numbers. For Marta, Daniela and Ander became the kinds of friends she seeks out whenever we move somewhere new: fellow foreigners with whom she can speak Spanish and joke about our crazy American ways: how polite we are, how easily we take offense, how early we eat dinner.

The night of the graduation party was perfect. An Argentinian friend of Daniela and Ander's barbequed in a corner of the backyard. An Italian friend had brought tiramisu. Our kids ran around while the adults talked about upcoming conferences or recent backpacking trips or how full the moon looked that night. Marta and I were still waiting to hear from the University of Michigan, so we welcomed the distraction even more than we would have usually. We drank and ate and talked and toasted

Daniela and somewhere in the progression of those events, I realized that Manuela had a wet diaper. I found Marta, and she said she'd go to the car for wipes and an extra diaper. But when she got back, she looked upset.

"I got a strange email," she said.

Manuela, on my hip, tugged at my hair.

"What?"

"Someone accusing me of sexual harassment."

I stared at her, confused, but Marta just shook her head. She took Manuela from me and said we'd talk about it when we got home.

"It's probably spam," she said, and disappeared into the house.

That night Daniela toasted Ander for supporting her while she finished her doctorate and we all toasted Daniela for her hard work. Then eventually it was time to leave, and suddenly I couldn't find Lucia. I looked all around the backyard and in the living room before I thought to check Daniela and Ander's bedroom. Opening the door, I found her standing on the bed with another little girl, the daughter of the Italians, surrounded by a snowstorm of toilet paper. I say snowstorm because that was my first thought: that perhaps they had been trying to make it snow in the desert. After that I wondered if there had been an accident, if one of them had peed her pants. Or maybe they'd had a toilet paper fight.

Only when the other little girl spoke did I understand the mess.

"We were trying to pull out her loose tooth," she said, clutching a wad of toilet paper in her hand and pointing to Lucia.

I laughed at that, picking up Lucia and carrying her out to the car like I used to when she was a toddler. On the drive home, I thought how much I loved that she could still surprise me, that her version of the world hadn't yet synched up with any number of narratives I might apply to it. You see a mess and try to explain it using whatever comes to mind first. But often, the story that answers a question is not the simplest one, but instead the one that turns that question on its head.

Later that night, once we were in bed, Marta forwarded me the email she'd received, the one she thought was spam. It came from an address called "burner account," and the person writing spoke in a formal way that did feel like spam, but with specifics that scared me. They said they didn't know Marta, but they wanted her to be aware that someone was posting about her on Reddit. The email included a screenshot of the posts.

"Feel free to use at-will and as you or your legal counsel see fit the screenshot or the body text of this email," the person wrote. "However, I would prefer to remain anonymous and ask that you omit this address and any potentially identifiable information from the metadata of both the email and screenshot."

The attached links were to a Reddit page dedicated to our university, a page normally reserved for students' complaints about grades or questions about housing and parking, a place where sometimes faculty chimed in to comment on a particular policy or controversy. Then, in the middle of all that were two posts about Marta.

The first was from someone called "asulinguistics."

"I am part of a Title IX case against Dr. Marta Tecedor Cabrero for her sexual behaviors with both advanced undergraduates and graduate students," it read. "If you, like me, have been harassed by Dr. Marta, please contact the anonymous email line with ASU's Title IX Office."

Twelve minutes later, someone called "azlgbtq" had posted in response.

"My situation has been very much the same. I attended a party at Marta's house one night, where she got several graduate students drunk and then asked me to her bedroom. When I tried to leave, she inappropriately touched me and I dropped her as my graduate adviser."

The girls were asleep by then, and Marta and I lay side by side, our computers balanced on our bellies, scrolling. Usually, this was the only time we spent alone together, or alone together without other obligations distracting us. Some nights, we were so tired we didn't speak. We'd both read our individual books or newsfeeds and then kiss before we fell asleep. Occasionally, we still tried to have sex. Marta pushed for it more, but when I gave in, I always felt thankful. I would lean into Marta afterward and apologize for resisting so much. I remembered how much

I loved her after we had sex, once we stopped being parents or teachers or academics and became bodies instead.

That night, though, we barely touched. Marta stared at her screen and I stared at mine. I read both Reddit posts through a second time, and then the email once more. It was like that scene in the bedroom with Lucia earlier that night, only this time I had no narrative—rote or inventive—to place upon the mess.

"This isn't spam," I said, touching Marta. She was still looking at her screen. Her face was angry, and I briefly wondered if she was to blame for whatever this was. Not that she'd done what they said, but that she'd somehow provoked someone into inventing it.

"What is it, then?" she asked.

6

I was supposed to teach the second person the following Monday. We'd read Ta-Nehisi Coates's *Between the World and Me* and followed it with Ocean Vuong's essay "A Letter to My Mother That She Will Never Read." In class, I planned to explain how the second person changes the relationship between narrator and reader. But instead of planning how I would teach that as I rode the light rail to my office in Phoenix that morning, I scrolled through Reddit, rereading the latest posts about Marta. Two new ones had gone up over the weekend. The first complained that the earlier posts had been deleted. That person wrote, "The university is being slow to protect students," and then added: "Lesbian professors, too, are capable of harassing students, despite common narratives, and I have been made so uncomfortable by this professor that I switched tracks."

I looked up from my seat. There was a man asleep across the aisle from me, and a woman in the handicapped section who had spread all the contents of her purse on the seat beside her and appeared to be organizing them by size and color. Through the windows, I watched Tempe slowly fade into Phoenix; we passed the Salt River and snaked through a landscape of industrial buildings and empty stoplights. I repeated that line in my head, "despite common narratives." It didn't sound like words an undergraduate would use, and yet the second new message on Reddit was clearly meant to have come from an undergrad.

"Hi y'all," that person had written. "I'm looking for advice. My linguistics professor has offered me wine several times in her office and acted inappropriately when I see her in various queer spaces in Tempe or Phoenix. Should I go to her department chair or someone else?"

I knew that Marta never went to her office—a small, dark space she hated using—and that she almost never drank wine, and yet the inconsistency I kept getting caught on in that post was the word "y'all." No one in Arizona said "y'all," at least outside of people online. It felt like a clue of some sort, if I could only figure out how to decipher it. But everything was starting to feel like a clue. I'd written the day before to my contact at the University of Michigan to see if there was any news about the offer, and he'd responded immediately: "I understand—and share—the wish for expediency here. I've been told the deans hope to wrap this up by the end of this week."

"That seems like an odd phrase, don't you think?" I'd asked Marta.

"Why?" she'd said, looking up from whatever was distracting her.

"'Wrap up,'" I said, "indicates a problem being solved."

I reread the Reddit posts the rest of the ride downtown, and I continued thinking about them and who might be behind them as I walked to my class that afternoon—still without a teaching plan. My students looked up from their phones or books when I opened the door, waiting, like they always do, for me to direct the action. If I had been Dr. Whiles, I would have started with a question. Maybe I would have plucked a pencil out of my bag and thrown it at the far wall. Maybe I would have pointed to the clock and asked if it was really there. But I wasn't him. For a moment, I couldn't remember who I was.

"Today we're going to write a letter we will never send," I said when I found myself. They looked back at me, confused. Our room was on the second floor of a three-story building with chairs and long tables bolted to the floor. Forming the circle I wanted for our discussions was impossible, so most days I sat on a tall office chair by myself in the open center of a hard U of tables—more like an interview than a discussion group. I tried again.

"Think about someone in your life you've disagreed with," I said. "Try to pick a substantial argument, something fundamental, and write that person a letter. The idea is to use that letter to tell the story, like Vuong does in his essay, highlighting the parts that are important to you. The goal here isn't to get angry, but to connect, to achieve intimacy within that misalignment. Write as if you would never send this letter, so you can say all the things you might never say in real life."

I watched as they pulled out their notebooks and pencils or pens, and I realized any one of them could be the person behind the posts on Reddit. Then I tried to erase that thought. I went to my desk near the whiteboard, dragging my tall chair with me, and pulled out my own notebook and pen. I always write alongside my students. I do so to encourage them, but also as a way of challenging myself to write from a different space.

"Okay," I said, "let's take ten minutes."

I stared at my notebook. I wanted to address whoever was behind the Reddit posts, but I still wasn't sure who that could be. An ex of Marta's who had it out for her? A former student mad about a grade or assignment? Someone who hated one of us for some reason I couldn't yet place? I had one more idea, but it seemed so far-fetched I tried to forget it, just as I'd waved away my brief suspicion of my students.

I put the date at the top of my letter. Then I started writing.

"Dear Dr. Whiles," I began.

Ten minutes later the timer on my phone rang, and I looked up at all the bowed heads in the room, the quietly moving pens and pencils. I told my students to stop writing. I had already stopped myself—in the middle of a sentence about Plato's cave, and the confusion I still felt.

7

Marta was in a conference room with the investigator assigned to her case. It was a Thursday, almost a week after that graduation party on a full moon night, and yet so much had already changed. Sitting in the waiting room in that building, the same one where Marta and I had attended a new employee orientation two years before, I kept picturing the fire safety video we'd been shown that day: a Christmas tree catching fire and burning down an apartment in a matter of minutes. I kept hearing Marta complain, afterward, about the American health system and how it never ceased to befuddle her, even after all these years in the United States. "Why so many options!" she'd said. I saw the Christmas tree burn. I pictured those tables of health insurance options. I remembered the Reddit posts. I closed my eyes.

When I opened them, a student worker was giving paperwork to the receptionist, who was shaking her head. As if to say the student was missing something. As if to say whatever he'd turned in was wrong. I tried to imagine Marta in her interview: what she looked like as the investigator asked her questions, how she moved her hands and gesticulated while she answered, what she might be saying in response, the tone of her voice, the seriousness of her gaze. I worried she'd come off as too aggressive, that her indignation at the accusations would be taken as further sign of her guilt. I wished I could be in there with her: to protect her, to speak for her. Or, if I were honest, to control her: make her more compliant, more polite, more like me.

Three days earlier, an administrator at the University of Michigan had emailed Marta to ask if they could talk. We'd hoped it was about a potential job for her. We were still waiting to hear about that possibility from the university, and it seemed likely that the call was to offer her something: a faculty spot or a staff position. I hovered outside Marta's office when she took the call, watching as she said hello and how nice it was to finally talk, watching as she listened for what seemed like too long. She looked at me at one point and shook her head. She said, yes, that she understood. When she started to talk, it wasn't about her research or teaching, but about the Reddit posts. I heard her say that as far as she knew, she wasn't under a Title IX investigation, which is to say an investigation for sexual harassment or assault, and that she had no idea why someone said she was. I heard her promise to figure out what was going on. Then she hung up and looked over my shoulder at a shadow on the wall. She told me that the University of Michigan had credible evidence she was under investigation for sexual misconduct.

We had assumed it was a mistake, or something worse, but either way that we could fix it by getting someone at our university to confirm that Marta was not being investigated. We called and called the Title IX office at our university, and later that day, Marta's cell phone rang. We were in the car, just having dropped off Lucia at choir practice and on our way to get Manuela from day care. I was driving, and again listening to Marta talk to someone I could not see. I heard her say, "How could I be under investigation and not know it?" I heard her agree to come in for an interview. Then she hung up and looked at me. "They say someone filed a complaint against me," she'd said. "But they won't tell me anything else."

Almost an hour had passed since Marta had gone into her interview. I checked my phone. There was a response from the secretary of a lawyer I'd contacted two days before, telling me he'd be glad to talk with us later that day. There was an email from a colleague asking for our help again with translation services for Spanish-speaking immigrants being released

from detention centers later that week. And there was a text from my
friend Lina about the conference I was supposed to present at in a few
days, the one I'd canceled as soon as Marta found out she was being investigated. The panel in which I was supposed to speak had been titled
"Reimagining Real True Crime." Lina told me everyone there missed me.
"You're handling this like a motherfucking pro," she wrote.

"I'm a wreck," I texted back.

In canceling my presentation, I'd told everyone but her that "family
issues" had made it impossible for me to fly out that week. It was a lie
that was also the truth.

When Marta reappeared on one side of the sweeping receptionist's
desk, she looked tired. She nodded at me like we were strangers both
waiting to see a harried doctor.

"She says she can talk to you now, too," she said. She meant the
woman waiting beside the desk.

"What happened?" I asked.

"I saw the actual complaint."

I packed up my things and Marta took the seat where I had been.

"They said I asked for sexual favors," she added.

I stopped.

Marta shook her head. She already had her computer open in front
of her. As if she might work.

I didn't want to leave her out there by herself, but the investigator was waiting. Her name was Melanie. She was young with amazingly
straight hair and a tight smile. I looked back at Marta once more and
then I followed Melanie back through a maze of desks toward an empty
conference room with no windows and a box of tissues on the table
between us.

8

A few days after I moved to Iowa City for graduate school, stories
began appearing in the local paper, the *Press-Citizen*, about a political science professor who had been accused of giving "extra credit"
to female students in exchange for sexual favors. His name was Arthur
Miller. Classes hadn't even started by then, and I remember thinking that
the news felt incongruent with the place itself. Iowa City, especially in
comparison to Houston, where I'd worked the previous two years, struck
me as pastoral, even boring. I'd rented a two-story clapboard house in
town with three other graduate students—all artists and musicians—and
we had a big porch that looked out on a quiet street and a backyard that
opened up onto other quiet backyards. There was a farmers market near
the co-op with some of the brightest tomatoes I'd ever seen, and a walk-
able downtown with a legendary bookstore whose name evoked the flat
landscape and silvery light of the Midwest. A river ran through the city,
passing the building where I would eventually take classes and teach.
Almost everyone I met was friendly, almost eerily so.

As I began mapping out my new life in Iowa City during those initial days and weeks, the details of the accusations against Arthur Miller
unfolded in the *Press-Citizen*. I registered for classes, and four former
students came forward to say he had asked to see, and sometimes touch,
their breasts in exchange for higher grades. I started preparing to teach

for the first time and Miller was arrested and put on paid leave. Soon after that, his wife reported that he'd disappeared with a high-powered rifle. His abandoned car was found outside the wooded park where I'd started to run with my dog, Finn, every morning, and soon that park was cordoned off. Nearly everyone I met mentioned what was happening—if only obliquely. "There's been an incident," one professor said to me. Others walked around with copies of the *Press-Citizen* in their hands and all of us avoided the woods. Then, one day, they found Arthur Miller's body. The woods reopened and his story moved off the front page.

Two months later, another professor at the university—this time from the music department, an oboist—was accused of sexual harassment by a former graduate student, and he also took his own life. The two deaths were enough of an anomaly that the *New York Times* ran an article about our university becoming "the gloomy setting of more trouble and tragedy lately than could fit in a single book." That characterization felt over-the-top, but many of us were spooked, perhaps particularly those, like me, who had only recently started teaching, and thus thinking about what it meant to teach well or, conversely, to teach badly. My first day in the classroom, I stood before the rows of young faces after a round of introductions, waiting to channel the best parts of Dr. Whiles or a handful of teachers or professors I'd had since: brilliant, charismatic, inspiring. But nothing happened. I looked at the clock on the far wall, and instead of asking my students if it existed, I told them we'd end class early that day. They shrugged and left, likely as relieved as I felt.

I met Marta the following semester, and in the months and years that followed, I became a better teacher because of her. She was one of those professors who thrives before a room of inscrutable faces, who makes students want to learn. She showed me how to plan my classes, but also to trust my instincts. By the time we moved to Arizona, I rarely felt nervous when I stepped into a new classroom. I had also completely forgotten about Arthur Miller and the twin tragedies in Iowa so many years before. But his story came back to me as soon as Marta told me the details of the accusation against her. We were driving home after the interview with Melanie, and Marta told me about the complaint. It was an email, she said, sent by a graduate student named Rebecca James who wrote that she was concerned about Marta.

"I have had two undergrads come to me and one fellow graduate student regarding Dr. Marta Cabrero," Rebecca wrote in a copy of the email we would later receive. "Dr. Cabrero has put these students in sexually compromising situations. Inviting them to meet her in her office late at night—when the building is mostly empty—she has offered to help their careers (grad student) or grades and standing in the department (undergrad) in exchange for sexual favors."

That term, "sexual favors," is what evoked Arthur Miller. Marta drove, and I watched buildings pass, but I could see the woods where he died. I could picture those four students. Then I tried to picture the three mentioned in Rebecca's email—two undergraduates and one graduate student. I tried to picture them in Marta's windowless office. I tried to picture her asking for sexual favors. But I couldn't suspend my disbelief. None of it made sense. Or rather, it made sense, but not in the way laid out in that email from Rebecca James, a student who Melanie had told Marta she hadn't yet been able to locate.

What Marta kept thinking about, she said, was how the complaint from Rebecca James had referred to her as Marta Cabrero instead of her actual name: Marta Tecedor Cabrero. In Spain, everyone has two last names. Hers are Tecedor and Cabrero. The first is the primary one, her father's last name, so people in her department would often call her Dr. Tecedor, though most of the time, per her preference, her students just called her Marta. No one in her department would call her Dr. Cabrero; only someone with no knowledge of Spanish-speaking cultures would do that. Marta said she had tried to explain the discrepancy to Melanie during her interview, but Melanie had seemed unimpressed. "I do think it's relevant to point that out," she'd said, before pivoting back to a long list of questions she had: Did Marta meet with students at night? Did Marta offer alcohol to students? Did Marta ask for sexual favors from her students? Did Marta know anyone named Rebecca James? No, Marta had said, no and no and no.

During my interview with Melanie that day, she'd told me she didn't have any questions for me, but that she could answer any questions I might have.

"We just want to figure this out as quickly as possible," I'd said. "It might have already jeopardized our job opportunities—" My voice broke, and I reached for one of those tissues in the box between us. Melanie's face had been impassive.

"You're fine," she said, though it was clear I wasn't.

9

Marta and I talked a lot about who might be behind whatever was happening—because we were both convinced that someone was trying to frame her. We both also assumed, or hoped, that if we could identify that person, everything would go back to the way it had been before. We wondered at first if one of her former students might have made the accusations, maybe someone misogynistic who had been put off by her bluntness, by her refusal to put up with anyone's shit. Or maybe it was one of her exes, someone who'd been holding a grudge that Marta never knew existed and had decided now was the time to seek revenge. But neither option made a lot of sense. Why now? Why such virulence?

I had another guess, but I felt paranoid, conspiratorial even, thinking that the person I suspected would go to such lengths over a job. After Marta got that call from the Michigan administrator, however, and after we learned that the accusations had been sent there as well, my instincts started to feel reasonable. None of Marta's former students or lovers would have known about the Michigan job offer. We'd only told a handful of people: my parents, who were thrilled; our good friends, who were as well; and a couple of colleagues in Arizona and back in West Texas. We hadn't even told the girls yet, because we still weren't sure it would work out.

"It has to be him," I told Marta after she got off the phone with the Michigan administrator that day. "He's the only one who has a motive."

Jay, or the person I'm going to call Jay here, was someone I had known for a couple of years at that point—mostly over social media. We were both queer writers working in the academy, so we knew a lot of the same people. We'd also hung out briefly at a conference for nonfiction writers the previous fall. Lina and I had been telling stories of memorable kisses one afternoon by the hotel bar, and he'd joined us, but notably didn't share one of his own. He laughed at our stories, though, and afterward I thought that maybe we'd be friends, that he seemed like the kind of person with whom I might have more in common than I originally assumed. Everyone I knew adored him. They said he was smart and charming.

When I ran into Jay at a winter wedding about a month later, I felt a rush of familiarity. We were by the drink stand in a crowded art museum where the ceremony would later take place. Sculptures of rabbits and satellite dishes hung precariously close to wedding guests holding plastic wineglasses. I noticed that Jay had grown a goatee. I asked how he'd been, and he said not bad. I was about to say something about the juxtaposition of drunk wedding guests and museum art when Jay spoke up. Instead of asking how I was, he asked if I was "on the market." It's a term in academia that means you're applying to jobs at universities that year, an ugly term that felt particularly unpleasant at a wedding, surrounded by friends and art. But I told Jay I was. Then he said something even odder.

"If you need a recommendation," he said, "I'd be glad to put in a good word for you."

I thanked him without meaning it, and we didn't speak after that. When I flew back to Arizona two days later, I told Marta about Jay's comment and she got mad on my behalf. "He thinks he's better than you," she'd said. "Like he's a professor and you're a student." I said I thought he was just prying, which wasn't such a big deal. He'd wanted to know if I had job interviews, maybe out of a slight sense of competition, but nothing sinister, especially given how competitive the academic job market can be. There are often only a handful of openings for hundreds of new graduates with PhDs and MFAs, not to mention the people, like Jay or me, who already had jobs but were out looking for better ones, or ones in better places. There were coaches for hire who helped candidates write application materials and prepare for job interviews. There were job boards filled with people's public insecurities about their search: "Has anyone heard anything about this job?" they'd write. Or "I've been on the market for ten years now, and it keeps getting worse."

I felt the tension myself, hearing from others who had interviews or job offers while I was still waiting for news. One of my interviews that winter had been at a university that eventually offered Lina the job, not me. It had stung, even as I was happy for her—which is to say, I understood professional jealousy and competition. When I later learned from a friend that Jay also had a campus interview at the University of Michigan, I'd felt competitive myself. But I also found job conversations tiresome, so after Jay had asked if I was on the market, I grew less interested in one day becoming friends—but I wasn't mad, or wary.

Then in early March, a couple of weeks after I received the offer from Michigan, he sent me a Facebook message, followed by a text: "Hi friend! Can I ask you a weird question?"

He congratulated me on the job offer—though I had no idea how he knew—and said he was writing to acknowledge the "weirdness" of the situation, which I assumed meant the fact that he had been a finalist for the job. I thanked him for the congratulations and he responded right away.

"I don't know if you plan on taking it, but they would be lucky to have you," he wrote. "And I just wanted to tell you that. I'm desperately trying to leave where I am now for my mental health, but yeah. Academia is weird like this."

"Don't respond," Marta had said when I told her about the texts. "He shouldn't be contacting you."

She was right. I knew that. But I also knew how anxiety producing the job search could be, and I remembered Jay's recent Facebook posts:

about how difficult it was living in the conservative town in the Southwest where he had a job, about his desire to get away. I remembered
when Marta and I lived in West Texas, the way we worried about holding
hands while walking with our girls in the neighborhood, how people we
met assumed we were sisters or friends but never spouses. Then I imagined being a gay man in a place like that, how it must wear Jay down,
how unbearable it would feel. I texted back that I was sorry things were
so difficult. Jay said thanks.

"And don't feel like you have to say anything," he added. "It's just
weird and I wanted to acknowledge that weirdness that we're both involved and say that I respect you, both as a writer and a person."

I went running, and when I got back, I answered the question I knew
Jay was asking: he wanted to know if I was going to accept the job. I told
him I wanted to, but that we were waiting to hear if Marta would be
offered a job, too. I said it would probably be a little while longer before
we knew anything concrete.

"Totally!" Jay wrote back. "That makes sense."

I told him I knew how excruciating the job search process could be.
He agreed. After that, I assumed our conversation had come to an end.
I showered and got dressed, ate my breakfast while I checked my email,
hoping that someone from Michigan would write with good news. But
there was no email from Michigan. Instead, a friend of mine wrote to say
she didn't get a job she'd been hoping for. "I hate the stupid job market,"
she wrote. "It's so humiliating."

Marta and I went shopping later that day—something we rarely had
a chance to do anymore. I looked for blouses and she tried to find gym
shoes. When I checked my phone, I saw that Jay had texted again: "I
really did mean what I said earlier: you're a phenomenon and I'm proud
to know you."

I thanked him, though the text felt excessive, and I told him again
that I understood how stressful the situation was.

"Keep me posted," he wrote. "And I will you. Queer solidarity and
love."

I thought that would be the last time I heard from him. But in the days and weeks that followed, Jay kept texting. He congratulated me on being a finalist for a book award and said he hoped negotiations with Michigan were going well. He asked for travel recommendations in Santa Fe and told me he was reading Jonathan Franzen's new essay collection. I assumed he was just anxious about the wait, as were Marta and I.

"Any news?" Jay wrote midway through March. "I've been thinking of y'all."

"I promise I'll tell you once we decide one way or the other," I responded.

"Thank you for being a good human," he said. "And I'm sorry I'm an anxious one."

"No worries," I wrote. "I'm super anxious, too."

"Totally. But you are strong. On the page and off! Really, sending you so much love."

I thanked him and recommended a new book I'd been reading, Ross Gay's *Book of Delights*, which I said helped distract me from the anxiety of waiting. But his comment about sending love unsettled me. His texts had felt disingenuous before—especially his compliments of my writing—but the intimacy in that final comment was eerie. I just couldn't quite place why.

I stopped responding after that beyond a brief comment or an emoji or two. But Jay kept checking in. He told me his trip to Santa Fe had gone well. He asked how my Wednesday was going. And my Monday. He said he was friends with a dean at my university, someone I didn't know.

"If you ever meet him," he wrote, "tell him we're friends."

Again, there was a presumption that felt off, but I tried to ignore my unease. Then on a Friday evening near the end of March, Jay texted again.

"WHY ARE THEY DOING THIS TO US," he wrote.

That night, the Reddit posts went up.

10

The same day that Marta had her first interview with Melanie, we scheduled a call with the lawyer we would end up hiring—an animated man named Rashaad who litigated libel and defamation cases but also specialized in technology and free speech. When we talked on the phone that day, we told him everything that had happened so far and our suspicions that Jay was behind it.

"But we can't prove it," I said, after we'd finished explaining.

In narrating the story to the few people we'd told, I'd started to feel like Dr. Whiles so many years before, tracing the connections of an elaborate scheme, one that made sense only if you were willing to believe that one person—or a cabal of people—had the power to manipulate the fate of ordinary lives. What is the rule of Occam's razor? If you have two possible explanations for a phenomenon, the simplest is always the best. What is one of the best arguments against conspiracy theories? Occam's razor. I realized that the simplest explanation for the accusations against Marta was that she had done something wrong. Maybe not everything she'd been accused of, but some of it. It's the story that made the most sense. But not the one I wanted to believe.

"There actually is a way to prove it," Rashaad said.

He told us that we'd need to file a lawsuit, a defamation suit, but not against Jay—we didn't have the evidence for that yet—against nobody, a "John Doe."

"Once we have the John Doe lawsuit in place, we can subpoena Reddit and get the user information for those posts," Rashaad told us. "Then we should be able to tie this all back to Jay."

Marta and I were sitting at our kitchen table, talking on speaker phone with Rashaad, who was on the other side of the city somewhere, in an office we'd never see, a face we'd never meet in person. He was charging us $325 an hour, a figure that had felt obscene at first but that slowly began to make sense in the days and weeks that followed. The facts necessary to expose the truth were available—they almost always are—but that didn't mean we had access to them. As Foucault had convinced me in college, the truth is far from an equally accessible good, not when systems of power regulate who can know what and when. We agreed to put down a deposit of $3,500 and Rashaad told us he'd file the suit as soon as he could.

"We're really anxious about time," I said before we hung up. "We don't know how long Michigan will hold the job."

Rashaad said he understood, but I doubted he did. He'd asked earlier if we stood to lose a lot of money if I couldn't take the job at Michigan, and he'd sounded disappointed when I said no. I tried to explain that the offer wasn't about money. The prestige mattered—the University of Michigan had one of the best creative writing programs in the country—but it was more about the place itself. I still looked some nights online at the thick green lawns and wide porches of houses in Ann Arbor. I still imagined a future that felt close enough to touch: the girls attending some of the best schools in the country, Marta and me walking among the brick buildings and towering trees of the university commons, all of us settling into one place, a place that wouldn't question a family like ours, a place that felt familiar, or as familiar as possible, to a couple like us.

That afternoon, both our girls came home sick. They stayed home the following day, and Marta and I did, too. All of us were on the couch together, one child atop Marta and the other snuggled against me. It felt that day like they were somehow embodying how Marta and I felt: fevered and lethargic, confused by circumstances out of our control. But by the afternoon, the girls' fevers had dissipated and both had enough energy that Marta took them to the park. I stayed home to prepare for my class the next day, but I kept checking my email, hoping for a confirmation that the lawsuit had been filed or that Melanie had changed her mind or that Michigan had realized the accusations were all a hoax. I kept looking at Jay's Facebook and Instagram pages for a confession or a clue. I kept reading and rereading the Title IX accusation against Marta, which Melanie had sent to us, and each time I got scared all over again.

Days passed and Rashaad still hadn't filled the lawsuit, nor had we heard anything from Melanie or Michigan. In the meantime, Jay continued to text, even though I hadn't responded to his all-caps message the Friday night before. He texted to ask if I was going to the writing conference that I had canceled because of the accusations. He texted to tell me he loved the essay collection I'd recommended by Ross Gay. And the following week he would text again: "How are you holding up, friend?"

His persistence felt like proof of his guilt, but then I would question myself. What if the story was more complicated? Or far simpler? I couldn't bring myself to consider what might happen if any of it were true. Instead, I cracked a beer each night after the girls went to bed. Then another, and another. At three, I felt the calm I craved during the day. Marta would sit beside me on the couch, snacking on something instead of drinking, and we'd talk through what was happening: what we knew and didn't know, what the friends we'd told the story to had said or hadn't said, and what we thought might happen next.

"When I told Maria Laura about this," Marta said one night, referring to one of her good friends, "she was like, 'You of all people!' and I'm like, 'Oh, come on, Maria Laura, how many people do you know that, if they told you so-and-so was accused of whatever, you would say, "Oh totally, I could see that."'"

We laughed at that, me snorting and Marta with her low laugh I love. I felt, but didn't say, that her attitude proved her innocence. But that night when we crawled into bed, I thought about Jay again, and how little I knew of him. The accusation we were considering had weight. I didn't want to make a mistake and blame him if it turned out I was wrong.

The following day, I got a text from a friend who I'm going to call Nan. She was someone I'd known before we moved to Arizona, someone who was also friends with Jay.

"Sarah," she wrote, "I feel pretty strongly that I need to talk to you but if I do, and you use the information (which is why I'm telling you, so you can if you need to), you must promise that you will wait two days before acting, and then tell people you learned it from somewhere where Marta works. You can never tell anyone you learned it from me. Is that a tenable condition to you?"

I showed the text to Marta.

"It's got to be about him," I said.

"Call her," she said.

I wrote Nan back.

"I have a pretty good idea what you might say," I texted before promising to keep her identity a secret. Nan called a few minutes later, and almost immediately she brought up Jay.

"He doesn't have your best interest in mind," she said. "You shouldn't trust him."

I was in our living room, walking in circles while she talked, staring out the window at the morning sky, then at the mantel where we'd taped some recent pictures Lucia had drawn: our family in stick figures, our family in blobs, a rainbow. Nan told me that Jay had been complaining for weeks that I'd been offered the job at Michigan instead of him. He claimed my offer was a mistake, that the faculty had wanted to give him the job but were overruled by an administrator who liked me more. Nan said she'd worried that something strange was going on when he told her that, but she'd only reached out to me when Jay mentioned that he'd heard Marta was being accused of sexual misconduct. He seemed excited, she said, because he thought that meant I'd eventually have to turn the offer down.

"If that's true, nobody should know that," Nan had told him. But when she asked Jay how he knew about the misconduct accusation, he had said someone at Michigan had let it slip.

"It doesn't make sense, Sarah," she said. "Something is going on."

"It is," I said.

I told her everything that had happened over the past week and a half: the Reddit posts, Marta's phone call with Michigan; the complaints at our university by women that no one could locate; our interviews with Melanie; and, of course, all the texts from Jay. Nan gasped. She sounded a little heartbroken. She and Jay were close. She was one of a number of middle-aged women I'd eventually realize had taken on something of a maternal role in his life, who were drawn to his story of growing up in a conservative community, of having a brother in jail, and another brother—or maybe that same one—who had committed suicide, and a father who was sick and possibly dying. He was the kind of person, I would eventually realize, that a lot of people wanted to protect.

"It's got to be him," Nan said when I was done talking. "But, God, I don't want to believe that."

I told her I didn't want to either. But that wasn't true. I needed it to be him; that way I didn't have to worry that it was someone else or that, far worse, it had been Marta all along. I knew we would need proof that he'd done it, but Nan's phone call had at least confirmed the facts in my mind. That night I snuggled into Marta as we fell asleep, my nose buried in her hair, my arm around her waist.

"Maybe everything will turn out all right," I said.

"Or not," she said.

She often retorted with that phrase when I tried to be hopeful. I loved that about her. Her enduring pessimism. Her ability to make me laugh.

"Or not," I said.

11

We emailed Melanie the following morning. Rashaad had advised us to tell her what we knew about Jay, and we explained that in our email. Melanie responded a few minutes later.

"I would actually like to meet with you both a second time," she wrote, "as I received some new information yesterday."

Reading that, I felt a flicker of hope. Maybe Melanie had been able to talk with administrators at Michigan, something she'd told us she planned to do, and they had figured out this was all a hoax. Maybe she'd been able to prove that Rebecca James didn't exist and was therefore dropping the investigation. Maybe she'd found out about Jay on her own and had the proof we'd sought to pin him to the accusations.

Or not.

That morning, we dropped off the girls at school and day care and drove straight to Melanie's office. We used the code she had given us to pay to park, just like we had done the first time. After waiting briefly, we followed Melanie through a series of cubicles into a conference room where we all sat down. Melanie didn't smile before she spoke.

"I've received another complaint," she said, pulling out a printed email.

She handed it to us to read. It had come from a different email account and ostensibly a different person: someone calling herself Jessica P.

Newman. The subject line read "Graduate Advisor Harassment." It had been sent on April Fools' Day.

In the opening paragraph "Jessica" said she was one of Marta's graduate students and then she repeated parts of the previous complaint and Reddit posts, though this time with more specificity: Jessica said that Marta had invited her into her office at night, had offered her wine, and spent hours poring over one paragraph in Jessica's dissertation draft. She said it made her uncomfortable but didn't know how to stop it. Then the email took a turn I should have expected but still didn't.

"One night, Marta and her wife, Sarah, had a party for queer students and faculty at their house and offered me glass of wine after glass of wine and eventually shots of whiskey. When most of the others had left, Marta asked to show me a painting in her bedroom, and when we entered, Sarah was on the bed, topless, and asked us to join her. I said I would be calling an Uber now, but before I could leave the room, Marta took my hand and placed it on her wife's bare chest."

The interview room we were in was smaller this time, and Marta and I sat on the same side of a table, reading the email together, while Melanie watched us. It felt like a test we were failing or a novel that had stopped making sense. I imagined everyone who would read or had read this email—Melanie, her supervisor, the university provost—and how they would all picture me topless on my bed, trying to seduce a student, while presumably my kids slept in their bedroom down the hall.

In closing, "Jessica" wrote: "I do not know how to proceed at this point, but thank you for your guidance. I do wish to remain anonymous at this time."

When we finished reading, Melanie said she wanted to talk to us separately. As I watched Marta leave the room, I set my phone on the table to record the interview. I had started recording everything by then, even a couple of conversations between Marta and me. It felt like a way to control reality, to prevent the manipulation of the present, at least. I'd always have a record.

Melanie told me I was now also under investigation and said she needed to ask me some questions as well.

"I want to talk about these parties," she said. "Tell me what that looks like."

I stared at her, surprised that she assumed there had been parties. Then I realized something I also should have known before: she wasn't on our side. In fact, she'd told me during our first interview that her goal wasn't to figure out what was true and what was false, but instead to determine whether or not there had been, as she phrased it, a "policy violation."

"So, there's never been a party," I said, trying not to sound defensive.

I told her the only thing close were two staid dinners we'd hosted for Marta's graduate-seminar students: one each year over the past two years. At the first one, a student brought fruit salad. For another, or maybe both, Marta made a Spanish omelet. I drank wine, but Marta had only bubbly water. We had all sat around our dining room table, chairs added for the extra bodies, and her graduate students talked about their classes, or their projects with Marta, or things going on in Spain or Latin American, while I had tried to keep Lucia and Manuela happy in our tiny section at the end of the table. The dinners were both rather dull, truth be told. At some point, both times, I left to put the kids to bed. After that no one went near the bedrooms.

"And I definitely was never topless on the bed," I added, interrupting whatever question Melanie had next. I wanted to move past that part of the interview as quickly as possible, but saying the words out loud only made it worse—as if by negating the accusation I had somehow reinforced it.

"I'm trying to think if we even have a painting," I added.

Melanie interrupted: "That's what I was going to ask."

I tried to picture our bedroom walls. It felt like safer territory than imagining my half-naked body on a bed. In my mind, I could see the print of a map of Galveston that hung above our dresser and the antique mirror I'd bought at an auction in Iowa on the adjacent wall. Then, I remembered the opposite wall, the one with a window looking out on an apartment building. Next to that window hung my favorite painting. I'd found it at a garage sale soon after graduating from college, when I was twenty-one or maybe twenty-two, and working as a newspaper journalist on a small island in Florida. It's of an androgynous kid in a flat cap smoking a cigarette, looking out with a brazen stare I immediately loved. So much so that I'd hung it in our bedroom—just as the email claimed.

That fact, or the fact that one fact in my life lined up with a fiction that was being built about us, disoriented me. I could see myself on the bed, just as "Jessica" had described. I was drunk, and laughing, as Marta led her into our room. Marta was laughing, too—at our audaciousness, at our power. On the wall hung the painting of that kid, defiant and bold, glaring at us in a way that seemed to say, I dare you.

"There is a painting, a small painting," I finally said, and Melanie took notes as I described it, as if what I shared might become evidence, as if it mattered to her, too, that one fact had aligned between these accusations and what we were claiming was the truth.

"Okay, so, never invited a student into the bedroom," Melanie asked at the end of our interview.

"No."

"Never invited a student into the bedroom and was topless on the bed?"

"No."

"Never asked anyone to join you in the bedroom."

"No," I said and then paused.

"I'm trying to think of other ways I can say no or disprove it somehow," I said, "but I can't."

12

I told Melanie about Jay, of course. It seemed to make a small difference. I could see her calculating possibilities in her head. I could see her rearranging probable facts. I also told her about Nan, and about our lawyer and the suit we hoped to file soon. I promised to share what we discovered whenever that time came, but I worried it would come too late. The end of the academic semester was only weeks away. The Michigan job would have to be figured out by then, and most likely we'd still be engulfed in accusations.

Marta and I drove home that morning, listening to her recording of her interview with Melanie. She'd been asked mostly the same questions as me, but Melanie had also pushed her for details on the dinners at our house, or the parties, as she called them. She wanted to see the email invitation. She wanted to talk to all the students who had attended. I thought about language, and how easily it can slip. A dinner can become a party. A painting, an assault. I thought how no graduate student at our university was named Jessica P. Newman—Melanie had confirmed that fact. She also couldn't locate an enrolled student named Rebecca James. But those details seemed not to matter. Or they mattered, but only as pieces in a larger puzzle Melanie had to put together. She said that both names could be aliases. The women behind them might be too afraid to come forward. She said that she'd written to Jessica, and someone from that email account had written back. Melanie and that person were figuring out a time to meet, and regardless of what proof we might be able to produce in the interim, she told us her final decision would have to wait for that meeting.

I kept trying to locate a frame of reference for what was happening. Sometimes, at night when I couldn't sleep, when I woke up and read the Reddit posts or accusations again, I would chide myself for nurturing so much self-pity. I knew that what we were feeling—that people didn't believe us, that we were assumed guilty from the start—was shockingly common. People are falsely accused of crimes, big and small, all the time, but the poorer or more socially disenfranchised you are, the more likely that you will be disbelieved. Black Americans are seven times more likely than whites to be convicted of a murder they didn't commit. Queer people have long been accused and wrongly convicted of sexual crimes. When I lived in Texas as a journalist in my twenties, queer sex itself was still illegal. We were a crime.

When I googled "false accusation" and "Title IX," however, what came up were stories about usually white, usually straight men. There was an organization called Save Our Sons dedicated to the idea that young men are under attack. There were websites for law firms in which promotional text explained that, while sexual assault is a problem, "what is equally alarming is the current climate of claiming sexual assault when none actually exists." I read through each of those pages and felt even further distanced from the words I needed to explain what was happening to Marta and me, and what it meant.

There was only one experience I'd had before, in high school, that resonated. It was a couple of weeks after Gina had broken up with me, my junior year, the same year that Dr. Whiles changed. The same year Mr. Garza died. It was late winter or early spring. We were at Gina's friend Dawn's house—me and Lucy and our friends Amy and Steph, and Gina of course—and suddenly Dawn found me.

"You need to leave, Sarah," she said.

She had a miniature bubble gum machine in her hands and she was crying. It had been a gift from someone important. She'd told us that when we first got to her apartment. She'd said that she had kept it sealed in its cellophane shell like that for years. It was from someone who died, I assumed, but wasn't sure. And now someone in the apartment that night had broken the seal and opened up the gift. She was saying that someone was me.

"You asked for gum earlier." She sniffled, wiping tears with her sleeve, staring at me.

Gina stood beside her, looking down at her feet. It was the first time I had seen her since we'd broken up. Dawn was her friend, but also her ex. Everyone seemed worried about her.

"I didn't do that," I said, but Dawn only shook her head and cried harder. She backed away like I was dangerous, moving toward her bedroom. Gina followed her. I felt the movement of my jaw as I mashed gum between my teeth.

"Dawn," I heard Gina say. "It's all right."

She'd written me a note a couple of days after we'd broken up, in which she apologized for ending things. She said that she had problems she needed to work out, that she could never commit to anything. What she hadn't mention was that she'd also started hanging out with Dawn again, and even though Dawn was dating my friend Steph, it was clear Gina was still in love with her.

"I'm never constant in anything I do except smoking my cigarettes and getting high," Gina wrote in that note. "You are such a beautiful person and I don't know why I run from you and have from everyone else."

I'd agreed to go to Dawn's apartment that night because I was still heartbroken, but also hopeful. I knew I'd see Gina there. I'd hoped she would see me, see my new short haircut, and fall for me all over again. But she hadn't.

"Oh," she'd said. "You cut your hair. I loved it long."

I'd asked Dawn for gum soon after that, and she'd told me about the tiny gumball machine she couldn't open. She even showed it to me. I'd said no worries, and later, I'd found gum in my bag, a pack I'd overlooked.

I'd unwrapped a stick and started chewing, still hoping Gina would look at me, or talk to me, or say something.

We all got high and maybe an hour passed before Dawn came out of her bedroom holding the busted-open gumball machine, crying and looking at me with something close to fear. I barely spoke at first. I'd forgotten about the gum. I was confused. And high. But once I realized Dawn was accusing me of opening it, I tried to defend myself. I explained how I'd found gum in my bag. I even pulled out the pack to show her, but she only shook her head and clutched the miniature bubble gum machine closer. I watched her disappear into her bedroom, Gina and Steph following, and I realized there was nothing I could say, or do, to prove that I was telling the truth. I stood there in the living room until Lucy put her arm around me.

"It's my gum, I swear," I said.

Behind Dawn's closed door, I could hear sniffles and whispering.

"Come on," she said, and Amy nodded.

"Let's go."

They walked with me toward the apartment door. I started to explain again, but Lucy shook her head.

"We believe you," she said.

I could hear Gina say something and then Dawn laughing as we left the apartment. Outside, I spit my gum into a wrapper from my bag and threw it in the trash.

I hadn't thought about that moment in years. It was one of those memories that might have slipped into the recesses of time and never reemerged—if we hadn't been accused, if I hadn't had that shock of reading a description of me naked on a bed, the shock after that of a moment in which I almost believed it was real, when I could see myself doing exactly what had been said in that accusation. Then, walking to the car to go pick up the girls a couple of days after that interview with Melanie, I reached for gum in my bag and suddenly it appeared— my memory of that night—fully formed. I remembered the hurt I'd felt when Dawn accused me, and I remembered, too, how it made me doubt myself afterward. In the days that followed, I grappled with two possible explanations for what had happened: that Dawn had opened up the gumball machine herself and accused me to make me look bad, or that I was a secret thief.

13

We decided to go camping. We needed to do something normal. We needed to stop looking at our email, waiting for the next shoe to drop, the gun to go off. We also needed to pay more attention to our girls, who had noticed the stress in the house and how tired both Marta and I had been, even if they didn't know what any of it meant.

The day before we left, Rashaad finally submitted the "John Doe" lawsuit.

"It's terrible what this guy is doing to you both," he wrote in an email before filing. "And yet, I'm not shocked."

Along with the subpoena sent to Reddit, he added ones for the email accounts used by "Rebecca James" and "Jessica P. Newman"—to Yahoo and Microsoft, respectively. But he told us it might be six weeks or more before we heard back from any of those companies. I tried to imagine waiting another six weeks for proof. What other accusations would arise during that time? What new women would be invented and sent out into our world to change the course of things? How else would I start to doubt myself? How else would I start to doubt Marta?

We left town early on Saturday, and as we drove into the mountains, I tried to stop going over the case in my head, like a mouse on a wheel, searching for a way off. We got to Prescott by midmorning and found a spot overlooking a pine forest bordered by a stream. On a hike that afternoon, Manuela tramped through brush and over rocks without complaints, and Lucia led us with a walking stick clutched in her fist. I realized I was thinking about something else, like how good a sudden breeze felt on my skin after sweating through my shirt, like Manuela's dimpled legs moving so fast through the brush, like the sound of water falling somewhere we couldn't yet see.

Afterward, Marta dropped Manuela and me off at the tent for a nap while she and Lucia went to buy marshmallows in town. I read Manuela a book in the tent about a butterfly and sang her a song about a boat that learns to sail. As she closed her eyes, I pulled out my phone. There was a text from Nan: "He's stalking you on social media," she wrote.

I'd blocked Jay before we'd left town. I had wanted to keep watching him, to see if he slipped up somehow and said something that might help me tie him to the accusations, but that desire was overpowered by the realization that I couldn't stand the thought of him seeing pictures of my kids. Before I had blocked him, he'd been posting again about being depressed and hating where he was. After, Nan told me he briefly posted and then took down the following message: "Queer family betrayal > bio family betrayal."

"Is he talking about me?" I'd asked Nan.

"I hope not," she'd said.

I'd also hoped he wouldn't notice that I'd blocked him. I didn't want to provoke him into doing something worse than what he'd already done, or what I thought he was doing. But he had noticed—within hours of my doing so, Nan said, and now she was worried. He'd been asking friends we had in common to check if I was still on Facebook and Twitter. He wanted to know if I had blocked him or just closed my accounts.

Manuela moved in her sleeping bag. I texted Nan that I was sure it would be all right, and I tried to convince myself that it would. But I felt the tightness in my chest reappear, and my thoughts returned to where they had been before we left town: sifting through scenarios and plans, like this was some sort of psychological warfare. Manuela held one of my hands, and in the other, I held up my phone again to see if Nan had responded. Instead, I saw a text from Jay.

"I'm genuinely sorry if communicating with you made you uncomfortable," he texted. "I had hoped admitting to the awkwardness of the situation would make everything ok. I guess I was wrong, and I apologized."

"*apologize," he corrected.

Manuela dropped my hand. I felt sick. There was a small part of me that worried, again, that I was wrong about Jay. Maybe there really was someone else behind the accusations. Or maybe they were true. Maybe Jessica and Rebecca were aliases, just as Melanie had proposed. But the rest of me knew he was responsible, and I was scared by how easily he could lie to me directly, and by what he might do next.

My biggest fear—one I told no one but thought about every day—was that Jay would call in a fake child abuse accusation against Marta and me. Sometimes the fear would come out of nowhere. I'd be watching Lucia draw a picture of a sun behind a mountain made out of a coffee filter, and suddenly it would be there. The knock on the door. The woman introducing herself to us. The panic as we tried to reach Rashaad. Some days I could almost smell the caseworker's perfume, hear her polite request to interview each child separately, alone in a room where we weren't. I thought about our house. All the toys we hadn't found time to pick up. The stink of Manuela's last diaper in the kitchen trash. The bruise on her knee from falling down at day care. The hysterical way Lucia cried sometimes when she didn't get what she wanted.

Manuela opened her eyes and snuggled into me. She asked me to sing her "Irene, Good night." It was a song I'd sung to her since she was a baby, a song my mom used to sing to me. I'd never told her what the song was really about: a person who's so sad about a lost love that he contemplates suicide. Just like I'd also never explained to Lucia the meaning of "Tom Dooley," the murder ballad that always calmed her crying when she was young. The stories within those songs never mattered to me if singing them succeeded in soothing my girls, in putting them to sleep. And they didn't matter to me in that moment either. Holding Manuela's hand again, I let go of my phone, of Jay and Nan and all of those stories, and started singing about Irene. I watched the trees make shadows on the walls of the tent and the sun sneak in between their weight. But neither of us could sleep.

14

When we got back from camping, Melanie wrote to ask for another meeting. She said she had new information. Again. And again, we hoped that meant she was closing the case, that she had caught Jay and that this would all be over and we could return to normal.

Instead, Melanie said that she'd been able to talk to someone at Michigan, and they'd sent her all the emails they'd received.

"Emails?" I thought. We had assumed there was just one.

Melanie had them stacked in a folder in front of her, though I couldn't see them, or her, or the rest of the conference room where she sat. I had to teach in Phoenix that afternoon, so I called from my office downtown, trying to picture it all while I stared at my neat desk. Marta was there, across the table from Melanie, facing the stack of printed emails. Like the stacks of conspiracy theories Dr. Whiles used to pick up and read to us in class.

"What are you going to do about this, folks?" he would ask.

The first email had been sent to an administrator at the University of Michigan on March 6, Melanie said.

"That was the day after Jay texted me about the job," I interrupted, and Melanie said she knew that. It had come from the same email account used by Rebecca James. Only this time the writer said she was a colleague of Marta's named Professor Orlich.

"I wanted to make you aware, especially in this moment of reconciliation for folks who abuse their positions, that we are investigating three credible allegations against [Marta] for putting students in sexually abusive and compromising situations," Professor Orlich wrote to that Michigan administrator. "That is all I can say, but I did not want our problem to become your problem, and I firmly believe universities need to be more in contact about these issues."

The next two emails were also from Professor Orlich to that same administrator: in one she claimed to be in Prague for a conference and wrote to say that she'd had a recent Skype meeting about Marta's transgressions. In another she said she wouldn't be writing again, but that she hoped her warnings would be taken seriously.

Listening to Melanie read those emails aloud, my brain kept getting tripped up on details, on the small inconsistencies that felt manageable if not egregious. Why was "Professor Orlich" in Prague? I thought. Why would she Skype into a Title IX interview? It was like a kid asking why Santa arrives via the chimney instead of the door. You want to deconstruct the larger fantasy, but you begin with small bits. Skype and Prague instead of that one line in Professor Orlich's final email that still upsets me to read: "Marta's behavior," she wrote, "has been abhorrent."

I later learned that the University of Michigan had been about to send me their official job offer when those emails from Professor Orlich arrived. Instead, they held off—while they debated what to do, I assume. In that interim, "Professor Orlich" disappeared and "Jessica P. Newman" showed up, emailing a different administrator this time.

"I hate to email you like this, but I could not remain silent any longer," Jessica wrote in her first email on March 14, almost two weeks before we learned about the accusations. "Dr. Cabrero should not be working with students, and I shudder at the thought that this problem will leap from university to university. It is, I have now found out through a graduate colleague, why she left her previous university as well—the sexual manipulation of students under the guise of mentorship."

That administrator responded—though Melanie didn't have copies of what he said—and at some point, he must have asked for more information because emails from Jessica over the following days and weeks included copies of the Reddit posts and a screenshot of a supposed email between two of Marta's colleagues discussing her removal from a dissertation committee "given the recent investigation into Dr. Cabrero's relationship with students in our program."

"This is getting crazy," Marta said at one point, after Melanie had finished reading the screenshot out loud. I wished I was there, holding Marta's hand under the table or leaning into her while we listened to Melanie read email after email, these stories that had been piling up in other people's inboxes, building a fictional reality there about Marta, for weeks.

"The reason I've called you both here today," Melanie eventually said, "is because Michigan just received another email from Jessica this past Friday."

That email, she told us, was titled "Text tonight," and in it, Jessica wrote, "I am turning this over to the authorities and wanted your administration to have this text message from Marta as well."

Over the phone, I heard Marta interrupt Melanie.

"Someone says they have a text message from me?"

She sounded concerned and confused. Later she would tell me that this was the moment in the meeting that she first felt scared.

Melanie said yes, and then she read out loud what she told us was a screenshot of that text:

MARTA: Jessica we need to talk.

JESSICA: Please stop contacting me. All communication needs to be processed through the Title IX coordinator, as you know.

MARTA: We will ruin your career. I will make sure you never get a job once your dissertation is done. My wife and I are well connected.

I heard Marta exhale loudly and I tried again to picture her face. I knew what she looked like when she was upset. I could tell, too, when she was mad. But this was something different. It was disbelief bordering on hilarity. It was bewilderment. And panic.

"I know," Melanie eventually said, her voice a little less professional, a little more consoling. "I understand."

She told us that she'd checked all the facts laid out in those emails and disproved them one by one: There was a Professor Orlich in Marta's department, but she hadn't sent any emails about Marta to Michigan. There was never a Skype call to Prague for a Title IX case—nor would there ever be, Melanie said. Marta's colleagues had denied sending any emails about her being taken off a dissertation committee. And Melanie still hadn't been able to find anyone at our university named Jessica P. Newman.

I felt something tight in me release.

"Does this mean," I paused, "that at this point you can actually close the investigation?"

Melanie paused, too, and I tried to imagine her face. Did she look hopeful? Apologetic? Concerned? I thought that she would say yes, that we would end that meeting knowing that this story had finally come to an end. But then I heard her say no.

Jessica had agreed to meet with her in person the following week, she reminded us. And even though we now knew that Jessica didn't exist, Melanie said she still had an obligation to see if the person who said she was Jessica would show up for the appointment she'd made.

15

I drank too much again that night and woke up early the next morning from a dream that Marta was having an affair—or I suspected she was. In the dream, she had plans to see old friends at the beach that she hadn't told me about, and she was strangely excited, like you are when you like someone new. I watched her smile as she packed a bag and I knew she was lying to me, but I didn't say anything.

Later that day, we both got emails from the University of Michigan letting us know that my job offer and the search for a job for Marta had been put on hold, "until the investigation by the Title IX office has been completed." I thought at first the email was a mistake. Melanie had shared all of her fact-checking with Michigan. I assumed that would be enough to prove our innocence, even if Melanie was still waiting to see if Jessica would show up for her interview. But it wasn't. Administrators at the University of Michigan had decided that they needed to see Melanie's official report clearing both Marta and me of any wrongdoing. And that wouldn't come until Jessica did or did not show up to talk with Melanie. Which meant we had to wait.

While we waited, Marta and I began to fight. It was mostly about strategy, or how to regain control of the narrative. She wanted to write to the president of our university. To get Rashaad to push the lawyers at our university to go after Jay for defamation or slander. She wanted to write Melanie again, and again. I wanted to hold back. To try to be nice.

"Nothing has changed," she said. "This keeps going on."

"We have to be patient," I said.

But the next day, it would be me who wanted to push: to write to the associate dean or the English chair at the University of Michigan and ask why they needed something official from Melanie when it was so clear that they'd been had. I drafted elaborate emails to each of them explaining again why Marta was innocent, why the job offer and search should be reopened, why this all needed to stop, but then I would show what I'd written to Marta and she'd shake her head.

"You sound desperate," she'd say.

"I am!"

I'd seethe afterward, angry at her for holding me back, for seeing things differently than I did. I'd say she was dismissing me for being too calculating. She'd say I dismissed her for being too anxious or enraged. One night that week, as we fought again over strategy, I got so angry I screamed.

"We have to stop fighting," I said into the silence that followed.

The girls were in the bath and they stopped playing, their splashing silent. Lucia called out, "What's going on?"

"It's fine," I yelled.

But it wasn't fine. We weren't fine.

We stopped talking at night, scrolling alone through the news or emails from our individual sides of the bed. In the morning we were rumpled and tired. I texted Lina that I was worried about Marta, and how fragile she suddenly seemed. But I was also worried about myself.

"I really feel like I can't keep doing this any longer," I texted at one point. "I'm just paralyzed all the time."

A few days after our interview with Melanie, I got home after dropping off the kids at day care and school and found Marta outside our house, pacing. She told me she'd been calling me for the past half hour, but my ringer wasn't on.

"What happened?" I asked.

"Melanie called again."

Her voice was flat.

She said that Melanie had called her soon after I'd left the house that morning. She told Marta that Jessica had written again, and this time she was claiming Marta had showed up at her apartment unannounced the Monday before and demanded she be let in. Jessica said she was so scared she was leaving the country. She told Melanie she planned to defend her dissertation from Spain.

"But we met with Melanie that same day," I said when Marta stopped talking. It was a Thursday. That Monday morning, Melanie had been reading those emails from Michigan to us aloud.

"Jessica says it was Monday afternoon," Marta said. "We met her in the morning, so now Melanie wants to know what I did that afternoon."

She was shaking. I wanted to reach for her, but for some reason I didn't.

"Sarah," she said, "I couldn't remember. I said I thought I was home working, but I really couldn't remember."

I stared at her. I knew that Marta hadn't gone to Jessica's apartment. I knew that Jessica didn't exist. But Marta also didn't know where she had been on Monday afternoon. That was only three days before. I'd been teaching in downtown Phoenix that afternoon. I rode the light rail home late after class, texting with Lina about our meeting with Melanie and my hope that everything would soon be resolved. When I got home that evening, Marta was already there with Lucia and Manuela, making dinner. But where had she been all afternoon?

We were in her office by that point, and I stood by her desk, looking down at her in her chair. I could hear the neighbors park their car outside. I felt the stick of my sweat from the morning heat. I tried not to say what I was thinking.

"My phone!" Marta suddenly broke the silence.

She pulled out her iPhone and began scrolling through the GPS data. After a minute, she found a little blue dot that showed that she had, in fact, been inside our house that whole afternoon. Until about 4:30, when she went to get the kids.

I felt my chest release and my shoulders lower. But below that relief was a feeling I couldn't shake. Because even though I knew Marta's phone had proved she was telling the truth, even though I knew I should have believed her without that proof, a tiny voice in my head kept asking insistently, "But what if she left her phone at home?"

16

What is true? And how do you know? Those were the questions Dr. Whiles asked us to ask ourselves my freshman year, the kind of questions that many teenagers ask themselves anyway. It is the most bewildering time: coming-of-age, we call it in novels. That spring, at forty, I felt like I had been wrested back into that world. It is easier to slip out of logic and into delusion than a lot of us want to believe. All you need is for one person to start lying, and a system—a high school, an investigation, a government—to legitimize that fiction. All you need is for that to go on for a little longer than you could have predicted. For you to get tired enough to doubt yourself, or others. Then suddenly you're a teenager again, writing frantically in her journal late at night: "I'm so confused. Is everyone?"

That doubt—of myself, and Marta, and our reality—only quieted when I focused on Jay: as a person, or a character. I imagined him some days in the conservative city where he lived, in an apartment alone with his dog, a pit bull mix whom he adored. I'd picture him after a department meeting or teaching, giving his dog a pet, hanging up his coat or putting away his books, and then opening his laptop at the kitchen table and pulling up the email account for Jessica. I wondered if he got drunk before sending each new email. I wondered if he told anyone what he was doing. I wondered how he'd thought to do it in the first place. Had he done this to someone else before?

I had obsessed in a similar way over Dr. Whiles—before Jay interrupted the story I once thought I was telling. I'd searched for him online. I'd scrutinized his reviews on Amazon, his photos of blue herons
and Texas flowers, his scant Facebook posts and short friends list, just
as I would later pore over Jay's social media posts—looking for clues.
I'd imagined him going about his life, just as I would later imagine Jay
doing the same. Dr. Whiles would live alone, I decided, in a tidy condo in
the small Texas town where he had retired. I saw him tromping through
mangroves, a camera in hand, or in his living room, reading, maybe from
a text he had once taught us—Dante's *Inferno* or *Brave New World*.
Whenever I pictured him like that, I rendered him tinged by remorse—
for what he had taught us, the way he had led some of us astray. I had
no idea if that was even close to true. Maybe Dr. Whiles never thought
about us at all. Maybe he was at peace with his acts and his beliefs.
Maybe Jay was, too.

"Make your characters want something right away even if it's only a
glass of water," Kurt Vonnegut famously advised. "Characters paralyzed by
the meaninglessness of modern life still have to drink water from time to
time." He was talking about motivation, what some creative writing teachers refer to as "the stakes" of a story. Characters need to want something
they can't yet have; that way we as readers will want to follow their story,
waiting to see if their wish is fulfilled—or dashed. But you can understand
what a character, what a person, wants, and still have no clue who he is.
With Dr. Whiles, I felt I understood who he was, at least as a teacher in the
1990s, but his motivation baffled me. Did he actually believe that a Jewish
cabal secretly ruled the world? Was he racist and homophobic? Did he
think Catholicism was the way out of the cave? Or was everything he had
done part of a plot to make us question ourselves and our beliefs? Was it
possible he wanted the best for us, in some twisted way?

With Jay, his motivation couldn't be clearer, but I still had no idea
who he was. I knew he grew up poor in southern Missouri, part of an
Evangelical community, and later wrote a dissertation on white hipsters
and literature. I knew he sometimes called himself a little otter, and that

at one point, he was learning to knit. People who knew him said he was sweet and funny, but that sometimes he could be catty. Once or twice, he had mentioned the idea of betrayal—that so-and-so had betrayed him—and Nan wondered later if that perspective allowed him to go after Marta and me without any apparent guilt. Perhaps he convinced himself that I had betrayed him, too, she said, by not letting go of the job when he thought I should have, by being offered it in the first place.

"He's completely delusional right now," Nan texted me in late April. "He must have convinced himself he's done nothing wrong."

Friends who didn't know Jay would hear our story and try to diagnose him from afar—calling him a narcissist or a psychopath, a pathological liar or sociopath—none of which helped clarify Jay in my mind, at least not beyond the two-dimensional character I already had situated there. But I collected all of the information I was given as if it were sacred. The better I understood him, I reasoned, the easier it would be to predict what he might do next. But also, the easier it was to remember that I trusted Marta, and myself, and that everything being built around us was a lie.

Then, around the middle of April—as we waited for Melanie to finish her investigation—Jay learned about our lawsuit. When Nan told me that he knew, I wondered at first if the news would scare him into confessing, or at least stop him from writing more emails, posting anything else about us, or doing something worse. Instead, he told Nan later that day that he had gone to the Reddit page for his own university and, to his surprise, found a post about himself there—one that had gone up that very day. It was titled "English Prof Gay," and the person posting called him a flamer who flirted with his students.

"God, that laugh of his is too gay," they wrote. "I bet he's trolling all that D-1 dick."

The next day, another post appeared, ostensibly by the same person—someone whose handle indicated they were a member of a local fraternity.

"Stop Hiring F*g Professors," that person wrote before naming both

Jay and another gay professor at his university. "You need to figure this out before the whole campus is gay."

"This is insane," I texted after Nan forwarded me the first Reddit post. "It's terrible," she wrote back. "He's very sick."

The day after that, Jay told Nan that he'd found an anonymous letter in his university mailbox that read "DIE FAG PROFESSOR." The university police showed up to investigate. People at Jay's college, especially other gay faculty, started to get scared. Jay began telling people that an anonymous Title IX accusation had been filed against him, too. It claimed he showed gay porn in his class and gave lower grades to anyone who refused to write about gay topics.

"That's a classic horror movie move!" Lina said when I told her what was happening. "The villain injures himself."

I laughed, but I was scared—for Marta and me, and more so for Nan. She lived in the same town as Jay, and she'd decided not to confront him about what she knew he was doing. That way, she told me, she could let me know if he did or said anything that seemed suspicious. She wanted to protect Marta and me, which had felt like a buoy in the night. She was someone who believed us, who could help. But for Nan, that position had started to feel untenable. Jay told her about each new attack he said he was facing, and she felt like she had to feign concern.

"I can't keep up this charade much longer," she told me after the Reddit posts about him went up. "He scares the shit out of me. As soon as he finds out I'm the betrayer, there's no telling what he'll do."

I told her to protect herself and that Marta and I would be fine, but Nan felt stuck. If she told Jay the truth, she worried he'd go after her—either online, as he had us, or possibly in person. She never thought he was capable of violence, but nothing he'd done so far had been predictable. She told me she'd keep up the ruse, at least until we had proof from our lawsuit, at least until there was something solid with which to accuse Jay, with which to make him stop.

17

O n the last day of classes that semester, a few minutes before 5 p.m., we received an email from the provost of our university: The case against us had closed. The attached two-page report spelled out all the facts Melanie been able to prove over the previous month and a half.

"The preponderance of evidence," she wrote, "shows that the person who submitted the complaints as R.J. and J.N. was pretending to be a faculty member and/or students and raised false allegations against Respondents 1 and 2."

She added that both Marta and I had "credibly denied all the allegations," which I realized was as close as Melanie would get to saying, "I believe you." We went to a friend's house that night and celebrated with a swim in her pool and macaroni and cheese for the girls. The next day, we drove up into the mountains again to camp. We roasted marshmallows, went on a long dusty hike, and read books together in the tent. Then that Sunday, as we were packing up our sleeping bags, I looked at my phone and saw an email from the University of Michigan. Attached was my official job offer—more than two and a half months after I got the call saying I was the top pick for the position. The job search for Marta had also restarted. We danced around in the woods after I read the email out loud, whooping like they do in movies following a big win. The girls whooped with us, though they had no idea why.

We drove back home later that day and FaceTimed my parents to tell them the news: of the investigation closing and the job offer arriving.

"Oh, Sarah," my dad said.

"What a relief," my mom added.

They'd been checking in on me every once in a while, worried, I knew, but also trying not to overwhelm us by asking for updates. I realized as Lucia showed them the rocks she'd been collecting and Manuela babbled on about the snake she'd seen on our hike that they had been part of a small team who had gathered around us over the previous month. We had Nan, of course, who I'd already texted with the news. We had friends in town who had made us dinner or offered to watch the kids. We had Lina, who sent me bags of popcorn and a little stuffed opossum, who texted me images of baby sloths to distract me from the looming threat of Jay and what he might do.

"Maybe it's gonna be all right," I told Marta before we went to bed.

"Or not," she said.

In the days that followed, we began to box up our house, the one with the arched doorways and wooden floors, but also the cockroach infestations. Our lease was up in June, and we still weren't sure if we would be in Arizona in the fall, so we'd decided not to renew for another year. We began putting books and toys into boxes, moving our way into a physical limbo after just having extricated ourselves from an emotional one.

One day, when more than half of our house was boxed up, we received an email from our law firm with the first response to our subpoenas. Attached was the user information from the Yahoo email account for both "Rebecca Newman" and later "Professor Orlich." The released information was a mere three pages and, at first, we thought it contained nothing important. I saw only an IP address and some basic information about the person who supposedly opened the account, someone named Rebecca Orlich. But just as Marta was walking away from the kitchen table, ready to give up, I noticed a line for a phone number. It said, "account verified by," and then listed a number.

"Marta," I said too loudly, "where's my phone?"

I was shaking as I tried to call up Jay's last message so I could scroll to his phone number. I was nervous I'd accidentally call him. I felt like I was doing something wrong.

Finally, I got it up, and there it was: an exact match.

Jay's phone had been used to verify the email account. The account had been opened the same day he texted me about the job in Michigan. And the IP addresses, when we checked, were all from the town where Jay lived.

"We've got him," I said.

"Motherfucker!" Marta said.

For a moment, I felt triumphant. We had discovered the truth, I thought, and now everything else would tumble into place. We would name Jay in our lawsuit and then he'd settle with us and apologize: to us, to Nan, to the rest of the world. Marta and I would accept jobs in Michigan, and we'd move into a cozy two-story house with a green lawn that snow would slowly cover that winter. The girls would build a snowman out front and we would watch them from the porch, drinking coffee and laughing, barely remembering the spring before when everything had turned upside down. We would stare up at the delicacy of the winter sunlight and maybe hold hands.

But that wasn't what happened.

We named Jay in our lawsuit in late May, and he was served while at a writing residency in Vermont. Nan said he texted her upset, asking why I was doing this to him. In the days that followed, he posted on Facebook about a stalker who he said had been defaming him on Reddit and filing false Title IX accusations against him at his school. He emailed the police at his university and attached a photo of a shattered back windshield, presumably of his car, along with a handwritten note that read "Stop Trying to Find Me." He told friends that the stalker had sent him an anonymous email via a burner account. The author of the email said he was in love with Jay and that being rejected by him earlier that year had caused "a mental break I cannot explain":

i began trolling you online, sent you death threats, broke into your house when you were gone and messed with you and your dogs medications, i tried to fuck up your job applications by getting into your university email, i trolled a friend of yours in Arizona, i trolled your writing partner in south Carolina, and i showed up at your office with a gun. i am in love with you but i also wanted you to die. i am sorry for what ive done, including following you to Vermont. i am dropping out of college and going to a mental health facility. i will not bother you again. i am sorry.

It read like the end of the *Scooby-Doo* episodes I loved as a kid, when the mask is pulled off and the criminal lays out his line of transgressions before he is carried off to receive his just punishment. What Jay was saying, I realized as I read that email, was that a stalker had hacked his phone, his computer, his everything, and, like those zombie ants that take over the host body of another insect, he had hurt us using the shell of Jay's identity—his online presences—all without Jay knowing anything. What he was saying was that our story of the truth was not true enough, because he now had a new story to contradict ours. It sounded like a conspiracy theory, this stalker who machinated everything, but as with all conspiracy theories, it created a counternarrative that questioned the facts just enough that some people, at least, maybe even some of you reading now, could still doubt that I am the one telling the truth.

PART III

"The Sun Itself by Itself"

1

Socrates was screaming at me. Marta was back in our hotel room, laid up with a broken toe while I sat in a lower Manhattan theater watching a writhing Socrates scream that he only wants to ask questions. "I am not wise," he yelled at me, at us, the audience: a stand-in for the jury of Athenian citizens who would eventually condemn him to death. "I know nothing!" he bellowed.

In the opening scene, Socrates had appeared drunk and surrounded by other men—Plato and Aristophanes among them—most of whom were drinking, too, and clearly worshipped him. The actor who played Socrates kept mussing his greasy hair, pushing it into a bird's nest before plastering it to his shiny forehead, pulling at the white tuft of his beard and asking question after question after question. Alcibiades, beautiful and regal, joked about trying to seduce Socrates once, calling him "a most unlikely deity among men," only to have Socrates respond to his caresses by asking more questions—by wanting to debate, that is, instead of fuck.

Marta and I had planned for a romantic date that evening. My parents had flown out to stay with the girls in Arizona so that we could take a red-eye in early June to New York, book a cheap hotel in Chelsea, and two days later attend an awards ceremony for which my first book was a finalist. We wanted to celebrate that honor, but also having survived the previous three months. That first morning on our own, we had met up with my uncle and aunt at a bistro near the Stonewall National Monument, then walked around the city, feeling like childless women, like the women we had been ten years earlier when we met in Iowa City. I could picture Marta in her leather jacket that day. I could almost see myself: making cookies, riding my bike through a Midwestern morning, not knowing that I'd run into a woman who'd make me laugh, that meeting her would eventually lead to all of this: the kids, the moves, the jobs, Jay. We wanted to celebrate that—our history and our survival—but when we made our way back to our hotel room that afternoon for a nap, Marta had tripped on a suitcase and her pinky toe swelled like a ripe grape. It hurt so much that once we woke up, she told me to go out that night without her. I wanted to stay. "This is supposed to be our night," I said. But she insisted, saying she only wanted some sleep, and eventually, I agreed. I walked to the East Village to see *Socrates* on my own, leaving Marta alone in the double bed of our Hollywood-themed hotel room, a poster of Doris Day smiling down on her, the sound of children screaming somewhere on a playground below. In the theater that night, the shouts of Socrates replaced them.

"Were you to say to me right now," Socrates addressed the audience at one point, "'Socrates, we will let you go free, but you must stop philosophizing or face death,' I would answer that I will not stop"—his voice grew to a growl—"but I will keep pursuing, questioning everyone I meet, saying, 'you, Athenian,'"—now pointing to one of us in the audience—"'why do you seek wealth and power and every comfort but refuse to ask what your life and the world around you might actually mean?'"

The first half of the play had mostly been men yelling, loudly, as they debated concepts like truth and democracy and what it meant to "corrupt the youth"—one of the charges against Socrates. I thought about Dr. Whiles, of course. All those questions. All that yelling. How he said he only wanted to make us think. How he, too, had amassed admirers. "Corrupt" was a word Ms. Ritter had used when I'd interviewed her about Dr. Whiles. "It's one thing to believe that on your own," she'd said of Holocaust denialism. "But it's another thing to try to corrupt young people." That distinction felt important at the time: the implication that we are free to lie to ourselves but not to others. I thought about Jay, too, of course. He was also a teacher, had also amassed admirers. Only he had accused us, accused Marta, of corrupting the youth. Or his cast of characters had: Jessica and Rebecca and all those nameless voices on Reddit.

Justice is the inciting incident in Plato's *Republic*, the impetus for a meandering discussion that eventually expands to include questions of truth; education; poetry; nation building; and, of course, the Allegory of the Cave. That connection confused me the first time I read the *Republic*, but it started to make more sense, watching that play. Truth alone—your ability to get out of the cave, our ability to prove that Jay had invented lies about us, my ability to identify Dr. Whiles's manipulations—has import, yes, but little resonance if it isn't shared with others, if it doesn't enter the public realm. The same could be said for lies. They have limited power as long as you keep them to yourself, as Ms. Ritter said. Once they are let loose, however, within a school or a society, there's a problem. But if we try to fix it, we first have to understand how. How can we justly handle a liar or a lie? What is justice?

"There's a Jewish saying, '*Tikkun olam*,'" the playwright of *Socrates*, Tim Blake Nelson, told an interviewer shortly after his play's debut, "which means to repair the world. I would like to think that's what this play is about, and certainly the spirit in which I wrote it, is an effort to participate in repairing democracy."

After the play ended, Marta hobbled out to meet me in the rain at a crowded Italian restaurant, where we shared pizza with a fancy name I no longer remember and ricotta doughnuts covered in a net of crystallized sugar. We then walked back to our dingy hotel, her leaning into me the whole way, and, once there, we had sex for the first time in months, maybe even the first time that year. Afterward I felt like something small had been made right, as we lay sweating and catching our breath beside each other in the double bed: the fact that we were still together, still whole, no longer under the thumb of someone else's storytelling. It wasn't justice, but it felt like something important had been rectified in our tiny universe.

But before all that happened, I sat alone in that theater and watched Socrates bellow center stage. I imagined for a moment that I was a member of the Athenian democracy, there to judge this raving, mussy-haired man for moral corruption and impiety. It's easy—maybe too easy—to say now that he never should have been put to death. But I tried to remember the context: Socrates had openly questioned the democracy—and a lot of other things as well—right before some of his students had helped overthrow it and install a violent oligarchy. His trial came soon after that democracy was restored. I could see how the Athenians might have viewed his ideas as dangerous. I could see how they would want to blame him, at least in part, for any fears they still felt about the world they were trying to preserve. I could also see, in hindsight—and after reading Plato's version of him—that they were wrong. But would I have known that then? Would I have been able to distinguish truth from fears from propaganda? Would I have sided with Socrates? Or those standing beside and among me who wanted to put him to death? The question of justice inherent to those calculations no longer seemed all that abstract. Neither Dr. Whiles nor Jay was a figure like Socrates—I knew that—but I still felt myself, both audience member and author of this much smaller drama, wanting not only to know what was true but also what was just.

2

There is a moment that complicates the narrative of Dr. Whiles as I have told it up until this point. It happened late my junior year, after Gina broke up with me, after the Holocaust debate video and me confiding in Ms. Ritter on the steps of her portable. This was sometime in late April or May, shortly before school let out for the summer. I still had Dr. Whiles as a teacher, but I'd become distant—at least as I remember the past—and I trusted him less, if at all. I also had other dramas to distract me. Lucy was about to leave for college, and I was already mourning the loss of that friendship. I was dating someone new, a twenty-year-old who loved Morrissey and left long black hairs in my bed. And then there was my own near future: colleges to apply to, tests to take, after-school service industry jobs to work and work and one day quit.

On the day in question, I was in trigonometry when someone in the front office buzzed our classroom via the intercom system, the same one the principal used to make morning announcements. It was a student worker, letting my teacher know that I was to attend an awards ceremony in the school library's media center that morning, for something called the Junior Awards, according to documents my mom sent me years later. I sat up in my seat when the disembodied voice said my name, and everyone else in the class turned to look at me, perhaps as surprised as I was. I was a strong student, but I wasn't one of the overachievers, not one of those fighting for a valedictorian or salutatorian spot. I always told people I liked the shape of a B over an A, and I meant that. No one would have expected me to be invited to an awards ceremony, especially when no one else in that class was being named. I stood up, packed up my books, and smiled at Mr. Bell on my way out.

"Congratulations," he said, pausing. "For whatever it is."

Outside of his class, my skin slowly sloughed off the air-conditioning permafrost. I took the open-air hallways toward the library, welcoming the morning heat and my brief solitude in a school of more than three thousand students. Walking through a building like that while classes are in session is a little like walking home after the bars have closed in a city. You're alone, but also not. The people are just elsewhere, sleeping or trying to sleep, and you know that the solitude you feel is dependent only on time. Wait a few hours until the sun rises, and people will spill from their apartments and houses and fill those relatively quiet streets in minutes. Wait half an hour until the bell rings, and bodies will flood that hallway with a swiftness that feels almost ecstatic. So much yelling and locker slamming. So much sweat and cheap cologne. So much closeness between you and them.

I got to the library and found the media center, a smaller room filled with chairs and a podium at the front. I saw Mrs. Morris first. My mom might have been there as well. She certainly remembers that day. There were several other students, some I knew and some I barely recognized, and then some strangers, all adults, milling about near the front of the room. Mrs. Axton, our principal, was with them. I took a seat and slipped back into my sweatshirt, adjusting again to the cold air, to the denial that we lived in a swamp. I knew I was getting an award, of course, but I didn't feel any real anticipation. I'd recently won a prize for a short story, and that had felt electrifying, because by then I knew I wanted to be a writer. Whatever was to take place in the media center that day seemed more bureaucratic.

Mrs. Axton gave a brief introduction and then handed the micro-phone off to one of the strangers, a woman who said she was presenting an Athena Society scholarship to a student I didn't recognize. After that, someone else from another society gave a different student an award. I yawned and looked around the room, which revealed nothing. Mrs. Axton introduced a representative from the Vassar Club of Tampa Bay, there to give out their Award of Promise, and a new woman stood up.

"This year we are awarding it for promise in the study of Theory of Knowledge," the new woman said, before looking over at Mrs. Morris, who smiled at me. "Sarah Viren. Congratulations."

I stood up, queasy. Theory of Knowledge was Dr. Whiles's course. I walked to the front of the room and shook hands with the woman. We stood for a picture, the paper certificate held between us like a prop.

"To further your education, this also comes with a seventy-five-dollar savings bond," the woman told me. She handed me what looked like a check, only bigger, more fake looking.

Dr. Whiles wasn't in the room, but I felt him there, staring at my discomfort. Instead of choosing Eric, or James, or Dale, or any of his disciples for this award, he'd picked me. It didn't make any sense. I returned to my chair, pretending to watch the rest of the awards, but in my mind, I was ticking back through the previous weeks and months. After I'd fled Dr. Whiles's classroom, he'd been markedly colder toward me, and I was distant in return. I still did my work. I still wanted him to respect my ideas. But I no longer looked to him for answers, while he no longer seemed all that interested in me, as a student or a writer. So why did he choose me? That question has haunted me ever since I started thinking about him again. I wish sometimes that it didn't exist. This story would be so much easier to tell if it didn't.

3

We returned to Iowa. After we flew back from New York, we finished boxing up our house and hauling everything we owned into two PODS parked in the long driveway out front. Then we packed our car with enough belongings to last us two months and drove across the Southwest and Midwest, before heading north toward the town where Marta and I met, where Lucia had been born, where a cheesy sign I love at the state line greets you as you arrive: Fields of Opportunities.

We rented a house that summer from a professor Marta knew and I borrowed the office of another professor we knew to use during the weekdays while our girls were in camp or day care. Like understudies, we filled the spaces of others. I wrote every morning in another scholar's office and when I couldn't write anymore, I poured water into her plants, looking out her window at the old state building, where Iowa had its first capitol, and where, at that rally ten years earlier, Marta and I had realized we liked each other. I've always loved the way shadows of the past reside in geography. It's a facet of place I first noticed in high school, as the landscape of Tampa peopled with memories I'd made once my friends and I could traverse the city on our own. The Bennigan's near the mall where Lara and I ate potato skins, her favorite, and fried mozzarella sticks, with Danny and Kevin. The empty lot near the university where Lucy and I parked one night and took turns recording parts of a story into a tape in my boom box. The apartment complex just past the river where I later realized Dr. Whiles lived all those years, his apartment with a balcony looking out on the Hillsborough River where he had his vision of the *Pietà*.

In that office in Iowa, I started writing again about high school, trying to draw together new scenes from the past based on memories resurrected from photos or interviews or the shuffling of old documents. I had finished a dozen new pages by mid-June, but the narrative of the past kept bumping up against the present. I'd be writing about a moment when Dr. Whiles had pounded his fist on the table, yelling, "You need to think!" and suddenly Jay would appear, that open-mouthed smile he has in so many photos, the way he had once texted me: "Thank you for being a good human." Or I'd be trying to narrate the scene of me confronting Dr. Whiles after that Holocaust video, but instead of conjuring up the curtainless windows and wood-paneled walls of our portable classroom, I'd see the interview room with Melanie, the tissue box between us, our phones both out, recording the present.

Other days, I felt too spent to write. By the end of June, we learned that the University of Michigan wouldn't offer Marta a job after all. Not a faculty position or a staff one. Nothing permanent or temporary. "It was too late in the year," we were told. And because we didn't feel we could move somewhere without jobs for both of us—not with two kids, not with a marriage that felt shaky—I turned down the offer. A few days after that, Rashaad said we should consider settling our lawsuit with Jay. We had the proof we needed to win it, he said, but it could cost close to $50,000 to go to court, and in the interim things might grow messier: Jay might make up new lies about us online, or spread new rumors, and each time he did, we'd have to file a subpoena to prove it was him before we could make him stop. If we settled, on the other hand, we could end everything right then. Except that no one else would know what Jay had done.

"Don't we have an obligation to out him?" I asked Marta one night as we lay in someone else's bed, talking again about the lawsuit.

"We don't have an obligation to anyone," she said. "The universities should have gone after him. Not us."

That was another difference between us: our sense of justice. Marta longed for institutional change, while I got caught up in the interpersonal. I wanted Jay to say he was sorry, to acknowledge that he'd been wrong and then reckon with what he had done. Marta wanted our university to apologize and commit to investigating Jay themselves—for harassing us and impersonating other faculty and staff, but also for hijacking Title IX, which was, after all, a law passed to protect women from gender discrimination in colleges and schools. I knew on some level that she was right. Real change happens when we change the systems that allow people like Jay to harm others, but my storytelling brain—or maybe just my brain-brain—kept getting stuck on character, and that edict of honesty that my parents instilled in me when I was young. A lie told should be revealed. The truth should be known.

We continued debating the ethics and costs of settling as June slipped into July; and at some point during that forward march of time, I stopped writing about Dr. Whiles and I started trying to tell the story of what had happened with Jay. My goal at first was simply to arrange the recent past into a sequence of events that made sense. That's what writers do, after all. We apply order to the randomness of life and memory. We create narratives out of chaos. What Jay did to us wouldn't have meaning, I decided, unless I crafted one. But once I started writing, I realized the impetus to do so came from a more primal need: control. As a woman, I had been forced to cede control to my own narrative innumerable times. As a queer person, the control I felt I had over that narrative was more tenuous still. I thought a lot about a day soon after Manuela was born, when I found a lump on my breast and went with Marta to get it examined. This was in Lubbock. We were at the Catholic hospital, and the nurse who performed the exam noticed Marta's obvious concern for me, saw her reach for my hand as the wet wand touched my breast and she smiled at us.

"Are you two sisters?" she asked.

"No," I said, and I felt a flash of anger. "She's my wife."

The nurse looked flustered.

"Oh," she said after a pause. "Congratulations!"

Marta and I laughed about her reaction afterward, which I suppose was a way of us reclaiming that story, rewriting that moment as a memory that is both funny and sad. I didn't have cancer. The tests showed that the lump was a milk cyst, one built up in my ducts from weeks of nursing, so that story, if you widen the lens, also ends happily. But the meaning it has for me, the stone of that story I hold in my hand, is that instant when the nurse asked if we were sisters, because for that second or two before I responded, Marta disappeared, and I was reminded how easily my reality might be overwritten by those imposing a version they'd rather see.

With the story of Jay, I decided I was no longer willing to cede that control. In early July, in an office that wasn't mine, facing a capitol that was no longer a capitol, I pulled out my recordings of our many interviews with Melanie and started listening to them again. I wrote to administrators at Michigan and asked for copies of the emails they had received about Marta. I began collecting documents and interviews, taking notes, looking back at all of Jay's texts. And each day when I got home, Marta would look at me and sigh.

"You're in a bad mood again," she'd say.

I'd see then that I was. I cried, listening to the interviews with Melanie. Reading the emails to Michigan—all fifteen of them—turned my stomach. The correspondence had carried on for weeks before we even knew it existed. I'd go back and read an email I received from an administrator about the job I'd been offered, and look at the date and realize "Jessica" had already emailed that very person four times by then, telling him that Marta was a predator.

What I kept thinking about, reading through those emails, and looking again at Jay's texts, was how close we had come to never knowing the truth. If the University of Michigan had never told us about the emails they'd received. If they'd done what Jay had likely hoped they would, if they'd told me back in early March, soon after that first email from "Professor Orlich" arrived, that they realized they had no job for Marta, I might have turned down their offer with a normal level of regret. Jay might have then been offered the job and thus never escalated his subterfuge, never filed the accusations at our university or written again to Michigan as "Jessica" or posted about Marta on Reddit. I would have watched on social media as he celebrated the job he had accepted and as others celebrated with him, and watching, I would have felt jealous, I'm sure, and then guilty for feeling jealousy, never realizing that he'd scripted the whole damn drama. My reality would have been a story in which I was offered a job I had to turn down, and he had the luck to be the next one in line.

Thinking about that alternative storyline some days scared me. Because it meant that similar machinations might have happened in the past, or might still happen in the future, and I'd never know. It meant no one person or series of events could be trusted. There could always be another Jay out there. A man behind the curtain. A New World Order. A conspiracy that I knew nothing of as I blithely went about my life, chalking each new turn up to either circumstance or chance.

4

We had gone to Iowa the summer before as well. Before Jay came along, back when I still thought I was writing only about Dr. Whiles. We stayed in the same house that summer, too, but I borrowed an office from a friend of mine that time, a woman named Inara who now was faculty in the same English Department where we both had once been graduate students. It was in Inara's office, during that first summer in Iowa, that I began calling up people from high school and asking them to share their memories from twenty years before: first Lara; then a woman named Carry, who told me who had dated whom and who had cheated on what test; then Mrs. Morris, who mailed me a package of documents and photos she'd saved for years; then Laura, who was researching her own family connections to the Holocaust but said that back then we just didn't question what our teachers taught; then Jamie, whose own son was about to enroll in the same magnet program at the same high school; then Gayle again; then Gayle's mom, Alise; then our European history teacher Mr. Kane; then my old friend Joel; then Ms. Ritter; then Marcus; and in the months that followed many, many more. Talking to them, I confirmed much of what I thought I remembered about high school, and I recovered some old memories; but I also occasionally learned about something new, some event or fact that I'd either entirely forgotten or had never known. Those moments excited me most, likely because learning them felt less like the work of memoir and more like journalism, as if I were reporting on my past rather than trying to rebuild it from memories alone.

The most significant of those discoveries that summer was a moment that Gayle told me about first and Laura and Eric later confirmed. All three of them remembered one day our senior year when Mr. Kane showed up in Dr. Whiles's portable and told all the students to leave. Our class no longer had Dr. Whiles as a teacher that year, but those three must have had him for study hall so they still saw him every day. They remembered being surprised by Mr. Kane's request, but they obeyed without asking why, filtering outside like dispersed sunlight. Or perhaps they were already outside, about to enter the classroom, when Mr. Kane told them to stay put. Either way, in their memories of that day, Mr. Kane and Dr. Whiles were inside the portable arguing while those students huddled together outside, straining to hear.

"I was sitting outside," Gayle remembered. "Mr. Kane came storming in and slammed the door and I definitely heard yelling coming out of the portable."

"I remember we were outside and they were inside," Laura said. "And Mr. Kane was not having it. We couldn't hear what they were saying; we just heard yelling."

Mr. Kane didn't put it that way. When I tracked him down that summer via a website for the YA historical novels he now writes on the side, and I called him up, he described what took place between him and Dr. Whiles as a "discussion."

"I had students coming to me, some of them were actually in tears because they could not handle the two conflicting stories," he said. "There were students who had families involved in the Holocaust."

Then Mr. Kane stopped himself. "I'm just going to keep it professional," he said, adding that he didn't want to say anything bad about anyone.

I was in Inara's office while we talked. It looked out on a parking lot that ran up against the banks of a river I couldn't see, but that I knew was there. I asked Mr. Kane if he remembered hearing about the Holocaust debate, because at that point, no one I'd talked to besides Gayle and Marcus had. He said that, yes, he remembered that. I asked what he did when he heard about it, and then he brought up the "discussion" again between him and Dr. Whiles.

"What did you say to Dr. Whiles?" I asked.

"He and I talked about it and we both agreed to just continue teaching as we were teaching," Mr. Kane said.

"Do you remember there being other complaints?"

"Vaguely," he said. "There may have been some administrative repercussions. The problem, and I say 'problem' in quotes, is that 'Theory of Knowledge' is such a wide-open curriculum and you could teach anything and still be within that curriculum, which had the goal of teaching students how to think. So, you could teach Holocaust denialism and say this is what people think, and use that as a teaching tool. The problem you run into is if you teach Holocaust denial as fact."

"Do you remember anything else specific that Dr. Whiles taught us?" I asked. I had forgotten so much, and hearing about the portable fight made me realize that there might be other stories out there still to learn.

"Do you remember reading a book called *The Bell Curve*?" he asked. I didn't, but I remembered why it's been criticized: for bolstering the lie that intelligence is determined by race.

"I believe you all had to read that for his class. It was also controversial."

He hesitated.

"If you and I were having a beer, this conversation would be different," he said. "One of the things I've always maintained is my professionalism. I will never criticize another teacher as long as they aren't harming students. We have a freedom to think."

What I thought, but didn't say, was that perhaps Dr. Whiles did harm us, or at least some of us. What is harm, after all? Gayle had used the word "grooming" when she'd first told me about Dr. Whiles, even though she did so in the negative, saying "I'm not saying he groomed me, but . . ." After watching the video of queer people breaking into a church my junior year, I wrote a screed in my journal that clearly showed emotional conflict, if not harm: "That bullshit video just attacks and sucks at my insides," I wrote. "It makes me nearly feel insane questioning my own intuitions, wondering if perhaps my morals are fucked." Then there was Marcus being told that Black people were happy while enslaved. He said he knew that Dr. Whiles was wrong, but he didn't yet have the confidence or knowledge to fight back. You could say we all grew from those experiences, that we are stronger because of them, but does that mean Dr. Whiles's teaching wasn't dangerous? They asked similar questions during Socrates's trial. They asked them after the fall of the Nazis. And we are asking them again today. Can words cause harm? Can ideas be dangerous? If so, in what contexts? And who gets to decide?

Instead of saying any of that, I asked Mr. Kane if he thought some students had drunk the Dr. Whiles Kool-Aid. It was an expression Gayle had used when we talked.

"Definitely, yes," Mr. Kane said. "I was very upset because there was one student who thought that *Brave New World* was a good idea and believed in eugenics."

Then he returned to that fight in the portable that he insisted wasn't a fight.

"I remember the conversation with Dr. Whiles vividly. I was upset that the student was upset. I was pretty much just questioning him on it, on why he was teaching it that way."

"What did he say?"

I assumed the upset student in this story was Gayle. I knew that her mom had gone to see Mr. Kane after Gayle had told her everything that night in the kitchen. Alise had wanted to go to Dr. Whiles directly, but Gayle had begged her not to. She'd said that would only make the problem worse. She was afraid that everyone would hate her for trying to take down a teacher they loved.

"I honestly can't remember," Mr. Kane said. "I just remember that—"

He stopped.

"Is this some sort of takedown piece?"

I flinched.

"No," I said, trying not to sound defensive. Then, I explained again why I was so interested in Dr. Whiles and the past.

"This all started after the election," I said, "when the main narrative I kept hearing was that only uneducated whites believed the lies that were being told. But I remembered us in high school, and how many of us believed what Dr. Whiles was saying. I started wondering why that was, how that happened."

"Do you want to know the answer, if I could be so bold," Mr. Kane asked. "I don't mean to be presumptuous because you are obviously an intelligent woman."

I flinched again but said nothing.

"But this is something I've been studying, and this is my line of work," Mr. Kane continued. "We can't escape who we are. There are people who believe that human beings should be treated well, who have a positive outlook on the future. And there are people who want other things, who have more hate in them, who have mistrust, who don't like the way the world is now. But up until ten or fifteen years ago, the side of those who believed people were equal was winning. Ever since World War II, the story that the Holocaust gave us is that everyone is equal, that segregation is wrong, and there is no difference between the races and everyone can rise to their potential. And academia supported that claim."

I typed his words as he talked, without really digesting them, just as I had once written down Dr. Whiles's words.

"But there are other people who don't like that version," Mr. Kane continued. "Your perspective—I don't know it, but I can imagine you're the kind of person who wants to believe that everyone matters and we should all be equal—even though you were fifteen years old and the intellectual person in you liked Dr. Whiles. When you got to the other part, that part hit you at the core. That leads to all other kinds of conclusions you didn't like, and you couldn't react positively to him."

I was about to respond, to say that characterization sounded close to true, because it did—in fact it sounded like that feeling of cognitive dissonance I remember so clearly from that time—but then Mr. Kane added something that stuck with me for a long time, for its neatness if not necessarily its accuracy.

"As a teacher," he said, "I've learned that there are three ways people can react to information: they can reject it, they can dive into it, or they can shrug it off."

He started telling me how he warns his students even today about Holocaust deniers, but I wasn't listening anymore. I was thinking about myself in high school. How I reacted to Dr. Whiles. How others reacted. Or didn't. Mr. Kane's theory would have us all neatly divided into groups: those who rejected the conspiracy theories; those who could ignore them; and those who unflinchingly accepted the lies. But the world feels messier to me than that, and his theory also didn't account for why: Why would some of us reject, and thus remember, and others ignore and thus forget? And which is the better approach when lies enter the public sphere? Should we all just shrug them off? Would that be the safer bet? Later, when I interviewed my friend Eric, he inadvertently offered me another idea—at least as to why some of us just can't seem to shrug off people like Dr. Whiles. Eric had also forgotten about the Holocaust debate, but when I told him what I remembered, he believed me and was immediately horrified.

"My suspicion is that those videos were toward the end of the year and Dr. Whiles had sort of lost me by then," he said, "but I will also just admit that I had less at stake. If I had had more at stake, I would have paid more attention. Mr. Kane was Jewish, so I can see why he tried to intervene. And then you had a lot at stake, too. I mean I can't imagine what it was like for you."

In other words, those of us who reacted, and those of us who remember what happened: we had the most to lose from the narratives Dr. Whiles propagated that year. Eric might have thought they were wacky. James might have doubted them at times, too. But neither of them was personally threatened by what Dr. Whiles was teaching. They didn't have as much as stake. And that made it easier for them to shrug it off—or accept it.

After Mr. Kane left Dr. Whiles's portable that day, the students drifted back inside. Gayle and Laura and Eric and the rest of them found their seats, pulled out papers or books from their backpacks to do homework, looking around at one another for clues to explain what had just taken place. Laura and Gayle don't remember anything else about that day, but Eric told me he remembers Dr. Whiles briefly addressing the class— offering an explanation that, to Eric at least, made sense at the time.

"I am not a conspiracy theorist," Dr. Whiles told them. "I just want you to think for yourselves"

5

Our good friends Phill and Caroline drove over from Chicago to see us in Iowa City that second summer—the summer after everything happened with Jay. They were a couple Marta knew from Beijing, where she'd taught Spanish for two years. Phill was from the United States and Caro from Germany. We'd asked them to be our kids' godparents soon after Lucia was born, and over the years, they had become a second family to us. Phill was tall and sinewy with long hair he kept back in a ponytail except when the girls wanted to brush and braid it. Caro was shorter, sharp, and slightly caustic like Marta. My parents would come to see us later in the summer, but that visit from Phill and Caro was when I started to feel the pieces of our life falling back into place. They had a normalizing effect, as if to remind us that we had a history before Jay and would have one afterward, as if to say, as my grandmother, my mom's mom, often did, "This, too, shall pass," which of course it would.

We had ice cream their first afternoon in town and then we all sat together on a blanket in the park and watched Lucia and Manuela soak themselves in jets of water on a splash pad near a city garden. The little girl Lucia was playing with became so sad at one point she threw herself on the ground and began crying profusely—though we had no idea why. Manuela had been playing with the little girl's sister—they were holding hands as they walked around the playground—but they stopped as soon as the crying started, staring at the wreck of human emotion. I thought, not for the first time, about the tiny tragedies we all carry inside us. You see this clearly when you raise kids: how their sadness and rage are distilled versions of what we as adults continue to feel, these aches at the injustices of life, at the solitude of living.

That night, we went to the same Italian restaurant where Marta and I had dinner with our families after our wedding six years before, and again I felt the past overlaid on the present. I remembered our wedding ceremony in her brother's living room, how my dog, Finn, followed me down the aisle, how my parents bought us matching Wife and Wife ball caps. My brother, Andy, was there via Skype, in a tie and shorts on the screen to my right, my sister, Jessie, inside the iPhone he held up for us to see. Marta's parents watched through another screen, while her brother and his wife and kids sat in chairs we'd organized into short rows. After Marta and I said our vows and kissed and had cake, we all went for Italian to celebrate. I don't remember what we ordered that night, but six years later with Phill and Caro I know we asked for the fried calamari. Manuela sang invented songs to the people at the table next to us while Lucia arranged the lemon wedges on her plate into an orderly design.

After the girls went to bed that night, Phill and Caro stayed up with us, talking in the living room, first about Germany and the rise of the Nazi party, and then about everything that followed that seismic shift in history. Caro said she felt like her country is often defined by that past in a way that borders on myopic, as if by vilifying one nation we might escape the potential in all of us to one day fall for an authoritarian ruler, to condone if not openly support a genocide. Marta talked about the dictatorship in Spain, and one of us mentioned the stories of kids locked in cages at the United States–Mexico border, how close we sometimes seemed to be moving toward a Nazi state in this country; and then at some point, the conversation wound its way from totalitarianism to Jay. I told Phill and Caro that I'd started to feel angry at him only once I began writing, to report on the recent past, which is to say reflect on it, and yet I didn't want to tell the story from that place. We talked about what to do with intense feelings now that we're grown and can't, like that kid at the park, lie on the ground and scream. Phill had trained in martial arts, and he said that when he was studying kung fu, he had a teacher who wanted his students to foster anger in their bodies but then remain calm and fight using the force of that anger against their opponent.

"But I thought that was stupid," he said. "And I wondered what it would mean to foster compassion for the world or for a person in your body and use that as direction."

Marta and Caro were sitting on the couch and Phill and I were on cushions on the floor. I glanced over at him and realized he looked a little like that guy Lara and I had snuck out with so many years before, the one we called Jesus, the one with whom we had paddled a stolen canoe into the middle of a lake below a full moon. I thought about the full moon the night that Marta first heard she was being investigated for sexual misconduct. I thought how for a long time I believed that my grandmother had invented the phrase "This, too, shall pass." Others have claimed it comes from the Bible or Abraham Lincoln, but its real origin is a Persian fable in which a sultan asks a sage to give him one sentence that will be true regardless of whatever wars or weddings or tragedies arise in the future. The sage gives him the phrase: "And this, too, shall pass away."

I went for a walk with a friend from graduate school a few days after Phill and Caro left: Inara, the same friend who had loaned me her office the summer before. It was a gorgeous summer day. We walked toward that same wooded park where that professor, Arthur Miller, had killed himself almost ten years earlier, and as we walked we talked about how his story seemed to haunt those woods, where both of us had jogged as graduate students. We entered the woods and I told Inara about Phill and his thoughts on anger versus compassion. I told her I was questioning my desire to write about what had happened with Jay.

"Is this about revenge?" I asked myself as much as her. "Or something else?"

Inara didn't say anything for a moment. She had also written a memoir about truth telling—I knew that. It was a story of recovering family history from the erasure of the past, particularly the erasure that came after Nazi Germany invaded Latvia, where Inara's grandparents had lived, and where Gayle's family had lived as well, I realized later—though their family histories traced opposing arcs. Most of Inara's book is about life under the Soviets, and the particular erasure that came with that regime; but there is a moment in the memoir when she recognizes that her grandfather, in being conscripted to fight for the Germans, must have contributed in some way, big or small, to the murders of the more than seventy thousand Jewish Latvians living there at the time.

"I think compassion can also be a force behind truth telling," she said. "We know it is better for us, collectively, to have the facts made clear, the lies documented and exposed."

We said goodbye at a corner outside the woods and I walked the rest of the way home, thinking about Inara's story of truth telling and then about something Gayle's mom, Alise, had told me when I interviewed her. We'd been discussing the audacity of denying the Holocaust and how that denial in the Soviet Union had eventually been dismantled. It wasn't via policy shifts, at least not from Alise's perspective, and at least not at first, but instead from a poem. In 1961, Yevgeny Yevtushenko published "Babi Yar," a poem about the genocide of more than thirty-three thousand Jewish people in a ravine with that same name outside Kyiv, Ukraine.

"He was the first who acknowledged that the Jews were killed in Babi Yar," she said of Yevtushenko. "We were told we could talk about it. That poem changed our lives."

A few days after my walk in the woods, Marta and I decided to settle our lawsuit with Jay. We knew that doing so meant giving up the right to name him publicly, which also meant ending our chance at telling the full truth of our particular story. But we traded that for the peace of closure. Before signing, though, I consulted with another attorney, one whom Nan had recommended and who, unlike Rashaad, had experience working with writers. After that lawyer looked over a draft of our settlement, he sent me back language to include that would protect my right to write about what had happened to us—as long as I didn't mention two things: Jay's real name or his current employer. We all signed the settlement agreement in late July as Marta and I were packing up the house in Iowa to return to Arizona. A month later, I finished the essay I had been writing about Jay.

6

When I finally read Plato's *Republic*, years after graduating from high school, I realized that Dr. Whiles's version of the cave allegory was slightly different from how Socrates tells it. The escape from the cave, at least in my memory of Dr. Whiles's telling, had sounded like a hero's quest, a solitary adventure, with little to no discomfort along the way. Whereas Socrates dwells on the pain and confusion, but also the prolonged ignorance, of each stage of the prisoner's escape: being unchained and discovering the fire, then leaving the cave and adjusting to the sunlight above. The prisoner is also freed by someone else—a detail I don't remember from Dr. Whiles's class—and then, according to Allan Bloom's translation, he is dragged "by force along the rough, steep, upward way" out of the cave and into the sunlight by that person, presumably a teacher, a figure like Socrates himself.

The bigger surprise of Plato's *Republic*, however, was not how different the cave allegory was from my memory, but that the encompassing dialogue centers on imagining an ideal city, a republic or regime depending on your translation (the Greek is πολιτεία, or politeia), that, when I first read it, sounded a lot like the one in Huxley's *Brave New World*. It is a city-state without families, one in which children are taken from their mothers and raised by the community, a world in which men and women are equal, but the citizens are divided into three distinct classes.

It is also a world in which much of the poetry of that era—Homer's epics among them—would have been banned, because, as Socrates explains, poetry of war and mourning and sex awakens the emotional part within us, "nourishes it, and by making it strong, destroys the calculating part." Ruling over this ideal republic are the philosopher kings, a class of citizens recognized for their ability to metaphorically escape the cave, which is to say to know the truth of things, and thus trusted to make wise decisions for everyone else. Their leadership would be ensured by what Socrates calls a "noble lie" told to the citizens of this world so they accept their lots in life.

"All of you in the city are certainly brothers," those citizens would be told, "but the god, in fashioning those of you who are competent to hold rule, mixed gold in at their birth; this is why they are most honored; in auxiliaries, silver; and iron and bronze in the farmers and other craftsmen."

The noble lie would justify the class system, in which those born with bronze in their bodies become the farmers and blacksmiths, or the Uber drivers and meat-packing plant workers; those with silver intermingled with their blood are the lawyers and government workers; and the men and women tinted with gold serve as the guardians, the philosopher kings, who rule over a city founded on a lie.

"This is a radical statement about the relationship between truth and justice," writes Bloom in the preface to his translation of the *Republic*, "one which leads to the paradox that wisdom can rule only in an element dominated by falsehood."

It is a vision of the world that more than one thinker, Karl Popper chief among them, have argued smacks of totalitarianism, but that Hannah Arendt tried to temper by calling a "tyranny of truth," a world designed in large part, she writes, out of grief: Plato's grief at Socrates's execution by the Athenian state. If a democracy could put to death the wisest man this world had known, the thinking goes, we need a better design for our ideal state. But do we need to lie to the people in order to get that? Do we need to replace a democracy with an authoritarian state?

Reading the *Republic* in that light felt demoralizing until I stumbled upon a book by Leo Strauss called *The City and Man*, in which he argues that Socrates didn't really mean what he said, or perhaps that Plato didn't mean for us to take Socrates quite so seriously. Strauss was also a controversial thinker and teacher: he's been linked to the rise in neo-conservative thought and authoritarianism in this country. (In his introduction to Bloom's translation of the *Republic*, the poet and literary critic Adam Kirsch writes that several students of Strauss were behind the Bush administration's push to invade Iraq based on faulty information, and, more recently, some Straussians, as they are known, have been among those advocating for regime change in the United States.) But Strauss's ideas on the *Republic* were and have been enormously helpful to me, most distinctly his reminder that Plato's dialogues are literature, not treatises, which means there is room for dramatic irony, for instances of saying one thing but meaning something else. Strauss finds evidence of this slippage in moments when Socrates takes the argument too far, when he pushes for what would have seemed like ridiculous ideas at the time: equal education for men and women, for instance, and shared child-rearing. His interlocutors, or readers, should have realized at that point that Socrates was goading them to push back, to think for themselves, to yell, "That's ridiculous, Socrates!" But, in the *Republic* at least, they don't do much of that. Which means that another lesson of Plato's dialogue could be how easy it is to manipulate and deceive even highly intelligent people—how vulnerable all of us are to false narratives and harmful fictions.

That reading of Plato's *Republic* eventually became the basis for one of my theories about why Dr. Whiles taught us conspiracy theories, but also why he had given me that award my junior year after I confronted him about that video denying the Holocaust. According to this line of thinking, Dr. Whiles never believed in conspiracy theories; he was just trying to goad us into pushing back. He didn't really want us to doubt the Holocaust. He only presented us with that lie so that we might then argue against it. It was a theory that fit with what Dr. Whiles told Eric

and others after that fight in the portable with Mr. Kane. "I'm not a conspiracy theorist," he said. "I just want you to think for yourselves." It's
also one a number of people I interviewed from high school posited, but
that my friend Joel articulated most clearly when we talked during that
first summer in Iowa. Joel and I had known each other since junior high,
played soccer together, and started a zine our senior year. He'd been a
tall and lanky kid, with a baby face and light freckles across his tanned
cheeks. He and Eric used to call me by my last name, Viren, and he did
so again when I called him up to ask about Dr. Whiles.

"He had his moments of deep frustration," Joel said that day. "You could
tell he was trying to instigate, that as a class he wanted us to come up with
our own ideas, and sometimes it seemed like he was über frustrated with
the fact that we weren't capable of doing that. You remember that?"

"Totally," I said.

I was at Lucia's swimming lesson when we talked. She was practicing going underwater with her teacher while I sat on the other side of a
plexiglass wall, watching her and listening to Joel remember.

"He had these outbursts," he continued. "He'd throw a book on the
desk and say, 'Come on, guys, what are you thinking?'"

I pictured in my head the Dr. Whiles that Joel was describing. The
way the book flew. The growl of his voice. Not scary, just insistent. It felt
accurate. Joel told me Dr. Whiles's class did for him what he thinks religion does for other people—it prompted him to consider those big questions we all eventually face about the existence of the self, the meaning
of life.

"So, his class changed you?" I asked.

"It changed everything. I absolutely think it changed everything. I
think everyone should take this course in their adolescence; I think everyone should be asking these questions."

I thought about a literature class I'd taught the semester before, how
at one point the students and I were discussing an essay we'd read; and I
mentioned that we've all had those moments in which we wonder who
we are and how we've come to be, in which we think about our own

existence and the existence of everything around us, these tiny specks on a spinning globe, and maybe even briefly doubt the reality of ourselves or this world. But as I talked, I noticed only a couple of students were nodding in agreement.

"I've never thought about anything like that," one kid said.

So maybe Joel was right. Maybe we all do need a class like Dr. Whiles's. But did we need Dr. Whiles's specific class? Is that kind of confusion, that cognitive dissonance, good for us? Am I stronger because, in the end, I did push back? I did what Strauss implies Plato ultimately wanted: for us to question the line of questioning, to see the irony or doubling inherent in many forms of storytelling. But Dr. Whiles was no Socrates. And so many others never pushed back. They believed what they were told. Or they shrugged it off, and then forgot it had happened at all.

Near the end of our conversation, I asked Joel about the conspiracy theories. He hesitated before answering, his voice less confident, or perhaps more pensive.

"There was always this kind of tension in the class because we didn't know if he was trying to give us the answers on top of the questions," he said, "and I think all he really cared about was getting us to think. I actually don't think he cared what our answers were as much as getting us to back up our ideas with some paradigm of thought."

We hung up soon after that, him calling me Viren one more time, me warming to hear it, and afterward, I found Lucia and helped her shivering body out of her swimsuit and into her summer clothes. I kept thinking about what Joel had said, and I would continue thinking about it in the months and eventually years that followed. His explanation was seductive because it erased the friction from my memories of high school. It allowed Dr. Whiles to return to the person he'd been our freshman year: odd, yes, and perhaps a bit temperamental, but overall an excellent teacher and mentor. Someone who just wanted us to think.

But an alternate theory, one more in line with Popper's view of Plato as the architect for a totalitarian world, and perhaps also in keeping with

Arendt's understanding of the tyrannical character of "truth" within Plato's dialogue, was that there was no irony to Dr. Whiles's teaching, no intention to nettle us into questioning the world. He believed it all. He thought the Holocaust had been invented. He was convinced a Jewish elite ruled the world. He saw civilization as a great accomplishment that our current "multicultural" world was quietly splintering. And he wanted us to believe these things along with him, to escape the cave as he understood it. If that were the case, if that second theory proved true, then Dr. Whiles chose me for that award my junior year not because I had spoken out as he'd hoped I would, but because he knew that doing so would make me question his motives less; he knew his tacit approval would make me doubt myself, and my interpretation of him and his class. And it did. I have. If that was his goal, he wins.

7

We returned to Arizona in August and moved into a house we'd bought over the internet soon after I turned down the Michigan job. It was Spanish colonial style with Saltillo tiles and a pool, and when we walked in that first day, I felt like I'd been yanked back to Florida, back to my childhood of suburban houses and individual pools and palm trees. I had to remind myself that I wasn't my parents, that eternal return was a thought hypothesis rather than a reality. But some days it felt like time was spinning on a tiny wheel. Or that I was standing still.

Lucia and Manuela went back to school and day care and Marta and I tried to settle into the regular life we'd had before the dream of clapboard houses in Ann Arbor. I began to write about Dr. Whiles again and Marta continued researching the way that people learn languages. We were both on teaching leave that semester—a benefit of reaching our third year at the same university—so we frequently found ourselves home together. I would wander into her office some days to talk about the past or the present and she would wander into mine, asking about the future: where we'd go for Christmas that year, how I wanted to renovate our house in the spring. Our minds had always worked differently when it came to time: I obsessed over what came before and she, quickly forgetting all that, fixated on what would eventually come to pass.

One day in the middle of September, I tracked down someone from high school I'd been trying to reach for a while: James, the smartest guy in our program, who'd taught me about astral projection. I'd reached out to him via Facebook that first summer in Iowa, but he hadn't responded to my messages. Then I thought to google him and there he was: an academic just like me. He had studied cognitive science in college and got a master's degree in religious studies before finishing a PhD in something called educational policy. I wrote to him through his university email and he responded right away. He'd be glad to talk, he said, "though we might need to get a hypnotist on the line to dredge up some of those memories. It feels like a very, very long time ago."

When we talked, he told me about converting to Catholicism in high school because of Dr. Whiles, but also falling from that faith later in college. He said that Dr. Whiles had been the most influential teacher he'd had, by far, but he also seemed open to acknowledging his faults. When I told him what Joel thought about Dr. Whiles and his conspiracy theories, James laughed.

"I got the sense that he believed them, or that he was entertaining them," he said. "I think what Joel said is a charitable interpretation."

James told me that a friend from his master's degree program taught Theory of Knowledge—Dr. Whiles's class—at a school somewhere else, and that his friend approached the course much more like an introduction to philosophy.

"Was that what it was supposed to be and we got this weird warped version of it?" James asked. "And yet it had the right effect on me in that it did get me to think about things."

I was in my office in our new house, a room with sliding glass doors that looked out on orange and grapefruit trees. James was the first person I'd talked to who was similarly conflicted about the past, and Dr. Whiles, and what it all meant. Gayle had been so badly hurt, she mostly was just angry; and Marcus seemed to feel a lot of resentment, too. Everyone else either didn't care or they'd forgotten what there was to care about. But James sounded of two minds, and that was consoling.

"I feel like shaking people up just to shake them up is not always great," he said at one point. "I think the problem is that you shake people up and you leave them with nothing. You can kind of leave people feeling like, 'Oh, it doesn't mean anything.' You might have to shake people up, but then you have to give them some material to rebuild. I think I ended up using Catholicism as that material, but it fell apart again. And then things did seem meaningless. Now I don't know what I think."

"I don't know what I think either," I said, and it felt good to admit that.

Before James and I got off the phone, I asked him about those conversations we'd had either my freshman or sophomore year, the ones in which he told me about leaving his body and I tried but failed to follow his instructions. I described what I remembered him saying about astral projection, but when I was done, there was silence on the other end of the phone. When James spoke, he said he didn't remember any of that. Not claiming he could leave his body, nor ever talking to me on the phone.

"This was what I remembered when you emailed me," he said. "I remembered you as a very kind person who I wish I had been better friends with at the time."

Later that night, Marta and I were watching *Stranger Things* on a laptop balanced on a pillow between us when I mentioned James and how he didn't remember our conversations about astral projection.

"He doesn't even remember talking to me on the phone," I told her. "So, I said, 'Well, maybe I made it up.' But that's not true. Why would I make up something so strange and specific?"

"You know I could leave my body when I was younger?" Marta said, as if we'd talked about this before. I shifted in the bed and recognized the creak it always makes when I move in that particular direction. The bed had been my parents' once, just like our kitchen table was theirs when they first got married. I sat with Manuela and Lucia at breakfast sometimes and looked down at the grain in the wood and suddenly remembered a Thanksgiving from thirty years before.

"You never told me that." I paused the show and turned to face Marta.

"I figured out that one day I could do it, and then it was easy."

"Easy how?"

"I had to have my neck in a certain way, I remember that, and then I'd be out and looking down on myself from above."

"That's exactly what James said happened to him!" I yelled, suddenly convinced that knowing more about Marta's story would help me understand my own memories.

"I did it for years, in high school and college, I think," Marta said. "But then I remember one day trying to do it and I couldn't anymore. It was gone."

A scene from the fictional Hawkins, Indiana, in the 1980s was frozen between us. I thought about myself in the 1980s and Marta during that same period: me in Columbia, Missouri, a quiet Midwestern college town, and her in Madrid after the death of Franco. I told her about my big picture moments, because that experience sounded similar to the way she had described being able to leave her body, the suddenness with which it would come on and mystical quality of it. As I described what used to happen, and sometimes still does, I suddenly sensed the feeling coming on again. We were there in my parents' old bed, our hands now touching, Hawkins still frozen between us, and I felt the creeping awareness of all of our selves waiting to take hold. I remembered Marta and me that day at that rally in Iowa, that same me, or at least the same body, lying beside her at that moment, a self like so many other selves in other beds, lying beside their partners or alone, already dead asleep or awake, making tea, or watching a movie, maybe masturbating, or reading. I never saw specifics when the big picture came on, but I felt each and every one of you as if you were a pulsing light, a presence I know is there without seeing it, a surety that we exist.

8

I was driving home after dropping off Manuela one morning in October when suddenly Jay was in the car with me. He was talking about memoirs and how there are too many of them, how they don't mean anything anymore. He sounded like someone young trying to appear sophisticated, but beneath that I could hear his real voice, the one he used to talk with friends, or with an acquaintance who might one day become a friend: a voice that was more playful, less slick. I passed the Bank of America and then a Starbucks and crossed the highway overpass and realized somewhere in that movement that Jay's voice was on the radio, not there, not real, in my car. An NPR reporter had been interviewing the author of a new memoir, and Jay had been interviewed, too, because he had reviewed it. He told the reporter the author's book stood out among the "glut" of memoirs on the market because he wrote like a poet. "Every sentence, every word, every paragraph is so painstakingly pored over," he said inside my Subaru; and listening, I remembered "Jessica" using that same phrase, "pore over," to talk about the way Marta read her dissertation draft. I remembered that I'd used it, too, at least once in the book I was writing, which is to say, in the book that you are reading now.

I thought I had found closure, whatever that means, when Marta and I signed the settlement agreement, but that moment in the car made me realize Jay still haunted me. I thought about him all the time. I had started to feel, sometimes, that he really might be present, that he still had a hold over my life in ways I wasn't yet aware.

A couple of days after hearing Jay on the radio, everyone in our house got sick. It started with Marta, who threw up one night, and in the morning kept saying she could no longer remember things. I got sick after that, with a sore throat and a rough cough. I stayed in bed and tried to write, but my head was foggy and I had trouble understanding what Marta was telling me. Soon the girls were sick, too, and in the week that followed, our individual illnesses lingered long enough that I started to have paranoid thoughts. I worried, late at night when I couldn't sleep, that Jay had poisoned us.

Thoughts like those scared me enough that I eventually talked to my therapist about my fear. I told her I wanted Jay to stop haunting me. I knew by that point that I would publish my essay about him. It had been accepted by a large national magazine and I worried what he might do once the story came out. I wondered sometimes if I should pull it, if telling our story would cause more harm than good. My therapist listened, she watched me cry, and then she talked to me about something called the state of unforgiving. It's when someone is stuck in your head, she said, a constant trigger. The opposite of that, forgiveness, is not about you letting that person off the hook. It's about letting them have less control over your life. You don't forgive as a form of absolution to them, you forgive as a means of lessening their psychic power over you. It's grief work, she said, and part of that work is considering what you would have wanted to have happened instead of what did.

"You mean to speculate?" I asked.

"Yes," she said.

For Jay, what I would have wanted was for him to never have existed, at least in my life. I had gained nothing by knowing him and I saw no point in a revision of history that included him. Thinking about that imaginary world, a world in which he just disappeared, did feel freeing, if unrealistic. But when I thought about Dr. Whiles, I couldn't imagine him out of my past. He had been too integral. I had learned too much from him. Instead of making him disappear, I began to imagine a world in which his religious conversion never happened. I imagined him staying close to the person he had been our first year. He'd talked about conspiracy theories at times, but without the urgency, without the moralizing and fear. If he had just stayed like that, I thought, I probably never would have felt as unsettled. Because it never would have gotten to the point where, as Eric put it, I had stakes in the stories he was selling us. I never would have felt like what he was teaching threatened who I was.

Soon after I began imagining a revision of our collective history, I had a dream about Dr. Whiles. I was in a portable classroom again, but this time for a writing residency. Dr. Whiles was there, one portable down from the one where I was staying, or writing, and I was trying to avoid him. When he found me, on the pathway between the two portables, he demanded to know what I was doing. I tried to explain without really explaining, but it didn't make a difference. I knew he knew that I was writing about him, and immediately he began machinating ways to interrupt me. He was nice about it, but he clearly wanted to stop me from writing anything else. He told me that none of this made sense, that no one cared, and that I should do something serious, like he had always hoped for me when I was his student. I had always been one of his favorites, he said. The portable classroom we were in was darker than I remembered it being. It had a closet, and other rooms. On the wall, there was a clock.

9

We flew back to Tampa for Christmas that year. My parents had moved from the house where we lived when I was in high school, the one in the suburbs that backed up against a swamp, the one almost indistinguishable from the other houses that surrounded it. But we drove out one day to see our old house and neighborhood, Tampa Palms: me, my mom, Marta, and the girls. In my mom's SUV, we took the same route I followed all those years, driving home from school in the afternoons or after going to see Gina or Lucy at night. We turned right at the first entrance to Tampa Palms, passing the apartments where we lived while our house was being built, a place once called Plantation Oaks but renamed Amberly Place, and then into a patch of dense forest. Marta joked with the girls that we were in a time machine traveling to the 1990s.

"There's Mommy now," she said as we passed a younger blond woman running along the same route I had run, right at the spot, in fact, where once I discovered a baby alligator sunning itself on the sidewalk and had to veer into the road to avoid it. We turned onto the main road and stopped at the country club where Lara and I had met Jesus, where we used to sneak Marlboro Reds behind the tennis courts and use the hair spray in the ladies' locker room. I stopped to take a photo in front of the gate where we once parked our bikes. Manuela wanted to get out, too, but Marta stopped her.

"This is a time machine!" she said. "You can't get out. It's dangerous. What if you meet yourself when you were younger?"

We drove by our old house after that, its red door now painted white, any hint of individuality erased. It was hard to summon memories just looking at it: a close match to the houses on both sides of it and up and down the street. Only the magnolia tree out front shook something in me. My mom loved that tree when it bloomed, and I did, too: the intensity of its flowering felt almost illicit in a place like that.

On our way out, we drove by Oak Park, where Lara and I used to meet up with boys when we snuck out, and I asked my mom to stop. I remembered a playground inside the park, and I thought the girls could swing or slide while I stood there for a bit, trying to reinhabit a space. My mom parked on the road beside a sign that read Danger: Snakes and Alligators.

"We'll get out here," Marta told the girls, "but you need your special time machine suits in case you meet your mom when she was younger."

Lucia and Manuela pretended to put on their suits and I looked around, open to the idea that maybe my former self would show up. We'd catch her as she was sneaking into a car with Jesus, perhaps, or one afternoon while she and Lara sat on the swings, swishing from side to side, secretly smoking. But when we got to the spot where I remembered the playground being, there was only open space, like a small helicopter landing pad. Surrounding it, Spanish moss hung from live oaks; and palmetto bushes burst like fireworks among stretches of St. Augustine grass. I had forgotten how much gray lay amid the deep greens of Florida, and how dark it could be in the woods. I wanted us to take a picture, but the girls started complaining about the mosquitoes and missing playground.

"Time traveling is hard because it affects your glands," Marta said, and my mom laughed.

We took the picture quickly and drove to another, larger park I remembered, one with a community center and pool that butted up against an artificial pond. The girls ran from the car toward the playground structures as soon as we unbuckled their car seats, forgetting all about their time travel suits. I followed them slowly, noticing a sign that neither of them had. It warned that only residents of Tampa Palms were allowed to use this playground. But Lucia and Manuela had already taken off their shoes like they always do at playgrounds and were sliding down the slides and swinging on the swings and pretending they were sleeping among the wood chips while Marta went to the bathroom and my mom and I sat on a bench nearby. I told her about picking shrooms in the cow fields behind us and boiling them in water and adding Kool-Aid so we could drink them and trip. She laughed and told me about the time Andy egged a house near this park. He'd swore to her that he hadn't done it, and she'd believed him until she found a pair of muddy shoes and an egg carton in the garage. After that, she drove him over to the egged house to apologize and he kept saying, "They're going to kill me, they're going to kill me." But they didn't. They just made him clean up the mess, which sounded like a manageable form of justice: you admit your transgression—you tell the truth—and you make amends. For my mom, though, the story was more about trust than justice. She had wanted to believe my brother, the baby in our family, so much that it took blatant evidence for her to see that he, too, could lie.

When it was time to leave, I asked Lucia how it was to play where I had played as a kid.

"Craaaazy," she said.

"Did you meet Mom when she was younger?" Marta asked. "Was she a bully?"

Both girls laughed, said they hadn't, and then we drove away, them talking about what parts they loved in the sprawling playground structure, and me thinking how awful our suburb seemed in the present, but what a fabulous place it had been when we were young, how we could ride our bikes along miles of bike paths and there would always be new places to explore outside, new ways to exist separate from our parents— and always in a world that felt safe enough for them to let us go. The dream of a planned community like Tampa Palms, I realized, was a little like the city Socrates dreams up in the *Republic*, only those in charge of

TO NAME THE BIGGER LIE

making the rules are the investors and designers, rather than philosophers. I sympathized with Plato, or one version of him: this man heartbroken that a democracy had killed his mentor, and thus determined to
plan a better, more just world, one that would have kept Socrates not
only alive but ruling over everyone else, their philosopher king. But how
do we know which rules will make for a just world and which will result
in a tyranny? One of the problems invoked by Plato's dialogue is inherent to suburbs as well: What is forfeited—truth; freedom; or, in the case
of our neighborhood, wilderness and diversity—in order to live in a community that is perfectly planned? Another is loss. Who suffers when one
segment of the population decides their utopia trumps everything else?

10

Our senior year, Ellen DeGeneres came out of the closet, Osama bin Laden declared war on the United States, and Tupac was murdered. I worked at Einstein Bros. Bagels and started a creative writing club at school called Club Zine. In my journal, I wrote that I was into Marxism. On my wrist, I got a tattoo of a sapling tree. And in the classroom, we had a new English teacher, a man named Mr. Lakatos, whose appearance felt a little like Mary Poppins arriving at the Bankses' house: mysterious and magical, if also a little suspect. He told us he had been homeless for a stint, living under bridges in Boston, before he became a teacher. He cried while reading us passages of Walt Whitman's "Song of Myself." He filled his portable with couches and an old stove, as if we were a family living in the prairie together instead of a bunch of teenagers in a portable classroom beside an urban high school the color of piss.

That portable, Mr. Lakatos told me years later, laughing into the phone when we talked, was a dump—"It was the third oldest portable in the county!" You could see the grass through holes in the floor, he said, and the chalkboard was so ancient it no longer accepted chalk. Mr. Lakatos bought chalkboard paint so he could write about literature on the board. He strung curtains in the windows because there were no blinds—that deficit that Dr. Whiles had complained about constantly. Instead of yelling, Mr. Lakatos brought in some curtains from his house and strung them up to block some of the intensity of the Florida sun. In that and so many other ways, he was the antithesis of Dr. Whiles.

I called him in June that first summer in Iowa, before anything had happened with Jay, and he and I talked about his memories of me and the other kids in our program that year. We were smart, he said, but overly text focused, and uncomfortable not knowing what to think. The first time he attempted a class discussion, he asked what we thought of "Song of Myself" and no one said anything for forty minutes.

"It was the break, and I said, 'I'll see you in ten minutes and we'll continue our conversation,'" Mr. Lakatos told me, laughing. "After that, when they came back, the house was afire with questions and interplay and I think the word got around because when each of the other classes came in, they were ready."

When I asked Mr. Lakatos if he remembered Dr. Whiles, his demeanor changed—from a sort of bemusement to something more somber.

"I was aware of what Mr. Whiles—I mean Dr. Whiles—was doing, of course," he said. "I was stunned that he was getting away with it."

He told me about the first time he realized something was off with Dr. Whiles.

"I was so busy those first weeks, I never even went down to the cafeteria; but the first week in October I went down and I was sitting next to Dr. Whiles and Will Beard"—our biology teacher—"and I don't remember who else, but at one point Dr. Whiles went riffing on one of his conspiracy theories and I thought he was one of the funniest people in the world. I was laughing so hard, but then Will sort of nudged me and said, 'He's serious.'"

Mr. Lakatos said that Dr. Whiles didn't believe in the lunar landing and that he told people the Virgin Mary had appeared to him as he was sitting on his balcony overlooking the Hillsborough River. He also knew about the Holocaust denialism.

"I think he got away with it because at some level he was such a charismatic and dynamic person," he said. "I sat in one of his classes and it struck me that it was the Dr. Whiles show. He had so much to say. But

I didn't feel I could confront him. Being the low man on the totem pole, I just kind of didn't want to make waves. He had built up such a reputation. With the students but also the faculty."

The following year, the year after we graduated, Dr. Whiles left our school, Mr. Lakatos said, so he also didn't have to confront him in the end. The area director for our program had opened up a new chapter in another county, and he wanted to create an "all-star" team there, so he invited Dr. Whiles to teach at that school.

"And in the ensuing years, the stories of what was going on there made their way over to Chapin," Mr. Lakatos said. "It was clear he had gotten worse."

I thought about all those students. One of them had later called him "a great being like Socrates" on that Rate My Teacher page. Another claimed he was "misunderstood by those who lack intelligence."

"When I took over his class, Theory of Knowledge, after he left," Mr. Lakatos said, "I taught a unit on the Holocaust as if it had actually taken place. We read *Man's Search for Meaning* by Viktor Frankl and there was a short documentary on the Holocaust before we read Frankl. We discussed his philosophy of logotherapy: what humans are looking for is not pleasure but meaning. I suggested that that's true. I think we can deal with anything as long as we have a 'why.' As long as there is meaning to what happened."

I thought about a quote from Hannah Arendt that I've always loved: "The need of reason is not inspired by the quest for truth but by the quest for meaning. And truth and meaning are not the same." One of the many things Mr. Lakatos's class taught me my senior year was to hold on a little less tightly to some of the questions that had anchored me in Dr. Whiles's class. Not that truth doesn't matter, but that what often matters more is the context in which whatever is true or false comes to our attention. That context is the story, the poem, the meaning we make from the raw material of a lived life.

11

In March, a plague hit, and we were trapped in our homes, talking about how nothing would be normal again. Amid the chaos, the story I had written about Jay the summer before went up online. I assumed at first that no one would read it. We were all too distracted by the rising death toll, by the lies our leaders kept telling, by reports about how easily the virus could spread: across surfaces, in the air, everywhere. But people read the story. Hundreds of them at first. Then thousands. Then more than a million. The comment section for the essay filled with nearly a thousand posts before they closed it down. People wrote things like "What a nightmare!" and "Truth is indeed stranger than fiction." They called the story Kafkaesque or compared it to Patricia Highsmith's *Strangers on a Train* and Lillian Hellman's *The Children's Hour*. One person posted a long comment about Foucault's thoughts on "parrhesia," or speaking truth to power, and another outlined a five-point plan for building a better world, including "a real need to deconstruct the meanings of truth, facts, narrative, subjectivity."

"The perfect 'story' for this moment in time, when fact and fiction blur and merge and reproduce a toxic sludge," wrote someone identifying themselves only as "counsel9." "Thanks for telling it."

People worried about us and they praised us. They said Melanie should have closed the investigation sooner. That Michigan should have given us jobs. "I wish Sarah and Marta a good life together with their daughters who have 2 very brave and courageous mothers," wrote one woman, whose words made me cry.

"As I read this, I kept thinking how, if this were me, I wouldn't have been able to remember all the terrible details," someone wrote from South Carolina. "I would have gone foggy. I would have been worn down by it all, would have just wanted to hide. The clarity of this account is an impressive feat. Just to put it all here, as it happened, requires strength."

Some people were bothered by my discussion of truth versus honesty in the essay. At one point, I had written: "So while truth may be subjective, its balustrades are always the facts at hand." And several readers had reacted with dismay.

"Truth is not subjective!" one of them wrote.

Others argued about whether our story debunked or supported the #MeToo movement. Someone wondered if the narrative would be read differently if told by a man. Many of those who were upset, though, had the same regret I had. They wanted a different ending.

"There's no justice in a story like this," wrote John in Michigan. "We think of the legal system as some sort of answer to personal injustices but it's not. The costs of legal action are exorbitant and the consequences for the perpetrator is often illusionary."

For a lot of these readers, justice would have been knowing Jay's real name. I had almost given it to them—encoded though it would have been. My original draft of the essay had ended with a line that would have shown readers how to find Jay without me saying his name out loud. It had read: "Our lawsuit is public record. You can search for it now." When I wrote that ending the summer before, it had felt like justice, in large part because it felt like the full telling of the truth—something our settlement agreement had prevented us from doing.

But a couple of weeks before the story ran, my editor emailed to ask if I wanted to reconsider. She said she had no sympathy for Jay, but she wanted to make sure I'd thought through the possible outcomes of what I wrote—but also that I was saying what I meant to say.

That question changed everything for me. In forcing me to reconsider the last line of that essay, my editor also pushed me to think through the premise of the story itself. It wasn't about outing Jay, I realized. That wouldn't bring me any real relief, nor would it provide actual justice. Because the story wasn't really about him. It was about us. Marta and me, but also all of us. Those reading that story then, and those reading this one now. We are the ones for whom this matters. Those of us trying to build a life that means something, that will remain standing, amid the towering lies.

I sat at my computer, alone in my home office, thinking about that ending for a few minutes before a new one fell into my mind. I revised the final line and sent it back to my editor. In the new ending, I explained to readers that I had told my story as honestly as I could up until that point. Then I wrote, "Now the story belongs to you."

"It has a different feeling but perhaps a more generous, thought-provoking one," my editor wrote back. I agreed. I still do. But many readers didn't. The lacuna left them stymied. They wished we hadn't settled. They wanted me to tell them who Jay was. Or who "J." was, because in the article I'd used only that initial for his name.

"J. does not deserve the luxury of privacy," wrote Lorenzo in Oregon.

"I understand the author's decision making process," said someone else named Jeff, "but how will they feel when 'J.' does this next time and the consequences are more than just a job offer and they realize they did nothing to stop it?"

Jay was no longer at his job by then. The last I heard he was living with his parents, working as an adjunct instructor, writing business copy on the side. He hadn't gotten the job at Michigan either. That all felt like a punishment to me, but did it make things right? I didn't know the answer to that, but I knew that I didn't want to make my story about naming him.

"The most interesting part to me is that the story didn't end in a great triumph or true vindication," someone named A. Rizwan Khan wrote in a comment that resonated the most with me. "This is how life is, most of the time, including my own experience. To realize that and to limit the damage and try to move on with life is key to a peaceful survival in this very imperfect world."

12

Within hours of my essay being published online, people on Twitter figured out who Jay was anyway. Our lawsuit was still public record, even if I hadn't alerted readers to that fact, and someone found it. They found his name, and they pasted it and photos of him online. One of him in a sweater and tie with a quizzical look on his face. One of him shirtless, a tattoo visible on his chest. They called him a "monster" and a "sociopath" and said he looked like a "creepy Truman Capote." They wrote to the university where they thought he worked and demanded he be fired. Then they wrote to the university where he did have a job and demanded the same.

"Drag him," someone wrote online.

"This man doesn't belong in academia," someone else posted. "He belongs nowhere."

I watched it all from my phone, amid the expanding lockdowns and rising death toll, and I began to feel a little ill. I knew that outing Jay was what those people, these readers, wanted—and they thought I did, too. I'd ended the essay, after all, by saying I had given my story to them. Many of them interpreted that as me saying I wanted them to name him. And maybe I did. I know I wanted the truth of what had happened known. That's always been my compulsion: toward naked honesty, transparency, that linen closet pried open and those cigarette butts revealed in their tiny, evidential line.

But that wasn't what I'd meant by "now this story belongs to you." I'd meant that the weight of our story, its burden, was now shared. The fact that Jay could briefly convince so many people to fall for a fiction meant that something was messed up in the world at large, not just within him. Which in turn meant that reckoning with that dysfunction, and so many adjacent ones, needed to expand beyond just a single individual. It should involve the universities that Marta kept pushing to take responsibility. It should involve our laws, and the way that Title IX had so easily been manipulated. It should involve the justice system and the racism and inequities that define it. It should involve the patriarchy, for god's sake, and all the legitimate stories of rape and sexual harassment that Jay had plagiarized.

But Jay was who everyone saw, who they wanted. And I understood that; I felt it, too. There were days I couldn't get him out of my mind. I thought about what he wrote about Marta and I wanted him to suffer. I thought about the way he had rewritten our future, and I needed some sort of punishment. But when he was outed online, I watched as Jay became a villain not only because of what he had done but because of who he had attacked: two women, two lesbians, people kept pointing out, with children. That was what made me feel ill: this need to turn us into helpless victims.

"Stop attacking moms," someone wrote on Twitter.

"This story made me Sick," someone else posted. "Imagine doing that to someone's family. They have fucking BABIES."

I felt complicit, and, even though I didn't want to, I worried about Jay. I worried he might harm himself or someone else. Nan wrote to me and said she was worried about him, too. But then a graduate student came forward online and said that Jay had sexually harassed him for months. Another man, also a student, spoke out after that and said more or less the same thing. A friend of mine posted that Jay had sexually harassed him, too, when Jay taught at his former university. He hadn't told anyone about it before, he said, because he'd blamed himself. These men posted screenshots of creepy and persistent texts from Jay. They talked about how they didn't feel like they could speak up—because everyone else thought he was so charming.

"I'm sorry I didn't tell anyone," one of those men wrote on Twitter. "I thought he was so well-liked and I worried about causing waves."

I thought about what Mr. Lakatos had said when we'd talked. How he didn't confront Dr. Whiles because he didn't feel like he could make waves. I thought about Gayle begging her mom not to complain. We all know this story: how difficult it is to push back against powerful men. This made sense to me when it came to Dr. Whiles. But I hadn't realized that Jay, in his short career, had already amassed enough power and respect to silence those he had wronged. I hadn't been thinking of him as another teacher, someone with the ability, and perhaps the propensity, to "corrupt the youth."

Reading those men's stories, I wondered if the added pressure might push Jay to come forward. To admit all he had done—to us but also to others—and talk about how he planned to try and make amends. I had hope, in other words: that thing with feathers. But instead of repenting, Jay disappeared—as much as that was possible. He closed his social media accounts. Erased his website. As if he'd never existed.

For a couple of days, at least. Then someone on Twitter posted a screenshot of an email he'd sent to friends.

"As many of you know," he wrote to them, "I'm going through the darkest time of my life (another death threat email? That's fun!). There's a lot of misinformation about me in the world. Feel free to text or call if you want to ask me questions. I'm sorry I've made some of you doubt me. As a writer, however, I try to always teach my students there are multiple points of view and narratives in a seemingly singular story. Be kind to one another. Spread light."

It was late at night when I read those lines. I couldn't sleep and I'd gone online, hoping to find a distraction. Instead, I found that screenshot, and reading it, I knew Jay would never confess. He had made the same moves that I'd been seeing politicians make more and more frequently: claiming there were two sides to every story, to every statement of truth, implying that the facts are never quite as clear as they seem. I felt the feathers molt, the weight return, as if the burden I'd tried to share with others had been hoisted back onto me. In the days that followed, that weight only intensified. The fact-checker at the magazine where my story had been published forwarded me a long text that Jay had sent him. Jay hadn't responded to multiple emails and calls from the fact-checker before my essay was published, but soon afterward, he began texting the fact-checker, saying he wanted to tell his side of the story, too. One of his texts included that story, a narrative that appeared to have been sent to others as well. "For anyone who cares to know, here is what happened to me," Jay wrote as an opening. He then retooled his story of a stalker, claiming now that the harassment had started in December, well before the job interview at the University of Michigan or the accusations against Marta and me. It was a change in his story's timeline that multiple people who worked with him told me wasn't true; they all said his story of the stalker had started in April or May, after the accusations against Marta and after Jay had learned about our lawsuit. Jay wrote that he'd also been too busy during the spring semester to have attacked Marta and me, and that doing so was out of character for him. "For those who know me," he wrote, "I think it is clear I do not have this malice."

More upsetting than his refusal to tell the truth, however, was a turn about halfway through that text, when Jay suddenly summoned a new villain: Nan. It was she, he claimed, who had "coordinated the campaign that turned so many people against me and my life upside down." This woman who had been among the first people to believe us, who had risked her own safety to protect us and keep me informed. I was so angry and sickened when I read that, I no longer felt sorry about Jay being outed online. I felt like he deserved it all, whatever it all became.

13

In May, we graduated from high school. Before we did, I fell in love
for the first time—or what I realized then was love. Not the obsession
I'd had with Lara, nor the infatuation with Gina, but a mutual feeling,
a shared desire to be with each other, to touch her hand and take long
drives in her Jeep with the top down, to listen to music in bed and com-
pare descriptions of our ideal house, a place where we might one day
live, together. Her name was Penny and she was three years older than
me, a college dropout from Texas who had enlisted in the air force to
get out of her hometown, someone who loved the same book I had as a
child, *My Side of the Mountain*, and the poet I loved then, Sylvia Plath.
She was gorgeous and funny and smart, but every time I visited her on
the military base where she had a dorm room, we had to pretend to be
friends. Don't Ask, Don't Tell had just gone into effect, and it meant that,
while queer people could now enlist in the military, they had to keep
their identity to themselves. I had come out to almost everyone at school
by then, told my sister and would tell my parents later that year; and yet
dating Penny, I found myself in a new closet. But at least I was in love, I
told myself. That's what I thought I wanted.

In the final weeks of school, those of us graduating from our magnet
program stood for a photo together in the courtyard beside the school
cafeteria. Right before the photo was taken, I stuffed a sweatshirt under

my tank top and pretended to be pregnant, smiling beside Mrs. Morris, who smiled, too, like a mother to all of us. We talked about our upcoming exams and what colleges or universities we planned to attend, where we would live the following year. I was going to Haverford in Pennsylvania, accepted for early admission based in part on an essay I'd written about honesty and the time my mom caught me lying about seeing Danny and Kevin at the library. James was going to Carnegie Mellon. Eric planned to attend a Bible college in upstate New York. Others were staying closer: Marcus went to Florida A&M and Gayle to New College of Florida, a hippie school without grades, the college to which I would eventually transfer, wanting to be closer to Penny, hoping to make that first relationship work even though it was fated, almost from the beginning, to end.

After graduation, those of us left in our magnet program—down to 85 from close to 110 that first year—came together one final time for a banquet. In the pictures from that night, I wear shiny red shoes and a black dress, my hair cut short, my eyelashes thick with mascara. Everyone else was dressed up as well; and we all looked at one another a little like we had that first year: evaluating, categorizing. Green Day's "The Time of Your Life" and the Cardigan's "Love Me, Love Me" played over a montage of photos of us projected on a screen. There was little Eric with his boyish face and that curly mop of hair. There was Gayle, with her gap-toothed smile. There was Marcus, so skinny that first year, his hair shorn short, trying too hard to look cool. And then there I was, beside Lara, in my mismatched clothes, looking happy, and lost.

Mrs. Rodriguez and Mrs. Adams, our government and English teachers, sang "I'm so excited" to us on stage, their huge personalities taking up more room than just their bodies. Keisha's mom said the prayer. Mr. Garza's parents accepted a gift from us in his name. At one point, a group of students put on a skit impersonating our teachers during a faculty meeting. My friend Erin was Ms. Ritter, complaining that the meeting was going on too long. Dale was Mr. Kane, speaking with a Kennedyesque accent so strong the real Mr. Kane's wife cackled up a storm in the audience. Keisha pretended to be Mrs. Adams practicing her kung fu moves.

Someone else stuffed a pillow under their belly and imitated our trigo-nometry teacher Mr. Bell. And James had become Dr. Whiles, his belly low and mustache white, while the real Dr. Whiles was "conspicuously absent," as Gayle later put it. Maybe because of the fight in the portable. Maybe because he was already on his way out, about to start teaching at that new school to a new set of students. Whatever the reason, he didn't show, and most of us never had a chance to say goodbye.

I was one of three students asked to give a speech that night. When it was my turn, I pulled out a handwritten essay I still have. It starts by talking about Lara, and how she was the only friend I had in school that first year, or the only one I thought important enough to have. I admitted that for a while the only things that mattered to me then were her friendship and whatever we were studying in Dr. Whiles's class. But somewhere along the line, I told the people in the room that night, those priorities changed. My world expanded to include much more than two obsessions. "So this program, and my journey therein, has not been the sterile intellectual escapade I expected at all," I told them. "It's been like a family I joined, or was adopted by. My memories of you guys are so rich and so fertile and I swear they will color all the experiences I've had and will have in the future."

14

That might have been the end of the story of Dr. Whiles. For years, it felt like one. We all graduated, went off to college, grew up, married or didn't marry, started our careers, maybe had kids; and with the passage of time, we stopped thinking so much about what had or hadn't happened when we were fifteen or seventeen. Like that scene from *The Wind in the Willows* I reread in ninth grade, time brought us "the gift of forgetfulness." Because of that, Dr. Whiles's story might have stayed there in the past forever. I know that. If I hadn't found that photo of us when I was seven months pregnant. If there hadn't been an election. If I hadn't called up Gayle and asked to hear her story. But also, if I hadn't started researching Dr. Whiles, following him through the internet, tracking down any mention of his name, until one day when I stumbled upon a document that rebutted any version of this story that might end neatly with our graduation and coming-of-age. Nothing ended there, even if we were convinced it did.

A month after we graduated, a website run by the Holocaust denier Ernst Zündel published a letter from someone in our magnet program, a kid one year younger than me, but someone who knew a lot of the same people and who had all the same teachers. The post started with a preface by Zündel in which he explains that "a goodly amount of our correspondence comes from youngsters in high school or even junior high." He writes that usually he advises those students to ask questions and speak out about what he called the lies of the past, but this time he decided to "let a youngster speak for himself."

"I too am a high school student," wrote the unnamed teenager in his email, "however my brain is not as deteriorated by liberal lies and Jewish rulings as others." His writing was awkward in its offensiveness, overly formal and at times grammatically incorrect, like a child pretending to be a neo-Nazi, but chilling nonetheless. "The following is a small story of how I became involved in the holocaust hoax, and how I became 'aware,'" he wrote. "Do with this as you see fit."

That small story started with Mr. Kane.

"It was my sophomore year in high school and I was under the influence of a Jewish history teacher," wrote the student. He said he paid little attention in class until the end of that year, when Mr. Kane passed out a newsletter from the Anti-Defamation League that addressed the topic of Holocaust denialism. The newsletter mentioned Arthur Butz, a professor at Northwestern University who had denied the Holocaust, and after reading that, the student went to Barnes & Noble and requested Butz's book, *The Hoax of the Twentieth Century*. From there he discovered the Institute for Historical Review, a pseudo-academic organization that publishes material questioning the Holocaust—but also Jewish history more generally. It's an insidious organization, so much so that in researching Plato's cave allegory online at one point, I found myself unwittingly reading an article on the organization's website. I only realized my mistake when I got to the line "Paleolithic barbarian Hebrew people." I looked up, noticed the URL, and quickly shut the page. But this student read everything from IHR that he could, and he wrote in his notes for Mr. Kane's class that year that Butz "sounded like a normal man suddenly made aware of truth." Based on that and other responses, he told Zündel, he was soon branded a Holocaust denier at our school.

"A few days later a verbal battle broke out amongst the teachers," he wrote. "As it turns out, my philosophy teacher, Dr. Whiles, had the same views as Butz and other Revisionist writers, and when he heard of K's

letter, he began some propaganda for himself. He told all his classes that
the holocaust did not happen—that 6,000,000 were not killed. Mr. Kane
exploded and the next day brought with him letters and other Kosher
paraphernalia which attempted to 'prove' the holocaust existed. I do
not know any more of the battle aside from Dr. Whiles's staunch and
unyielding views and the Jew which weeped [*sic*] in despair as memories
of the holocaust were brought back to his mind."

Reading that section of the letter, I had the feeling one sometimes
has when a friend or family member recalls a shared memory differently. Parts of the story feel familiar, but there is a disparity that makes
the whole telling strange. I had heard about the fight between Mr. Kane
and Dr. Whiles from three different people, but here it was, being told
again, by this kid who saw Mr. Kane as the villain and Dr. Whiles as the
vanquishing hero. I tried to imagine this anonymous student as he would
have been then. I even looked through my yearbooks for his face, as if I
could have recognized him. What scared me most about that letter was
not what he said but the fact that he existed in the first place.

"Now I have many conversations with my friends about the Jews," he
wrote near the end of his email. "There is a group of around 10 of us who talk
all the time of the holocaust, of international bankers, of Eustus Mullins [*sic*]
and other revisionists, and even of Dr. William L. Pierce. What's funny about
the latter is we are not even all White—two or three are Indians . . . ! The
point is, we are out here, and there are more of us than you think."

That last line stayed with me. Because it sounds a lot like what others
had been saying in the years since I started working on this book. There are
more of them than you think. The throngs of marchers in Charlottesville
shouting "The Jews will not replace us" the first summer after Manuela
was born, the men rushing into synagogues and shopping centers with
guns aloft in the years after that, all because they believe the stories about
being replaced, the thousands who are convinced that parents would fake
their children's murder, that politicians were trafficking in sex, that an
election had been stolen, that the earth was no longer round. There are
more of them than you think. This is bigger than we want to believe.

15

Summer came and we watched the rising body count. We watched the fights over what was real about this virus and what had been made up. We watched as a policeman in Minneapolis knelt on the neck of a Black man who kept saying "I can't breathe," and then "Mama," and "Mama" before he went quiet. We watched the police lie about what had happened after the fact, issuing a press release that tried to rewrite the order and details of events. We knew they would have gotten away with it, too, if there hadn't been a video, if someone—a teenage girl—hadn't thought to pull out her phone, record it all, and make sure this time there was proof.

Fall arrived and with it another election. We watched as that election was disputed, and we waited to see what would happen next. In January, two days before my birthday, I talked to someone from high school I barely remembered. Her name was Audrey. In the memories I did have of her, she'd been there our freshman and sophomore years, but after that she had dropped out. Something about drugs, I thought, or getting fed up with all the work—though none of that ended up being true. I got ahold of her through another classmate I also barely remembered but whom I had found on Facebook. That classmate, when we talked, kept mentioning Audrey and what a great memory she had, and I knew immediately I'd want to talk to her. I had no idea that what we eventually discussed, though, would simultaneously resolve and unravel so much.

Audrey and I talked at first about the books we'd read our freshman year—*Hitchhiker's Guide to the Galaxy, Brave New World, Fahrenheit 451*—and she told me that Dr. Whiles's class had been transformative for her, which wasn't rare to hear. Lots of people told me that his class was the one they remembered, that he had changed them more than anyone else. What was different with Audrey was what happened when I asked what else she remembered about his class.

"Like the revisionist history?" she said, and I laughed, surprised, but also relieved, that she brought it up on her own.

"Yes," I said. "What do you remember about the revisionist history?"

"I think we were calling into question that the Holocaust was as terrible"—she paused, seeming to look for the right word—"an atrocity as it actually was in terms of the number of people that had died."

She remembered the debate video that we watched and how it led to a "heated passionate discussion" between Dr. Whiles and Mr. Kane in the portable sometime after that. She remembered it having shocking material, but when I asked how she had reacted after watching it, Audrey said she hadn't been that upset. She never thought, she said, that Dr. Whiles was a Holocaust denier himself.

"I think he was using it to expand our minds," she said, echoing Joel, "not necessarily to say this is what happened, just to show that there was this different viewpoint out there. I think it was a challenge to a group of kids who should have been able to handle it."

That last line stopped me again, though I tried not to let on. I obviously hadn't been able to handle it. I'd broken down in tears. I'd stormed out of the classroom. I was still grappling with it twenty-five years later. I wondered what handling it would have looked like. Laughing at Dr. Whiles and how weird he was? Or seriously considering the story as he had presented it to us? I wonder that today as well, when crying and leaving no longer feels like an option. Because it's not only one country, or one problem attributable to one politician: it's everywhere and everything.

Instead of saying any of that, I changed the subject. We talked about reading *The Sound and the Fury* and debating NAFTA and watching the O. J. Simpson trial in class. At some point something Audrey said reminded me of someone else I had almost forgotten, a kid named Blake. He was one of the smartest kids in our class that first year, handsome and witty, but he'd also fallen under Dr. Whiles's spell—more so than me or Lara or James or Gayle or anyone else. I knew he had been close with Audrey but also that he'd eventually disappeared.

"What ever happened to him?" I asked. "I remember a rumor that he'd had a psychological break."

"He did have a mental breakdown," Audrey said. Then she said that she and Blake weren't just close friends, they had been dating, were dating when he started to act erratically, when he got caught stealing, was sent to juvenile detention, and eventually when he dropped out.

"He was one of the smart ones," she said. "It's a shame that he wasn't able to cut it. He would actually be a good person to talk to. He took a lot of what Dr. Whiles was saying at face value."

I went looking for Blake on Facebook after we hung up, and I eventually found him: overweight, balding, and kind of a prick: the type of person who posts memes about the absurdity of transgenderism and the criminality of protesting for Black Lives. But looking at his profile photo, I could see the kid he'd once been, and staring at that face, I realized I'd made a significant mistake. James wasn't the person I'd talked to on the phone in high school about astral projection. It was Blake. Over the years, I realized, and especially after Blake disappeared, I must have merged the two of them in my mind, a composite character of sorts: both uncannily smart, both with so much potential, and both always hanging on Dr. Whiles's every word. James, though, had ended up a success story—at least in the most traditional ways: a university researcher, married with kids. While Blake was some dude ranting on Facebook about how fact-checking is another form of censorship.

Their divergent trajectories said something important, I was sure, about Dr. Whiles, but the resurrection of Blake also said something about

me: I had been wrong regarding at least one detail in the story I was trying to tell. I could correct that fact, though, and I am now—even though
Blake never responded to my requests for an interview, I know this is the
truth. He and I had talked on the phone for hours in high school and at
one point he brought up leaving the body; he'd said he could do it, and
I'd been jealous of him. Now look at us. We're on opposite poles of a
spinning wheel.

Two days later, the U.S. Capitol was stormed by a mob of people
who believed the election had been a hoax. I was parking outside the
grocery store when I first heard the chaos on the radio, at a point before
anyone was willing to give that chaos a name, and when I went inside
to buy milk and coffee, I shopped in a trance. I worried someone in the
store might pull out a gun. I remembered the race war predicted in *The
Turner Diaries*, that novel by William L. Pierce. I thought about the pre-
dictions of insurrection that cinched so many conspiracy theories. We
hadn't taken those lies seriously, we'd thought we could "handle" them,
and here we were. In the middle of an attempted coup that within days
would be rewritten by those who supported it as just another protest,
as something orchestrated by the left, or as a false flag manipulation
that would be used to "strip Americans of their basic rights." When I
checked again on Blake from high school, he was in the middle of that
thicket, posting almost every day, sometimes multiple times, about how
the story being told in the news, the story of what had just happened in
our country—an attempted coup—was a lie we were being fed to keep
us quiet. This isn't a democracy we're fighting over, he argued in one of
those posts. It's a republic.

16

There's a final part of the allegory of the cave that I never knew existed until I read the *Republic* in full. The man standing in the sunlight at the end of the story does not stay there forever, reveling in the truth he has discovered, as Dr. Whiles had implied. Instead, Socrates imagines what might happen if that man left the open sky and bright sunlight and returned to the shadow world below.

"If such a man were to come down again and sit in the same seat, on coming suddenly from the sun wouldn't his eyes get infected with darkness?" Socrates asks.

The answer is yes, but worse. Socrates hypothesizes that the other prisoners, upon seeing their disoriented companion return from above, would likely laugh at him, jeering that he has come back to them delusional and unable to comprehend the reality they so plainly see. And if this man were then to attempt to explain his new knowledge to his companions or to set them free, loosening their chains and dragging them up toward the sunlight so they, too, could see the truth of things, "wouldn't they kill him?" Socrates asks.

"No doubt about it," says Glaucon, Socrates's primary interlocutor throughout most of the *Republic*.

To those prisoners, the freed man would appear more mad than enlightened, puttering on about something called sunlight and how the things and ideas that populate the world of the cave were, in fact, a fiction. This man might resemble Socrates, at least as he was seen by many Athenians before he was put to death. But he also sounds a little like how Dr. Whiles appeared to so many of us in high school. Which is not to say that Dr. Whiles was anything like Socrates but that allegories are tricky forms of storytelling. Something is always standing in for something else. The question is who represents what? Who are the shadow makers? Who are those freed from the cave? What is the cave even? And what is the sunlight?

A problem inherent to this ending for the cave allegory is how, or if, truth can exist in the collective. Socrates presents a world in which those who have been led up to the sunlight—which in his telling means those educated to know the essence of things, the Forms—cannot easily communicate what they've learned with those in the cave caught up debating shadows. It is an elitist scenario (Plato has often been called an elitist), but it also speaks to a problem that feels familiar today. Try convincing someone who believes in a secret Jewish cabal that they've been duped, and they'll likely either pity your ignorance or decide you are part of the cabal yourself. Try to fact-check misinformation and you may be called a censor or compared to Hitler. Agree to debate the Holocaust with a denier and your commitment will be used to bolster the idea that such history is still up for debate.

The real damage to Holocaust denialism, in fact, came not from a debate but a lawsuit—though one that centered on questions of truth. In 2000, soon after we graduated from high school, a British Holocaust denier and author named David Irving sued Deborah Lipstadt, an American Jewish historian, for libel after Lipstadt called Irving a denier in her 1993 book *Denying the Holocaust*. Lipstadt won in court, after five weeks of detailed testimony by experts who picked apart Irving's misleading and at times inaccurate research. That slow, methodical dismantling of a false narrative—along with the accompanying public humiliation of one of the key tellers of it—is now seen as a major reason for the waning power of Holocaust denialism over the past two decades. But people still deny the Holocaust. People still cling to conspiratorial thinking. They are still enamored of lies despite our professed allegiance to the truth. And one reading of Plato's allegory, especially the way it ends, is that this is a condition we will never escape.

I don't want to fall into that kind of cynicism. Nor do I want to return to that moment in which I longed to see the Twitter mobs tear Jay apart. Or to that state of panic in which I worried that everyone in the grocery store had a gun. I know hope can be debilitating, that it can keep us from seeing the truth of things, but I also remember Gayle's story of escaping the trap of Dr. Whiles's conspiracies and I briefly feel it: those feathers, that potential for flight. It's not easy for me to think of Gayle as a conspiracy theorist, but she was one, briefly. And her transformation from delusion to truth didn't happen immediately after the conversation with her mom, or even the following year when she went away to college. Gayle knew something had gone wrong with Dr. Whiles, but she still felt confused, and his ideas lingered, as did her guilt for having been taken in by them. She might have stayed like that forever, in the limbo of unresolved beliefs that can happen when time passes and you chose to forget instead of address the past. But then by chance in college, Gayle went up to visit a friend who was at Emory University, and there, she met Lipstadt, the Holocaust historian.

"That was the first moment I began to process what happened," Gayle told me. "She was the first person I really talked to about that. She was so kind. I remember her telling me that it wasn't my fault that I got hoodwinked."

Gayle worked herself free from those shadows, in other words, by having conversations: first with her mom; then with Lipstadt; and, later, I assume with others, including me. In that way, her story is a counter to Socrates's caution that the shadow watchers might kill whoever tries to show them the truth. Her story demonstrates the value of conversation, of discussions—of what Socrates was trying to do when he questioned everyone in the agora of Athens, and what Plato was arguably hoping to do when he wrote: to seek the truth, or move closer to it, not through propositions or fact-checking, but through dialogue.

PART IV

"A Tale Was Saved and Not Lost"

Dear Reader,

I am at a writing residency. It's May. It feels like it is always May in this book. Or April—the cruelest month. This residency isn't a real residency; it's a tiny backhouse in Arizona that Marta and I rented for three weeks so that I might secure some time away from Lucia and Manuela to finish writing. I think sometimes that I started this project when Manuela was still part of me. I was seven months pregnant when I found that photo from high school. She's now four years old. We've passed through an entire presidency. A global pandemic has come and gone and come and gone and come again. I think about how I wrote that this is not a "real" residency as if I had a handle on what is real. Even as I write "real" now, my computer has other opinions. It's developed a lag and my words appear more slowly than I type them: r e a l n o w.

The delay reminds me of the first time I saw a shuttle launch as a kid in Florida. It was soon after we moved to Tampa from the Midwest. Jennifer Pierce's mom took several of her friends, including me, in their minivan to watch the launch from across a body of water—a swamp or maybe a small lake—in Cape Canaveral. It was dark that night and I felt awkward like I often did in sixth grade. We sat on blankets and slapped slap bracelets on our wrists and waited for so long that, when the launch began, I questioned whether it was real. Across that body of water, we watched the rocket push itself into the air, more slowly than I thought possible. Then we heard the rumble of its ascension, and a couple of seconds later, we felt it: the ground below us began to tremble even though the rocket had already left the earth.

Those delays in our perception that night were what Dr. Whiles had been referring to when he said we could never know if the clock is real: we are unreliable sources, in part because our senses leave us out of sync with the real world, the things in themselves, if they exist at all. The true clock is buried somewhere underneath all those sense perceptions, inaccessible to those of us sitting in the classroom, just as the launching rocket was unknowable to any of us watching that night. Both the clock and the rocket are even more unknowable to me now, this "I now" trying to excavate my "I then" from bits of memory and interviews and scarce documentation. Though I imagine that Socrates would remind me, if he and I were in dialogue now, that I might inch closer to understanding all of this—the clock, the rocket, my past—by thinking the subject through, by asking questions, by having a dialogue.

There is a giant tortoise at this residency that isn't a real residency. He lives in the backyard of the front house, which means I can see him out the front windows when I write at the kitchen table. Every morning, I wake up, pull back the curtains to see if he's out yet, munching on grass. He's the size of a golden retriever and likes to have his back scratched. Some afternoons, when I need a break, I go out to the yard. I bring him some kale or, a treat, strawberries, fill his water bowl. He moves faster than I thought a tortoise could when he hears me coming. He sidles up to the tiny fence that keeps him off the sidewalk. His name is Lemmy, which feels like the perfect name for a backyard tortoise at a writing residency that is not quite real.

I've been calling this book an "autobiography of shadows," but I mean "autobiography" in an allegorical sense and "shadows" as a metaphor. The shadows are everything I believe is real in this world. Like Lemmy the tortoise. Like the clock. Like Jay and Dr. Whiles. But the shadows are also everything that's been invented here so far: the lies that Jay and Dr. Whiles and others have told, and perhaps the ones that I've unwittingly spun myself, here at my desk, trying to rake the past into neat piles. An autobiography of those shadows, then, would be an autobiography of everything in my life except what's true, which frankly feels like a relief to say out loud. Because writing about "the truth" gives me the creeps. Even as I keep trying to do it.

Dear Reader,

I had the idea just now, as I went to take a nap, of placing Jay in Dr. Whiles's classroom, and having him confront some of the questions we were asked our first year. What if he'd had that when he was young? Would it have made a difference?

The setting, then, is this: our classroom in Chapin High School my freshman year. Dr. Whiles is up front, like he always was. He's flipping the toothpick in his mouth. He's leaning back in his chair and putting his feet up on the desk, sucking his teeth and talking about Steak 'n Shake—how much he loves it (a detail Eric remembered)—while the students file in and take their seats. This is a different student body, a different world than the one I knew. And Jay is there. He's a small kid, wiry, but the teachers tend to like him. He's sweet. The kind of kid who, in college and grad school, would bring his professors coffee (a detail I gleaned from an essay of his online).

Dr. Whiles, though, thinks differently.

"Jay," he says, nodding his head. "You decided to join us today."

Jay comes every day, so it's not clear what this means or why Dr. Whiles says it on this particular day—let's say it's a Tuesday. But Jay knows enough not to question Dr. Whiles.

"I wouldn't miss your class for the world," he says. He's smiling, hoping it can be a joke they share. But Dr. Whiles only grunts. He closes the door after the final student arrives, then remains on his feet. There's a poster behind him that reads Visualize Whirled Peas. It always made Jay laugh. He's the kind of kid who likes wordplay. Who likes getting praise for the way he uses words. Just the other day, he wrote that phrase down and asked his mom to read it out loud. When she did, she guffawed.

"Where'd you hear that?" she asked Jay.

"I just made it up," he said.

She stared at him for a second but didn't say anything else.

In class, Dr. Whiles is staring at the clock. It says 1:30, a time of the day when most students grow tired, start to yawn and stretch, perhaps even fall asleep atop folded arms on their desks. But Jay is alert. He's waiting for his chance to impress Dr. Whiles. He needs this approval.

"You see that clock on the wall," Dr. Whiles says now, looking at everyone and no one in particular. Everyone turns toward the wall, including Jay. He sees the clock and he wonders what will happen next. Maybe he even respects this move, the way that Dr. Whiles slowly builds suspense. Like the teller of a good story. A literary thriller. A philosophical heist.

"Does it exist?" Dr. Whiles asks.

There is silence. Jay wonders what he should say. The answer is clearly not yes. But it doesn't make sense to say no either. As he waits, a girl raises her hand.

"I can see it, so it exists," she says.

Dr. Whiles moves through his spiel, drawing from Kant or maybe Schopenhauer's take on Kant, how we can never know if anything concrete exists because we are confined to our bodies and limited by our individual perceptions, blah, blah, blah. The clock, the backpack, the boy, it's all phenomena, not the "thing-in-itself."

Jay listens. But what does he think? I want the idea of our shared unknowability to rock him like it had me. I want to know the unknowability of him.

I see him staring at the clock. I see him sneaking a look at Dr. Whiles when he's sure he's not looking. Maybe he's thinking that one day he'll get a PhD, too, and then he won't have to think back on this shitty school and this crazy teacher and all these fucked-up kids. Maybe he's thinking, like Thrasymachus does in the *Republic*, that justice is only "the advantage of the stronger." Maybe he's assuming he can just shrug it off. The cave. The videos Dr. Whiles will eventually show. The award he might one day give him.

But then Dr. Whiles does something I hadn't expected. He looks at Jay.

"What do you think?" he asks.

The room grows quiet. Dr. Whiles never does this. He jokes with students. He teases some of them. But he rarely forces one of us to answer a question if we haven't volunteered ourselves.

Jay shifts in his seat. He looks from the clock to Dr. Whiles, from Dr. Whiles to his toothpick, which keeps flipping. The second hand ticks, but there is still so much more time before this class ends.

"Why did you lie?" Dr. Whiles says when Jay still doesn't answer.

Jay looks up. He's confused.

"Why did you lie and once you were caught, why didn't you come clean?"

"I don't know what you're talking about," Jay says.

"You do."

"I think the clock exists, okay. We all see it. It's there."

"That's not what I'm talking about."

"I didn't lie. I was hacked."

"Stop lying. It will feel better."

"I feel fine."

"Well, I don't."

Dear Reader,

One connection between Dr. Whiles and Jay, but also Marta and me, is that we all are, or were, teachers. My mom was a teacher, too. My dad was one as well, but he was bad enough at the other part of academia—dealing with administration—that he quit. Lucia will also likely grow up to teach; she's pretended to be a teacher ever since she was toddler. After coming home from day care some days, she would line up the condiments from the fridge and teach them lessons in our kitchen. Then she'd place them facedown on the tile for their nap and pat their backs until they fell asleep. We have a video of her moving through this routine that I watch every so often to remind myself what I love about being human. How imitative we are. How caring is learned. How much I love Lucia. And Manuela. And Marta.

Plato was a teacher, too, as was Socrates, and the cave allegory is also a metaphor for what education is or could be. Socrates describes the process of educating the guardian class of his ideal city as a "turning of the soul" toward the sunlight, one in which future rulers, those philosopher kings, are taught to know what is good and just and to use that knowledge to protect those virtues within the republic or regime. He lists a series of subjects that said students should study—calculation, geometry, astronomy, etc.—all aimed at helping students to use the visible world to think more deeply about the intelligible one. Let's say you have a triangle. You may see that triangle in the visible world—a slice of pizza, say—and you could also draw it on a piece of paper—like the rooftops Manuela often puts on her tiny crayoned houses—but Socrates wants his students to know what properties comprise a triangle, what makes it a triangle and not, say, a square, and thus to reorient their understanding from the concrete to the abstract, so that the visible world is understood in terms of the true Forms, or patterns, that underlie it.

That education is only a prelude to what Socrates calls "the song itself," the dialectic: the art of investigation through dialogue that Plato re-creates in his books. But not just anyone should learn the dialectic, Socrates argues: only the steadiest; the smartest; and also, oddly, the best looking should be given that education. (Socrates is said to have been the ugliest man in Athens.) He warns, too, against teaching young people how to investigate the truth through dialogue—because, he says, they are like puppies who tear apart an argument for the fun of it.

"Don't you notice," Socrates says in the *Republic*, "how great is the harm coming from the practice of dialectic these days?"

It's an argument that Dr. Whiles summarizes in his dissertation, that study of the potential harms of philosophy for young people that I read my first year in Arizona. But he concludes—after a qualitative and quantitative analysis of student work and feedback from a philosophy class he taught years before he taught us—that his teaching, at least, doesn't harm students (though he also couldn't prove that it did them any good). Reading that dissertation four years ago had felt revelatory to me because it was the first time I had read what Dr. Whiles had written. He'd read our essays for years, but we'd never seen how his mind worked on the page. Reading his dissertation again recently, though, it felt significant for another reason: it was proof that, at one point at least, Dr. Whiles had also wondered whether his teaching might cause harm.

I think about him now and how much I want to interview him for this book, though really what I hope for is a dialogue. I want the same with Jay, but Marta told me she might divorce me if I reach out to him. "We finally have him out of our life," she said. "Don't do anything that would bring him back in." My focus, then, has to be on Dr. Whiles. I want to write to him. I need to write to him. But I'm scared.

Dear Reader,

Another moment of conjecture: Dr. Whiles is a boy, a young man. He lives in a tiny town that we'll call Athens, about an hour's drive from Lubbock, and maybe one day I drive out there. Maybe I drive right up to his house. I get off the two-lane highway and pass through downtown, driving by brick buildings filled with shoe stores and pharmacies and banks that decades later will hold only meth heads and prairie birds trying to nest. When I find Dr. Whiles's house, he is sitting on the front porch. Seventeen years old. A towhead. Nerdy and a little unkempt. His mom is inside. She'll live with him again years later, before she dies, but he can't know this now. He's only looking ahead a year or two, when he sees himself going to college, maybe studying philosophy, one day getting a job.

He's been taught to be polite, so he stands as I get out of the car and walk toward the front porch. I'm seventeen again. Long blond hair I will chop off when Gina breaks up with me. Birkenstocks. Ratty jeans. He thinks I'm a hippie, most likely. Lost in West Texas. I think he looks just like all the other kids my age: boring and nondescript.

"Hello?" he says, now on the porch steps. It's windy. It's always windy in West Texas, and the sun comes through a filter of dust.

"Hey," I say.

I sit down on the porch step and he hesitates a moment before sitting beside me.

"I'm lost," I say.

"You're in Athens, Texas," he says, looking less confused.

"No," I say. "I'm talking allegorically."

Dan. That's his name. (It's not his name.) I can't call him Dr. Whiles. Not when he's so skinny and nervous, like boys his age are when they're smart but suddenly don't understand something.

"Do you know how to get out of the cave?" I ask, because why not?

He stares at me. Maybe he thinks I'm on something. PCP. Acid. Grass.

"There aren't any caves around here," he says. "There's cotton. And oil. For caves, you'd have to visit Austin. They've got bats there, too. I heard about them from a friend. A bunch of them live under a bridge and fly up at dusk, dappling the sky with darkness."

"I always knew you wanted to be a writer."

"What?"

"You're going to be a teacher when you grow up, but I always knew you were like me. You wanted to grow up and write."

"Are you on drugs?"

"Have you read Kierkegaard yet?"

"No."

"He writes philosophy in the form of a story. You'll love him one day. He believed in God."

"I believe in God."

"You won't when you're older. Then you will again, many years after that."

"You *are* on drugs."

He stands up, but he doesn't move toward the door.

"Dan," I say. "Please sit down. I need your help."

He doesn't sit back down.

"With what?" he says.

"What do you think the cave is?" I ask.

"Something that's got something to do with you being high."

"I'm not high."

"All right, then something to do with you being crazy."

"I'm not crazy."

"What are you, then?"

"I'm lost. I already told you that."

"This doesn't make any sense."

He turns toward the door, like he's committed to leaving this time.

"Wait!" I say too loudly. "The truth is, I'm here because I'm avoiding you in the future."

He turns back toward me.

"Miss," he says, "that makes even less sense than the stuff about the cave."

"I know, but trust me. I don't mean any harm. I'm just trying to work up the nerve to write to the future you by better understanding the boy you once were."

Dan sits down on the steps again. Together we stare out at the thundering flatness.

"I want to be a writer," he says. "You were right about that."

"See! This is great. What kind of writer? What do you want to write?"

"I want to write novels. Like Larry McMurtry or Hemingway, but I also love sci-fi. My dream is to write a sci-fi novel where humans are so advanced they no longer need their brains or even their bodies to communicate. Anybody will be able to write like Shakespeare or think like Socrates and they'll be able to solve all the world's problems—only something will have to go wrong, obviously, or it wouldn't be a good book. I haven't figured out that part yet."

"Maybe they'll elect an evil ruler who tries to ruin the world?"

"Too predictable."

"Maybe they'll all get super sick and there will be a cure but half the population will refuse to take it?"

"That doesn't make sense."

"Maybe they'll realize they're all stuck in a cave together, staring at shadows, and instead of just letting one or two of them out into the sunlight, they'll conspire to free each other, and then they'll make a mad rush for the mouth of the cave, but they'll end up trampling their fellow citizens to death on the way there and only a few of them will get out in the end?"

"You really are weird."

"I feel better about you."

"We just met."

"I know, but I've been thinking about you for a long time."

"Why?"

"Because of these questions I need to ask you."

"Why don't you just ask them now?"

"You can't know the answers yet."

"Then why are you here?"

"I told you. I'm procrastinating."

"But what are you scared of?"

"I don't know. That I'll feel like I used to feel in your classroom when I was your age."

"You look like you're my age now."

"I mean in the future when I'm still your age."

"What did you feel?"

"That I had no control, and you had all the power."

He starts to laugh, slowly at first but in a way that builds until it's almost scary.

"I'm not powerful at all," he says when he catches his breath. "Look at me. I'm a seventeen-year-old kid living with his mom in Athens, Texas."

I look at him, really look at him, like he's asked me to do. He's smaller than me, and so skinny I can see his collarbone. He looks a little scared.

"You're right. You're not that powerful anymore."

He smiles, and it's a nice smile.

"You feel better?" he asks.

"I do."

"Can I go now? I'm getting hungry."

"Yeah, sure, go inside. I'm just going to sit out here a bit and then I'll leave."

"Okay."

"Dan?"

"Yes?"

"Can you try to remember this talk, when you grow up?"

"Sure," he says, and then he disappears behind a slamming screen door.

Dear Reader,

Today, I've committed to writing to Dr. Whiles—to attempt a real dialogue with him instead of inventing ones in my head. I try the email address I have first, the one from some high school records that Mrs. Morris sent me two years ago, but my email bounces back. It bounces back once, and I do nothing. It bounces a second time, and I still do nothing. On the third notice, I start searching for another way to contact him.

I remember the website where I found Dr. Whiles's photos, where there was a picture of him, too, dressed in the safari wear of rich people who visit Florida or Texas for fishing trips or birding expeditions. All beige and ripstop nylon. A brimmed hat, an expensive camera strapped around his neck. He stands beside a live oak, almost smiling, hair neatly trimmed—the mustache now gone. Beside the photo of him are his photos of blue herons. They are taking flight. They are standing in pairs on marsh grasses. They are wading with fish in their beaks. They are carrying twigs to a nest. They are leaving a nest. The website offers an option to follow the artist, and then another for sending him an email. I click on that link and paste my original email into the message box.

Dear Dr. Whiles,

I'm not sure if you remember me, but I was in your class at Chapin High School (class of 1997). I'm a writer now (and a professor) and I'm working on a book that looks back on high school, and in particular a number of the questions that were raised in your class (the shadow text for the book is Plato's Allegory of the Cave).

I hoped you might be willing to be interviewed for this book. I have lots of questions about what we learned during our two years in your classes, and also about you as a teacher. (I'm a teacher now, and I often wish I could be half as inspiring as you were.) I've already interviewed a number of my fellow classmates, including Eric, James, Carry, Keisha, Bobbie, Marcus, and others, and also teachers like Ms. Ritter, Mr. Lakatos, Mrs. Perez.

If you'd have some time in the next few weeks, I'd love to talk, either via phone or Zoom.

Best,
Sarah Viren

I press Send. Then I wait.

Dear Reader,

Virginia Woolf conceived of the construct of "I now" and "I then" when she was nearly sixty. It arose from her first attempt at memoir, a genre she had read widely but practiced little. She began her sketch, as she called it, in April 1939 and the last day she worked on it was November of the following year, four months before she killed herself. In that sketch, she begins by considering memory and structure, which is to say: how to decide which memories to include and also what structure to give to a sequence of memories. In discussing the former, she writes about memories she classifies as moments of "shock" from her childhood, often moments when something seemingly insignificant happened but she remembered them forever, moments she distinguishes from the rest of her past, which she calls non-being, or "cotton wool," which is to say forgotten time.

"Perhaps this is the strongest pleasure known to me," she writes of bringing a memory to life on the page. "It is the rapture I get when in writing I seem to be discovering what Belongs to what; making a scene come right; making a character come together. From this I reach what I might call a philosophy; at any rate it is a constant idea of mine; that behind the cotton wool is a hidden pattern; that we—I mean all human beings—are connected with this; that the whole world is a work of art; that we are parts of the work of art. *Hamlet* or a Beethoven quartet is the truth about this vast mass that we call the world. But there is no Shakespeare, there is no Beethoven; certainly and emphatically there is no God; we are the words; we are the music; we are the thing itself. And I see this when I have a shock."

I had a shock that day in the portable with Dr. Whiles after he played the first part of the Holocaust debate but refused to show us the second half. I hadn't thought about it in years, but then we elected a president who lied about almost everything and used those lies to bully people into place, and I was thinking about that president while running one afternoon with my old dog Finn through the barren streets of Lubbock when I remembered my confrontation with Dr. Whiles in the portable classroom. It was a shock in the Woolfian sense, and writing into it, I did begin to see patterns behind the cotton wool.

A couple of years later, I experienced another shock, when the Reddit posts and then the accusations started coming in. That was shocking in the traditional sense, but within that drama, there were smaller moments—the day in the tent with Manuela, the interview with Melanie when I realized we had a painting in our room, and the moment with Marta in her office when I wasn't sure she was telling the truth—that felt more akin to Woolf's account of the memories that, when we dig into them, help us see the larger patterns connecting all of us.

Woolf describes writing about what belongs to what as the "strongest pleasure" and even a "rapture," and I feel that now, in this residency that isn't a residency, writing these imagined scenes, piecing together an alternate reality birthed from the one I live with every day. I can start to see the pattern sometimes, behind the wool, and it's exhilarating.

Dear Reader,

The next day, while I'm making coffee, I look at my phone and see that Dr. Whiles has already responded. His name in my inbox gives me a start.

Sarah,

Sure, I remember you and your classmates at Chapin High School.

What have you been doing since then? And I'd like to hear about any classmates that you have kept up with!

Best wishes,
Dr. Whiles

Hi, Dr. Whiles,

Thanks for getting back to me. It's so nice to be in touch.

I've been doing a lot since then, so it's hard to summarize, but I went to New College of Florida, then I was a journalist for a while, working in Boca Grande at a tiny paper and eventually in Houston at a very large paper (the *Houston Chronicle*). I got tired of the politics and lifestyle of newspaper reporting, though, and then went back to get my MFA (master of fine arts) in creative nonfiction, and after that a PhD in English/comparative lit and now I'm an assistant professor of creative nonfiction at Arizona State University. I'm married and I have two kids, 4 and 8.

As for everyone else, we might have to save that for when we talk, if you're up for being interviewed, but off the top of my head: Eric and Dale are pastors. Clara and James are academics like me. A lot of people are either lawyers or doctors. Carry is doing something corporate. Luke is a colonel in the navy. Laura was a high school teacher for a while as well, but I don't think she is anymore. Oh, and Lara (my really good friend who left after two years) is an art archivist. Erin does something in art as well. She was a gallery owner, I think, but is also an artist.

I look forward to (hopefully) chatting soon. I'm pretty free for the next couple of weeks, so let me know a time/day that works best for you. Oh! and I love your photographs of blue herons! Were you always a photographer? Or is that something you've taken up more recently?

Best,
Sarah

Before pressing Send, I debate whether to add that I am married to a woman, or just say that I am married. I want to be honest, but if Dr. Whiles is homophobic, I know I might lose my chance to ask questions. In the end, I elide the truth. I write that I am married and leave it at that.

Sarah,

Thanks for the update on your activities!

I taught at Chapin for 4 years, then was invited to help the new program at —— get going. I taught Theory of Knowledge and Inquiry Skills there for 13 years and retired.

After I retired, I became a volunteer with the —— in their —— program, which I've done for several years. I took up photography, and those are a few of my blue heron photos you saw on ——

Thanks again for the updates, but I don't want to be interviewed.

Best wishes,
Dr. Whiles

Dear Reader,

I ride my bike home that afternoon to walk our dog, Oki. The backhouse we've rented for my residency is a fifteen-minute ride from where we live in real life: me, Marta, the girls, and Oki. Marta wanted Oki home with her while I was gone—he keeps her from feeling scared at night—but having Oki also means more work for her, on top of the kids and her own research and teaching, so every couple of days, I bike through the searing May heat back to our house to walk him.

Today, I arrive before the kids are home, so Marta and I have a chance to talk. We're in the kitchen when I tell her about the last email from Dr. Whiles.

"He said he doesn't want to be interviewed," I say.

She looks up from making herself a snack.

"Are you relieved?"

"No. I mean, a little bit, yes. I wasn't looking forward to facing him and asking all the questions I have. But now I still have those questions. And what do I do with them?"

She looks at me like she's about to say something, but then she stops.

"I've gotta go get the kids," she says, because real-life dialogues often go nowhere.

We kiss and she disappears through the garage doorway.

On my bike ride back to the residency, I think again about Dr. Whiles and the disappointment of his saying no to an interview. The heat bears down on my neck and the afternoon traffic crowds me off the road and onto the sidewalk. I feel frustrated, stymied, until I remember who I am. I'd mostly been researching this story like a memoirist, but I am also a journalist, and a journalist wouldn't give up the first time someone said no to an interview. She'd push a little. She'd ask Dr. Whiles if he'd be open to answering questions via email, and if he was, she'd hope—I'd hope—that a written conversation might lead to questions over the phone or on Zoom, and maybe one day in person.

When I get back, the sun is setting and Lemmy has disappeared into his turtle house. I open my laptop and type up my plea before I can change my mind.

Hi, Dr. Whiles,

I'm so sorry to hear that! Would you be open to a few questions via email? In particular, I'm interested in Plato's Allegory of the Cave. Did you always teach that to students? And did you have any particular goals when teaching it?

If you'd be open to answering that and a few more questions, I could send them via email. It would mean a lot to me.

Thanks for considering.

Best,
Sarah

Plato and Dr. Whiles walk into a bar. They take a seat. I'm the bartender.

"What'll you have?" I say.

"Ambrosia," Plato says.

"Bud Light," Dr. Whiles says.

I pour and watch the men drink. Plato's hot. He's got a great body, even if he looks a little odd in the robes. His hair is impressively thick and luminescent—such a contrast to Dr. Whiles, who is overweight and slightly unkempt. The beer head sticks to his mustache.

"Where's Socrates?" Dr. Whiles says.

Plato stares at him, as if they've discussed this before. I imagine Socrates is sick.

"And Jesus?"

Dr. Whiles sounds desperate. Plato blinks.

"Isn't there still one other possibility, Daniel?" He pauses dramatically. "That we two alone must reason our way out of this question?"

I want to ask what the question is, but I decide that a bartender wouldn't do that.

"That's fine. I already figured it out." Dr. Whiles notices the beer head on his mustache and wipes it off with a napkin. "What everyone has to do is exactly what I did. If you haven't found a way out by the time you turn fifty, you realize that the noble lie already exists and its enforcers are keeping the truth from you, and then you spend the rest of your life trying to unmask the workings of the New World Order."

He slams his empty glass on the counter. Plato exhales with obvious exaggeration.

"What you say is fine, Daniel. But as to the truth, shall we simply assert that it is thus, at this point in history, rendered unknowable?"

"Plato, you're not listening to me."

"Not at all, best of men." Plato winks at me. "Just tell me more clearly what you mean."

"All right. You were born somewhere between 428 and 423 BC. Correct?"

"Certainly."

"And how many people were living at that point in time?"

Plato opens his mouth to speak, but Dr. Whiles keeps talking.

"I'll tell you: around one hundred and fifty million. Do you know how many people are living on this planet right now?"

"Tell me, Daniel."

"Seven point nine billion. You think we could manage a philosopher king or guardian class with all those people, Plato? You think things weren't bound to get incredibly messed up around, say, the Middle Ages, which is exactly when the Illuminati got its start!"

Dr. Whiles slams his glass again, but I've refilled it so some of the Bud Light splashes across the bar.

"Apologies," he says, and looking up at me, he suddenly seems almost dignified, closer to the teacher I remember from high school and less like the crank I'm conjuring up at this bar. The shift is so quick I wonder who is imagining whom.

"No worries," I say. I pull out my rag, a stained one I keep under the counter for moments like this, and wipe away the spilled beer. I know this is my cue to say something that will shore up this conversation. But I can't stop staring at Plato. He's so much better looking than I thought he would be.

"Do you live around here?" I ask him.

Plato looks at me, disappointed. Then he looks to the spot where the spilled beer once was.

"My, my, my dear," he says. "How vigorously you polish this bar—just like a statue—for our judgment."

"Thanks," I say. He smiles and I feel better than I have in years.

"Plato." Dr. Whiles is impatient. "You've got to listen to me. The regime plan you dreamed up has been hijacked in the centuries since. It's like they heard you. They did everything you said. We've got people believing in shadows. We've got a class system. We've more or less banished the poets from the city. We don't have the free love and equality between men and women, but that was a bit too much, don't you think? But the noble lie exists, only the people controlling that lie—they are not philosopher kings!"

Dr. Whiles is yelling again. Plato sips his ambrosia and looks around the room. It's a mix of dingy and kitsch. There's a railroad train track running around the ceiling because I saw one of those in a restaurant in Madison as a kid and have never been able to forget it. There are booths and a jukebox like we had in a bar I loved in graduate school in Iowa. Other features have clearly been pulled from movies or TV shows: the curtained windows looking on a parking lot filled with motorcycles and pickup trucks (*Thelma & Louise*) and a strong smell of yeast emanating from a hot guy in one of the back booths (*Made for Love*).

Plato turns back toward me, disappointed again.

"How would you have written it?" I ask.

He sighs again, louder this time.

"One ought, in my opinion, to include more men," he says.

"Noted."

"But this is not a bad beginning," he says. "That Daniel character"—he then nods at Dr. Whiles, who is finishing his second beer—"he, in my opinion, is good. The discussion you've set in motion as well, from the beginning again as it were, about the question of truth—that is very fine. But as to the scenery, I remain unconvinced."

"Also noted."

"We can all acknowledge that you are not me." He smiles.

"Not trying to be."

"Certainly."

"No, seriously." I start cleaning glasses, but I find a clean rag this time. "I don't want to be Plato—or any philosopher, really."

"Of course. Not at all. For who am I? Only the thinker to whom all of subsequent philosophy is but a mere footnote?"

"Can we please get back to the dialogue at hand," Dr. Whiles says. His mug is empty. I pour him an IPA this time. I make Plato a stronger drink as well. Maker's, neat. Then I pour myself a glass of Tempranillo.

Plato smirks.

"First we must understand what you mean, Daniel," he says, finally turning his attention away from me. "For as it is, I don't yet understand. You say my plans for a city have been perverted over time. Whatever do you mean by that—"

"Ridiculous idea," I interrupt.

"It's not ridiculous," Dr. Whiles says. "No, no, wait! What do you mean . . . by ridiculous?"

"Daniel!" Plato almost screams. Then he pauses and takes a deep breath. "Let us accept that you are not Socrates," he says.

"But seriously," Dr. Whiles says, only slightly subdued. "What is ridiculous? What does it even mean for an idea to be ridiculous?"

"It means we ridicule it," I say. "Like a joke."

"And why do you do that?"

"Because it has no basis in reality."

"Because you've been made to believe that it has no basis in reality!" Dr. Whiles says. "The air of ridicule is part of the cover-up. That's key to the new noble lie!"

"For money's sake!" Plato finishes his Maker's in one gulp, then clears his throat. "Yes, it is ridiculous, but all the same, since we've come to this place, we mustn't weary. Tell me, Daniel, according to your argument, this brave new world order is under the leadership of whom?"

Dr. Whiles starts to speak, but Plato interrupts.

"Ah, yes! The Jewish people. Who according to said theory control everything and yet have been persecuted and killed throughout much of your recent history?"

Dr. Whiles tries again to speak, but Plato keeps talking.

"How much discussion you've set in motion, Daniel, about the regime, my ideal city. You don't know how great a swarm of arguments you are stirring up with what you are now summoning to the bar. Tell me, Daniel, do you think you're wise? Or is it that you are angry at your lack of wisdom and thus you turn to this story of a new world order cabal so that you might feel as if you are scraping your way out of the cave and toward the place where the sun is itself by itself?"

Dr. Whiles looks overwhelmed. The IPA was likely too much for him. I pour him another.

"I'm not stuck in the cave," he says.

"You want to carry out that dispute, do you?" Plato says.

"I'd actually like us to go back to the whole noble-lie-cabal thing," I say. "I think that's where the problem lies in, you know, modern society. It's doesn't really matter who Dr. Whiles is or whether or not he's stuck in a cave, but it matters whether or not people like him believe in the cabal. What I mean is, it matters that we figure out a way to convince them not to believe in the cabal."

"Sarah." Dr. Whiles stares at me. "You were always a good student—I'm not saying that you weren't. But if you're saying your goal is to convince others that the cabal doesn't exist, then it's going to be clear to all of us that you've already been tricked by the new noble lie, and we're not going to listen to you. I mean, I'm not, at least."

"Sarah," Plato interrupts. "The real lie is hated not only by the gods but also by human beings."

"But how do you identify a lie?" I feel pathetic asking this.

"Is it a fact that whether one falls into a little swimming pool or into the middle of the biggest sea, one nevertheless swims all the same?" Plato is talking to me but looking out the window at a biker dude in leather chaps.

"Yes?"

Plato turns back to face me and for a moment all the movement in the room stops. Dr. Whiles shimmers as if he is about to disappear.

"Then we, too, must swim and try to save ourselves, hoping as we do that some dolphin might take us on his back or for some other unusual rescue," Plato says. "Come, then. Let's see if we can make our way out."

When I wake up, there's a new message from Dr. Whiles.

Sarah,

OK for email, then.

Dr. Whiles

Thanks, Dr. Whiles,

I appreciate it. And I'll try to be brief. I have one more expansive question and then some specific ones. Here they are:

1. You are by far the most memorable of our teachers, and I heard that from almost everyone I talked to. They said that you challenged them or pushed them to think in new ways, and that you got them to consider questions or ideas that they might not have otherwise. I completely agree. But I'd like to hear what you see as the difference(s) in your approach to teaching when compared with other teachers'. Also, what or who made you the teacher you were?

2. I'm also curious, as I mentioned, about Plato's Allegory of the Cave. What were your goals in teaching us that story? How did you hope students would respond? How did we actually respond?

3. Related to that, a lesson that almost everyone mentioned from your class is the clock on the wall. I later assumed you'd been talking about the Kantian idea of a thing-in-itself, but others thought you were commenting on time. So, a similar question: What did you hope students would say or ask or think after you had us question the clock on the wall? What did we actually do?

4. You may not remember this, but in my junior year, you chose me for the Theory of Knowledge Award from Vassar College, which surprised me because I clearly wasn't your "best" student. If you do remember, can you say why you chose me? If not, then a more general question: What, in your eyes, makes for a strong student?

5. Lastly, another expansive question: Do you think philosophy is a subject that should be taught to all high school students? Or are there some students who might not be ready for it at that age (or maybe never)? And, if so, why?

Thank you!

Best,
Sarah

Sarah,

1. My approach to teaching was shaped by my educational and experiential background. I started reading Schopenhauer as a senior in high school and became enthralled with his writings about The World as Will and Representation—the difference between the "inside" and the "outside" of our reality. I was fortunate to be a philosophy major at —— in the '60s, when they brought in some really talented philosophy professors. My main influences were ——, the Philosophy Department Chair (who later became President of ——) and —— the Existentialism teacher. —— taught us that Kant was important, and —— taught by introducing a question at the start of each seminar—like "What is Real?" —— was my introduction to Wittgenstein and Kierkegaard.

After I got my BA in Philosophy, I joined the Navy and served as a Naval Officer for 4 years. I spent 2 years at sea, then my last 2 years on shore duty, where I was able to go to grad school. My main influence there was ——, a fantastic teacher and my Thesis advisor. My Master's Thesis pursues the same ideas of the difference between "inside" and "outside" reality. Schopenhauer called the "inside" Will and the "outside" Representation. Freud thought the "inside" was hostile and called it the Id. Freud got many of his ideas from Schopenhauer, but usually failed to cite him.

I started teaching in 1982, teaching AP English, Humanities, and Philosophy (Dual Enrollment). My Philosophy class was the basis of my PhD Dissertation, which was "——."

2. My goal in teaching Plato's Allegory of the Cave was to encourage thinking about the problem that all we can actually know are our own perceptions, since something has to be in time, space, and subject to the law of cause and effect to be "knowable." Whatever "reality" is in itself, we can't "know." That is one of Kant's antinomies, but subject to a priori

(Kant said held in place by God) knowledge. Plato implied that perceptions are held together by Forms, which we have intuitive knowledge of. Schopenhauer said what underlies perceptions (Representations) is Will, which is not necessarily hostile, but Freud said it is hostile. Most students thought of television as the shadows which we assume to be reality.

3. The "clock on the wall" was just to show how the clock appears differently, depending on where it is viewed from. We somehow assume that a real clock underlies (a priori) all our different perceptions (a posteriori). This has been one of the main questions in the history of philosophy.

4. I remember that you had already developed a nice writing style, and showed independent thinking by questioning some things we discussed in class.

5. Please look up my PhD Dissertation in Dissertation Abstracts for my view on teaching philosophy in High School.

So, in summary, I had an enormous advantage in teaching since I had several fantastic teachers in my own education.

Best wishes,
Dr. Whiles

Dear Reader,

I was dreaming of death. I woke to a train rattling and then thundering from behind this tiny house, and something in those sounds launched me back into Schopenhauer, who I'd been reading the night before, and this whole week, in fact, as I decide how to answer Dr. Whiles's email. (I responded briefly to say that I would order a copy of his dissertation and write back once I'd read it, which was a lie, and yet one for which, amazingly, I don't presently feel any guilt.) Schopenhauer said that death, or the knowledge of death, is the reason we are philosophically minded (an idea he likely got from Plato's *Phaedo*). It's the one experience we're all aware of but can never fully understand, but also the experience that makes us aware that we, too, are objects in this world. By this I think he means that we are like the clock, in a way, or the rocket, or any aspect of physical reality. Our bodies are physical objects that we can see, smell, touch, taste, etc., and thus come to know through our senses, and yet unlike the clock, our bodies are also known to us from the inside because we—whoever we are—are embodied beings.

This felt revelatory to me when I read it last night, though now I am struggling to articulate what it is I thought I understood—and I know I am getting distracted from the problem at hand, which has to do with Dr. Whiles and by extension Plato and his republic, as well as ours. What feels relevant about Schopenhauer, however (and exciting, in a way that Plato's cave was exciting to me in high school), is his argument that the things-in-themselves that Kant discusses, which is to say those features of reality—the clock, rocket, pencil, lover—that we can't fully know outside of how they appear to us, instead of being many, are really only one thing: the thing-in-itself, which Schopenhauer calls the Will. It is a force or energy, the Will, like the qi in Taoism (which I was also obsessed with in high school), though Schopenhauer's primary influence was the

Hindu text the Upanishads, which he read before bed most nights, and the concept of Brahman, or ultimate reality.

Another thought that came to me while reading Schopenhauer is that Dr. Whiles may have been an ascetic. He never had relationships, as far as we could tell, and he lived alone. He must have indulged in eating, but he never talked about drinking or drugs after his religious conversion the summer before our junior year. Schopenhauer similarly advocated the ascetic life—and an appreciation of music and art—or that was my understanding, reading him late at night, not quite grasping everything. He says that standing before a breathtaking painting, for instance, can momentarily calm our awareness of the fact that the world is rife with crisis and strife. Because even though Schopenhauer believed we are all made of one thing, he also argued that the Will is manifest as multiple things, representations, and those representations are always in competition, always fighting and waging wars and trying to take each other down, never realizing that they are in essence one thing. Schopenhauer felt that we're better off escaping from the din of this world than trying to engage with it.

That's the point in his argument where he lost me, or perhaps where I lost him. And maybe it's where I lost Dr. Whiles, too. Because it seems to me that knowing that we are all one—or believing that to be true—should draw you toward others, rather than away. It would also follow that the embodied experience, rather than the abstract or intellectual experience of looking at art or listening to music, is what would draw you closer to knowing the physical self, and thus the Will within all of us. I think of Marta's eruptions of laughter sometimes after we make love. I think of that second when Manuela was born and the mirror dropped to the floor. We don't control those reactions, but I'm not sure control is the point. The point should be to know what it means to be, to sing those two notes—knowledge and being—at once.

Another scenario: we are in the waiting room from *No Exit*—Sartre's play that we read in high school. Lara is Estelle again. I'm still Inez. But now Jay is here, too. He's Joseph Garcin: the only man. We've all realized by now that this is a form of hell, and Jay/Joseph has warned us not to talk to each other. We'll only torture each other, he says. But Lara/Estelle wants a mirror. She misses being able to see herself, so I/Inez offer to let her look in my eyes. I/Inez want her to look in my eyes. The intimacy would be excruciating—almost closer than sex: for someone to look at the part of your body that you use to look at them, to see themselves there, reflected faintly within you.

"I can't see myself," Lara/Estelle says and I want to pull her closer but don't. I want to make her into Marta because it's difficult to remember wanting Lara, so I do that instead.

"Come closer," I/Inez say.

Marta/Estelle tries.

"Sarah." She sighs, breaking from the role. "This makes no sense. My anxieties are about other things. Like death."

I pull back, look at her from a greater distance.

"You're afraid to die."

"Exactly," she says, and increases the distance between us even more.

She finds a couch and stretches out. Jay is on the other couch, not looking at us. But we are both aware he is in the room.

"You know," I say, turning to Marta, "I once had a theory that people
are either afraid to die or they want to die. And you're the former and
I'm the latter."

"I had a theory that there are people who come up with theories like
that and people who don't."

"And you're the latter."

"Exactly."

"That's why you don't want to look at yourself?"

"Probably."

"Because you don't want to know yourself?"

"I don't see the need."

I squeeze into the small space at the other end of her couch. The
room is sparsely furnished. Only the couches, both velvet, French Em-
pire, uncomfortable. And a grandfather clock. I let my toes touch Marta's
toes. We are both wearing wool socks.

"Why?" I ask.

"I'll start thinking about dying."

"Is fear also the reason you don't want to understand Jay?"

Jay raises his head. He'd been sitting upright on the other couch,
which is indigo instead of green, with his eyes closed, as if meditating,
or sleeping.

"I also don't want to understand myself," he says.

"But I want to understand you," I say.

"And myself," I add when neither he nor Marta responds.

"I refuse to participate in this scene if he's also participating," Marta
says.

"Why?" I ask.

Jay closes his eyes again. I wonder what he's thinking. Is he maneu-
vering to hijack this scene? Does he feel remorse for everything he's
done?

"Sarah, we can hear you think," Marta says. Jay nods.

"I'm not planning anything," he adds. "There's no point."

"Do you mean there's no point because there is no one here you want to impress?"

"Kinda," he says. "There's also nothing to be gained. We will be here forever and none of what I wanted before—prestige, sex, money—is possible in Sartre's waiting room."

I think on that for a moment, before sitting up on my end of the couch. Marta has her eyes closed, as if to will both of us out of existence.

"Actually, they are," I say.

"I don't want to have sex with either of you." Jay sounds more disgusted than seems necessary.

"I know. We don't want to have sex with you either. But imagine we are here forever. I could see a world in which we invent money, maybe it's the best couch or something else like our clothes, and bartering with those objects becomes a means of accumulating power. And sex doesn't always have to mean sex. Maybe we start giving massages—"

"Sarah." Marta opens her eyes. "There is no way I will let him get close to me. Being in a room with him is already maddening. I want to hurt him. Don't you?"

"I can't think about violence," I say.

"That's your version of death."

"I suppose."

"I guess that's something Marta and I share," Jay says.

"Shut up," Marta says. "Don't say my name."

"In therapy, we talk about violations," I say, but I wonder if I'm changing the subject because violence makes me nervous.

"You are," Marta says.

"I think I might be the id in this scenario," Jay says. "I mean, I'm the one who wants everything, and who will do anything to get what I want."

"Oh, God," I say. "I hadn't realized we were moving in that direction. Marta, you've got to be the superego."

"Why? So you can be the ego? I think if anyone is worried about rules, it's you."

"True, but this is my scene. I can't let you be the self."

"Fine. But I am going to be a shitty superego."

"I think they're shitty most of the time."

"What do we do?" Jay says, standing up, now engaged. "Should I try to want something?"

"I think the whole point of the id is that it doesn't think about what it wants," I say. "You're the Will, the thing-in-itself that we'll never understand."

"That's depressing," Marta says.

"Schopenhauer was a pessimist," I say. "He thought the world was a miserable place where we're all inherently violent and treat each other horribly and thus people suffer."

"Then Jay is like the epitome of that world."

"I like that," he says, now frighteningly animated. "I didn't think I could accumulate power here, but this feels close."

"I think so," I say to Marta, trying to ignore Jay, who is starting to feel out of my control. "It's strange, because all this time I've felt like I needed to figure out Jay, like understanding him would bring me closer to mending that violation that my therapist keeps talking about. But maybe he's been knowable all along. Because whatever he did or does, I'm capable of as well. If he's the Will, and there is only one Will, that means that whatever potential in him for nihilism or sadism or just being a con artist is with me as well. Which means that understanding him isn't the way out of here."

"Wait," Marta says. "Are we in the cave?"

"Probably," I say. "I mean, what story isn't a cave? But an interminable waiting room certainly feels like one."

"But if we're the parts of the self, is the cave also the body?"

"Maybe."

"Which would mean there's no way out?"

"It seems a little out of character for you to care so much."

"You forget that I read a lot of philosophy and literature in college," she says. "I cared about these things a great deal then."

"I know," I say. "I think about that version of you a lot."

"You don't have to sound so morose."

"It's just that all of this feels so impossible that I understand why you decided to leave those questions behind."

"I'm hungry," Jay interrupts, rubbing his hands together as if the friction alone might manifest a meal. I remember that he is supposed to be the id, and that makes me laugh, one of those eruptive, gorgeous laughs that bursts out before you can control it.

"I'm hungry, too," I realize. I've been up since four this morning, when the train came through again. It's only 5:30 now, the sun is still not up, and yet I can feel my stomach wanting. That's the thing about the id: you feel most united with it in moments of desire. But giving in to those desires doesn't result in an answer.

What feels closer is what I am doing right here, right now: making connections, or trying to. I realized the other day that Virginia Woolf's essay on memoir, at least the part in which she writes about "the rapture" she feels sometimes in writing, sounds oddly as if she were in a conversation with Schopenhauer's idea of the Will.

"From this," she writes—and I am repeating this quote for a reason—"I reach what I might call a philosophy; at any rate it is a constant idea of mine; that behind the cotton wool is a hidden pattern; that we—I mean all human beings—are connected with this; that the whole world is a work of art; that we are parts of the work of art. *Hamlet* or a Beethoven quartet is the truth about this vast mass that we call the world. But there is no Shakespeare, there is no Beethoven; certainly and emphatically there is no God; we are the words; we are the music; we are the thing itself."

We are the thing itself. The way out of the cave is to write!

Dear Dr. Whiles,

Thanks again for your answers. I tracked down your dissertation (still waiting on your master's thesis) and I have a few follow-up questions. If you have time to answer them, I'd be grateful:

1. Do you think there is a way to measure if a class has "changed the way" students "look at things," as you phrase it in your dissertation? I mean is it ever possible to show that a philosophical education is "working"?

2. Do you ever feel like your classes or philosophy in general was harmful to specific people even if it wasn't harmful in general? And, if so, what are the harms? I remember our freshman year, for instance, feeling so distraught at times by the realization that there was no way to confirm my own reality. I eventually stopped thinking about that as much, and I moved past whatever desperation I felt then, but I wonder if other students got stuck in that mental space in a way that could be harmful. Was that something you ever witnessed? And if so, how did you deal with that?

3. You said that you chose me for that award because I'd questioned some of the things we talked about in class, and I remember doing that and how hard it was, but also how formative it felt in the long run. I'm wondering, though, in your experience, if the best way to educate is to present students with material or lessons that will prompt them to push back and/or question what is said in class?

4. Related to that, did you actually believe the conspiracy theories that you told us about in class? I've thought a lot about that lately because of the attention now being paid to those kinds of

theories, but also because that was the reason that I ended up questioning things we discussed in class—especially the video we watched questioning the Holocaust. I've always wondered if you actually believed some or all of those conspiracy theories. Or were you only using them as a teaching tool? But if it's the latter, did you also see a potential danger in that?

5. Do you think Socrates's plan for the ideal city in the *Republic* was one he wanted to see enacted in reality (i.e., a class system, no families, gender equality, and a "noble lie" at the center of things— kind of like *Brave New World*) or was he also trying to get his readers/interlocutors to push back?

6. Related: Do you think it is possible to metaphorically "get out of the cave"?

Thanks again for your time.

Best,
Sarah

Sarah,

What do you plan to do with whatever input you get from me?

    Dr. Whiles

Hi, Dr. Whiles,

I can't say for sure because I'm still working on the book. I've mostly been using interviews to help inform and at times fact-check memories I've been writing about, though in some cases interviews have helped me remember something or think about something I'd forgotten. For the most part, I've also changed people's names, so I planned to do that with you as well, if that helps to know. The Allegory of the Cave is sort of a through line within the memoir, so some of my questions in that regard are really more about me trying to think about the various ways that that story, and Plato's *Republic* in general, have been interpreted.

Thanks for considering. I'd love to hear your thoughts.

Best,
Sarah

Dear Reader,

I have a confession to make—or rather, two. The first is this: the correspondence you are reading here between me and Dr. Whiles is not an exact replica of the actual correspondence that took place in real life. I have removed small portions of our exchange that felt redundant or unnecessarily distracting within the context of the story I am trying to tell. I have also excised references that might make Dr. Whiles identifiable, wanting to believe I've learned something from Jay's public outing. I haven't added any details or changed the words or phrases that Dr. Whiles used (beyond tiny changes to protect his identity), but this is still a mediated, curated version of reality, not reality itself. When it comes to storytelling, to making meaning from facts, that's always the case. But I think we should be honest about that fact.

Secondly, when I said earlier that I wanted a dialogue with Dr. Whiles, I may have been lying to you, but also to myself. What I often feel I want from him is what I wanted from Jay: for him to confirm my version of reality and then apologize. I feel that desire acutely these days, writing alone in this tiny house, thinking about truth in the stories I am trying to tell and how it is or is not connected to the realities we are witnesses to in the world today. "I." "We." "Reality." "World." When I can't grapple with those concepts anymore, or my own flustering need for an apology, I sometimes play a game of pool (there's also a pool table in this residency that isn't a residency), briefly soothing myself with the soft clink of balls and the swoosh followed by a thundering roll when I make one in the pocket. Other times, I step outside, carrying strawberries or kale for Lemmy. When he eats, Lemmy's mouth opens wide and I can see the thick pink of his tongue and that's when I am sure he's almost human. Then his jaws snap shut and the pointed beak of his lips reminds me that he's not.

My desire with both Jay and Dr. Whiles is, I think, to mend the tear in what Hannah Arendt calls the "fabric of factuality," a phrase that comes from an essay she published after the "so-called controversy"— her words—around her 1963 *New Yorker* article "Eichmann in Jerusalem." People were upset about the way Arendt wrote about Jewish victims of the Holocaust, but also about Adolf Eichmann, who Arendt refused to characterize as either a monster or psychopath. Most journalists would have responded by proving their article was fact-checked or by defending the logic in their argument, but Arendt's retort was a long essay, "Truth and Politics," that excavated several questions about the relationship between those two concepts, in particular this one: "What kind of reality does truth possess if it is powerless in the public realm?"

In talking about truth, Arendt points out that the truth Plato was referring to in his cave allegory—knowledge of the Forms, or what Arendt calls philosophical or rational truth—is not the same kind of truth we are bickering about today. In fact, philosophical truths mean little to those of us caught up in debates about conspiracy theories or political lies. What we care about are the facts, or what Arendt calls "factual truths." A single, directed lie only tears a hole in the fabric of factuality, she writes, and afterward, we all see that tear, we know the lie for what it is, and we can fix it. Or at least we can point to it—note that over there is a lie tearing at the fabric of our daily lives. But when the lies become all-encompassing, when even the liar starts to believe them, the result is "a complete rearrangement of the whole factual texture—the making of another reality," she writes. I think of how Jay attempted that for Marta and me—a complete rewriting of our reality—and how close he came. But I don't think he ever believed his own lies. He may, in fact, have been a little like Eichmann, in Arendt's interpretation of him, which is to say, someone lacking the ability to truly think, to achieve what Arendt calls "the silent dialogue carried on between me and myself" about right and wrong. But in the end, his lies were exposed and the tear in that fabric was mended. Dr. Whiles, however, may have believed the lies he told us—he might believe them still. Arendt compares this type of person to Antonio, Prospero's traitorous brother in *The Tempest*, who "made a sinner of his memory, to credit his own lie," which is to say, who ignores what he once knew was true because it conflicts with the lie he's committed to believing. Which feels infinitely scarier—for Dr. Whiles's students back then, but for all of us today as well. Because while Jay was shocking, a figure who so many people readily despised, Dr. Whiles no longer feels like an outlier.

Sarah,

If you do look through my Master's Thesis, you'll notice that it's mainly just comparing passages from Freud with similar passages from Schopenhauer—not very profound. My original idea was that Freud "stole" almost all of his primary concepts directly from the earlier works of Schopenhauer that Freud had studied in his own education.

I was dissuaded from this direct accusation since I was comparing translations in English instead of the original writings of both in German. So the thesis is called "Parallel Thinking" in the history of ideas.

Anyone can see that Schopenhauer is the deeper and more original thinker about the "thing in itself" and the impossibility of knowledge of it, since anything "knowable" has to be located in mental or physical time and space, and subject to the laws of cause and effect. That's why the cave has to be envisioned with allegory, not as Freud tried to do with dream interpretation.

Dr. Whiles

Dear Reader,

I don't respond right away and when I wake up the next morning, there's a second message from Dr. Whiles waiting in my inbox. The subject is "More Responses to Your Questions." No salutation.

1. The only way I know of to show that a philosophy class "worked" is to find out whether or not the student has put any of the class content into practice in later life. In my case, I contacted my main professors several years after taking their classes and expressed my appreciation for what they had done.

2. Yes, I have seen and heard of students going into a kind of "crisis" after or during one of my classes—especially TOK. But the natural stress of junior year in the program produces effects on its own, because of the sheer volume of work expected of students. So, I think only a very few students would have an "intellectual" crisis. However, a doubting of religious belief or a skepticism about religion was pretty common with TOK and Inquiry Skills. I had a mystical vision myself, while I was teaching at Chapin, and became Catholic—which I still am. So I was able to explore the underlying mysticism which is the basis of true faith, and to share it with those students who were having doubts. This became the most cherished aspect of teaching, for me. While I was teaching at Chapin, I was also teaching the Eastern Humanities course at ——. This course was a survey of Buddhism, Hinduism, and Taoism. After my Pieta vision, I stopped teaching Eastern Humanities, as I could see that those viewpoints just resulted, pretty much, in a dead end. I don't think you could meditate your way out of the cave.

3. The two main tools I used in TOK and Inquiry Skills were the results of the Psycho-epistemological Profile and feedback from students on Herman Kahn's Three Systems of Truth. I used these to figure out the dominant viewpoint of each student. Those who scored highest in a metaphorical understanding of truth usually had a positive approach to my teaching, a sense of humor, and were willing to question whatever was going on. Those who scored highest in the empirical viewpoint were usually not apparently affected by my class—except being glad to get an A.

4. I used several different conspiracy theories in the 17 years I taught in the program. I usually "believed" the one that differed the most from commonly held belief. Overall, I really think this approach to teaching is effective—but every teacher I have discussed this with always says they are not willing to "take the chance" of upsetting parents, administrators, other teachers, etc. I had the advantage of having a PhD, which kept me pretty much immune to criticism.

5. I took a whole "in depth" seminar on the *Republic* one summer, and I never was able to decide about Plato's intentions. There have been volumes of discourse on this, as you probably are aware. So, I really have no idea about Plato's intentions.

6. Yes, it is possible to "get out of the cave." In my case, it was through a mystical vision of The Pieta by Michelangelo, followed by a vision of a dove and subsequent conversion to Catholicism—with the reception of Holy Communion, which bridges the gap between the shadow world and the inner world. All my ideas on this are shaped by the works of G. K. Chesterton. I was/am so lucky!

Dr. Whiles

H ey, Lemmy, got you a strawberry."
 I squat beside the low fence that keeps Lemmy on the grass
section of the backyard and scratch his shell while he looks up at me and
cocks his long neck-head slightly, like a scaly puppy.

"Here you go." I put the strawberry on the grass. Lemmy takes it in his
mouth and moves it around, trying to squash it before swallowing. For
a moment I worry he'll swallow it whole, and that I'll have accidentally
killed the giant tortoise everyone loves. But this is not his first strawberry.
It's smashed and disappears in Lemmy's mouth, leaving behind a ring of
red on what you might call lips.

"I love you, Lemmy. I know that sounds weird because you're a tortoise and we've just met, but I feel a strong tenderness toward you."

Lemmy returns to the grass, which he chews in slow, thoughtful
bursts before lowering his long neck-head toward the ground for more.
The other day I was watching him from the window and he stopped
chewing grass for a moment and sank into the lawn, his two strong, scaly
arms forming arcs beside his head. He waited like that for quite a while,
just watching the world.

"Why are you trying to work everything out via dialogue?" Lemmy
says now, his lips still pink.

"I knew you'd speak eventually."

"I'm not really speaking," he says.

"Of course. But I feel like you are. Like you're more human than I am." I look at my own body then, my human form, which I know so well but can also never really know.

"Then answer my question," he says. "Why not just leave me silent? And figure out your shit another way?"

"No other way is working."

"What do you mean by working?"

"Are you getting Socratic now, too?" I smile, but Lemmy remains serious, if a tortoise can be serious.

"No," he says. "But how can you know why you're doing what you're doing if you don't even know how to define what you'd see as success?"

I think about that.

"I guess by working," I say. "I mean moving things forward, getting closer to that pattern behind the cotton wool that Virginia Woolf talks about."

"But what about Dr. Whiles and Jay? Are they even real to you?"

"That's a good question."

"I'm a good tortoise."

"You're the best tortoise."

A train comes through, so we stop talking and feel the way it rumbles, its whooshing cars sucking static from the air. It's evening and Lemmy will return soon to his boxed house on the porch to sleep. In a few days, I'll leave this residency that is not a residency and never see him again. I give him a stalk of kale and watch as he expertly snaps it in two and folds it into his mouth, that thick, pink tongue present for a moment, then gone.

"You know I can also hear you thinking."

"I'm sorry. I'm obsessed with your tongue."

"It's fine."

"Also, your arms and legs. They're so nubby yet strong."

"Answer the question, Sarah."

I exhale (I really did just exhale writing this). "Dr. Whiles feels real to me—especially after what he just wrote. It was so earnest and vulnerable that I started to feel deceitful myself. I asked all those questions about what he thinks when all I really wanted to know was why he taught us conspiracy theories, and if he feels guilty for having done so. But I'm glad I asked the other questions. His answers make him more complicated and more human, even if he's not the human I want him to be. Whereas Jay was never anyone I knew all that well or cared about, and then he did such pointedly cruel and selfish things that he feels less redeemable, but also more pathetic. Some days it's almost like I dreamed him up, unless I search his name on the internet, and see that creepy smile again."

"Wow," Lemmy says. "When you get started, you can really talk."

"Sorry."

"It's cool. I don't have anything else to do."

Lemmy chews some grass.

"It's also possible that I'm talking to you right now to avoid responding to Dr. Whiles."

"You're scared again?"

"I think so. I know that I need to push a little more, to ask directly about the conspiracy theories, and I don't know how he'll respond, or if he'll respond at all."

"Why do you care?"

"I think because if he doesn't respond or if he responds badly, like the bully he sometimes was in our classroom, then it will feel like a failed dialogue, like I lost."

"But why is this about winning?"

"It's not, but if he doesn't engage, I don't know how else to grapple with the story about him."

"Yeah, but does that mean there's nothing else to grapple with when it comes to that story?"

"No. But I feel like this book is about men who tell lies."

"Is it?"

Lemmy chews more grass.

"I mean, that's how I've always thought of it. Our president's lies got me thinking about Dr. Whiles's conspiracy theories, and then when

I was writing about those, Jay stepped in and used lies and con artistry in a much more fucked-up way—for us, at least. I think of each as being an allegory of the next or maybe parallel stories of lying men and the ways their lies tear at the 'fabric of factuality'—which I'm realizing feels connected to the 'cotton wool' that Woolf talks about."

"So maybe your book isn't about those lying men at all. Maybe it's about the women who make sense of moments of shock?"

"Lemmy, that's a little cheesy."

"I'm a tortoise, Sarah. I can't be cheesy."

"I'm not sure that's true. But I hear you. You may be right."

"I also could be lying."

"I don't think you lie."

"I can't even really talk."

"Exactly. That makes it easier to trust you."

"So maybe the answer to the problem with truth in this world is for everyone to stop talking?"

"Turn us all into tortoises?"

Lemmy laughs, which is an odd sight. His neck-head bobs a little and he opens his mouth and these huff-hisses escape, like that image of The Little Engine That Could, chugging.

"You should see the way tortoises talk about human laughter," he says when he's done.

"I'm sure."

"You guys shake like trees in a hurricane."

"Did you know that in the nineties we had a whole show dedicated to home videos of people falling down or tripping or spilling things, and my family watched that show religiously, cracking up together on the couch. It feels so ancient now: a family watching home video compilations on an actual TV."

"Now you have TikTok and you crack up to that in bed with earbuds in so you won't bother Marta."

"Yeah. It's hard not to think that things were better once."

"They were pretty fucked-up before, too."

"I know. But do you think truth was more prevalent or powerful back then? I mean, are we actually living in a post-truth world? And who invented this 'post' idea, anyway. As if colonialism or truth might end on a specific year."

"Which of those questions do you want me to answer?"

"None. It's fine. Do you want more kale?"

"Do tortoises have shells?"

I give Lemmy the rest of the kale and watch him eat it. I wish, watching him, that this were all that life required: watching a tortoise eat. There's no deception in that act. It just is.

"Stop simplifying me, Sarah."

"I'm sorry, Lemmy. I'm going to miss you."

"I like you. You bring me strawberries and scratch my hard shell."

"I should go back and write."

"That's a lie. You're writing right now. I'm imaginary and so are you."

"I know, but in this imagined scene, I'm going to stand up and walk back to my writing residency and try to finish this book."

"Are you going to respond to Dr. Whiles?"

"Yes."

"Will you bring me more strawberries and kale?"

"Of course." I stand up. "Thank you, Lemmy."

"Sarah. Write."

Dear Dr. Whiles,

I had forgotten about Herman Kahn, but when you mentioned him, I looked him up, and I immediately remembered our discussions of the stages of art/culture: Idealistic, Integrated, Sensate, and Post-Sensate. I remember you saying, I believe, that we were living in a sensate culture or perhaps a post-sensate one. Are those the stages of truth you're talking about? If so, I remember feeling some resistance to those categories, or at least the way they were framed, in part because the sensate and post-sensate cultures seemed to be disparaged, and yet they also tended to include developments that I saw then, and now, as positive—including expanded rights for those who have traditionally been subjugated—but also because I thought the interpretation of art felt too simplistic, i.e., that I could also feel the sublime when staring at a Rothko painting or listening to Deee-Lite or Tori Amos (or any number of bands/singers I liked then). But I'm curious how those stages of culture and/or our reaction to that theory relates to questions of truth or how truth is conceptualized.

I also had many questions about Catholicism, so thank you for mentioning that. I remember your conversion between our ninth and eleventh grade years, and the vision you told some of us about, and I'm glad to hear that, for you, it has meant escaping from the cave, so to speak. As a nonbeliever, it's still hard for me to see how that is any different from meditation or studying the Vedas. All of those practices/choices feel like they are wrapped up in a form of mysticism that might be tied to Schopenhauer's ideas about the Will as a force/thing we could access when/if we become "one" with our physical self, so to speak. So, what, for you, feels different about Catholic mysticism than those other approaches to metaphorically leaving the cave?

Finally, my biggest question is still about conspiracy theories and using them in the classroom. I'd love to hear more about what, from your perspective, are the benefits of teaching conspiracy theories. To me, it feels like the danger outweighs any benefit, in part because so many of those stories—including Holocaust denialism—are embedded within larger narratives that are prejudiced in nature. But also, because conspiratorial thinking doesn't feel helpful if we're talking about teaching students how to be and do what you value in your dissertation: thinking critically and increasing or at least maintaining self-esteem. So, for you, what is the value of conspiratorial thinking? I wonder, too, if any of your thoughts on conspiracy theories have changed in the past five or so years, as we've seen them become much more popular than they were back in the 1990s but also, arguably, even less logical. You said that you tended to "believe" the one that differed most from the commonly held beliefs, so what happens when those theories become more common and more commonly believed?

Okay. I know that's a lot, but you gave me a lot to think about! Thanks again for taking the time to discuss all of this with me. The dialogue means a lot to me.

Best,
Sarah

Dear Reader,

I send that email on a Thursday, and when I don't hear anything on Friday or Saturday, I assume I've pushed too hard, been too honest about what I thought. Then late on Sunday evening, Dr. Whiles writes back:

Sarah,

Well, I'd say the underlying attitude of your last response was "skeptical" or doubt, which was the desired effect of Theory of Knowledge, according to the official description of it, which follows: "How is TOK structured? As a thoughtful and purposeful inquiry into different ways of knowing, and into different kinds of knowledge, TOK is composed almost entirely of questions. The most central of these is 'How do we know?,' while other questions include: 'What counts as evidence for X?,' 'How do we judge which is the best model of Y?,' 'What does theory Z mean in the real world?' Through discussions of these and other questions, students gain greater awareness of their personal and ideological assumptions, as well as developing an appreciation of the diversity and richness of cultural perspectives."

So, that's what the program wanted, and that's what I did, for several years. I finally got tired of TOK and went back to teaching Inquiry Skills for the last 3 and a half years of my teaching career. Inquiry Skills was a lot more fun, and the freshmen were more spontaneous. You didn't mention the novels we read—*Brave New World, Fahrenheit 451*, and *Hitchhiker's Guide*.

I really don't have any interest in conspiracy theories or Kahn's Three Systems of Truth or Plato's Cave anymore. Or in defending or justifying my religion.

Dr. Whiles

Dear Reader,

A photographer came to our house once, before the plague, to take a picture of me for an award I had won, and while he set up his equipment, he and I started talking about this book and about conspiracy theories more generally. He told me he had a friend who had fallen into conspiratorial thinking—first through Holocaust denialism, which surprised me. I assumed you'd start with JFK or the moon landing "hoax." I thought you'd begin with aliens and then go to flat earth. But his friend began with the Holocaust as myth and then transitioned to flat earth, and now he can't be convinced of anything.

The photographer told me he takes a picture of his shadow every day, or almost every day, of the year as a way of documenting how it changes with the passing of days and seasons. I was standing in the heat of his studio lights while he described this. He took photos without audible clicks, so I had no idea when he was capturing me. He said the project of documenting his shadow had the secondary effect of proving the roundness of the earth to his flat-earther friend. He could show by the changes in the shape and length of his shadow that the earth curves like a globe rather than running flat toward empty space. But his friend didn't care. At least you tried, I said, and he agreed. At least I'm trying, I tell myself now.

I saw an installation at the Phoenix Art Museum with my kids once, also before the plague, that featured a table of mirrors with mirrored shapes constructed atop it: a cube, a triangle, a sphere. From a distance, the installation lacked the immediate allure of art. The mirrored surface made the whole piece appear dull white with dark blue hues and, compared to the other works on display that day, it felt uneventful. But Manuela and Lucia were on a scavenger hunt set up by the museum and the hunt included that art piece, so we drew closer to have a look;

and a docent standing there, guarding it, asked us, "Do you know what is special about this piece?"

"No," Lucia said.

"What do you think it's made of?"

She paused, her eyes passing over its shining surfaces.

"Mirrors?"

The docent nodded.

"But where are the shadows?"

We looked then, and for the first time, we noticed their absence. None of the shapes cast shadows onto the ground, because that ground was a mirror, too, and it would cast them back off. But off where? For a minute at least, we looked around the artwork, on the ground, on our bodies, confused until one of us thought to look up, and there they were. A distorted square. A globe askew. A stretched-out triangle. They glimmered on the ceiling, like a cave wall.

Shadows are like mirrors in that both are replicas of the real thing: through them, we see ourselves, but also the world, in the broadest of strokes. A tree outside the front window of this backhouse where I am writing right now has cast its shadow on the stucco wall and it looks like an extension of the tree itself. A dialogue between the tree and the double the sun makes of it. I do not know how to respond to Dr. Whiles. But I will.

Dear Dr. Whiles,

Thanks for these responses. I agree that I'm skeptical. I think that's always been my nature. But in this case, I think "curious" is a better word. In writing this book about high school, I've been thinking a lot about how influential your classes were, on me as a thinker and writer, but also as a teacher, and I've been trying to figure out why. But I also want to understand why I started to feel resistant to some of what we were being taught; and when I look back on those years, that shift in me seems to center on the use of conspiracy theories. And so, I really am curious about how you conceived of those as a teaching tool.

I also feel like, from the tone of your email, that I offended you with my questions and that wasn't my intention. I was and am curious about Catholicism within the context of our class, and Plato's cave, but my aim wasn't for you to defend your religious choices. You brought the subject up, so I thought that was a topic you might be open to discussing more generally.

I am also curious why Plato's cave is no longer something you're interested in discussing. Maybe it's because you've found your answer and, as you wrote earlier, you feel lucky for that. And maybe it's still interesting to me because I haven't yet—and I don't think I ever will.

If you later decide you're open to talking more about any of those topics that no longer interest you, I'd always love to hear from you. Either way, thank you for taking the time to answer my questions. I don't think I would be the person I am now without your classes, and so even though I'm curious and/or skeptical about some components, I will always be grateful I had you as a teacher.

Best,
Sarah

Dearest Reader,

I woke from a dream just now in which the end of this book was a woman looking into a mirror that became a lake turned on its side and held up to the sky. Every time the woman peered closer, she fell in, like Lemmy diving his head into the bowl of water I put out for him on the lawn. There was more to the dream, but I've lost it. A line kept passing through my head as I was both trying to wake up and hoping to remain asleep.

I'm sure the dream came on because, as I fell asleep last night, I thought to myself, I will imagine this book as if it were the body of a person, and sleeping, I slipped inside that form. She was young and not me and the lake she leaned up against reflected the rest of the world. Like that lake in high school, Lara and I canoeing to the middle, but also like that boat on the shore in the painting behind the podium during the Holocaust debate. Is a lake the inverse of a cave? When you are in a lake, you are almost always on the surface of things. There is no fire to make shadows. Only the moon reflecting on the surface that holds you. Out there, without a boat, your options are limited to two possibilities: what you see reflected on the surface of the water and what you see when you look toward the sky or shore. Maybe there's a woman at the waterline, waving. Or a man coming toward you with a boat. Maybe you climb inside. Maybe you tread water and wait.

I've been thinking lately about what I would do if I were in Plato's cave and someone let me out. That question is implied in the final part of the allegory. Would you return to the prisoners below? If you did, what would you say? It's hard to imagine not trying to engage. Just like it's hard to believe that the cave dwellers would love their lies so much they'd kill you for telling the truth. I think about that poem Gayle's mom, Alise, told me changed everything for her: "Babi Yar." Yevtushenko was not Jewish, did not have stakes, as Eric might have put it, in the story of the more than thirty-three-thousand Jews murdered in that ravine after the Nazis invaded Kyiv, and yet he imagined his way into those stakes. The poem starts with the history of Jewish people and Yevtushenko embodies specific moments within that history before eventually inserting himself within the genocide along that Ukrainian ravine. "We are denied the leaves / we are denied the sky," he writes of those who were murdered during the Holocaust and then had their murders erased when the Soviets refused to acknowledge that history, "Yet we can do so much— / tenderly / embrace each other in a darkened room."

That "Yet" is the moment where that poem turns for me. Because it's the moment in which those in the darkened room—or shadowy cave or eternal waiting room—turn toward each other instead of away. Yevtushenko's poem is not a tale of one man's escape, not a hero's quest. It's a story about shared suffering but also, in sharing that suffering, acknowledging the truth of one another's lived experience, and fighting to keep that truth from being erased or forgotten. That's what stories and poetry can do that Socrates buried or wouldn't acknowledge when he banned so many of them from his republic. They remind us that the division between those trapped in the cave and those released into the sunlight is also a fiction. That we are in this cave together. That any of us can end up in a ravine. That all of us have stakes in the story being told.

Arendt had a theory I like to explain the dark ending to Plato's Allegory of the Cave and the fact that the man never tries to "persuade his fellow citizens" as Arendt puts it, to leave the cave themselves. It has to do, she writes in "Philosophy and Politics," with Plato's understanding, not of truth but philosophy—a study he says begins with wonder and ends with speechlessness. Speechlessness is the philosopher's only response, Arendt tells us, to the shock of experiencing "that which is as it is," the thing in itself.

"In this shock," Arendt writes, "man in the singular, as it were, is for one fleeting moment confronted with the whole of the universe, as he will be confronted again only at the moment of his death."

I think of Woolf and her ideas on shock, and of me as a kid and my "big picture," of Marta briefly feeling like she could leave her own body through a turn of her neck, but also of Dr. Whiles on his balcony witnessing a vision of the *Pietà*. Arendt says that the experience of wonder isn't limited to the philosopher. It's a feeling that all of us, everyone in the cave—if the cave metaphor even makes sense anymore—can access and likely have. The difference is that the majority of us "refuse to endure" the shock of it and the speechlessness that follows. And even if we do, what do we say afterward? How do we communicate? Socrates refused to write and when he spoke, he asked questions. Plato wrote but he did so in dialogues that keep us from knowing what he actually thought. Which perhaps is the only way of going about these things. Obliquely. Metaphorically. Telling stories in ways that open up meaning, that elicit questions rather than tendering answers. Like I no longer trust what Plato wrote because I've realized he was never after my trust. Like Dr. Whiles was a transformative teacher because he was so destructive. Like, god damn the conspiracy theorists and con artists for complicating our world and thank god for their thorniness against which we struggle and even suffer. A utopia would be a far scarier place.

Dr. Whiles never responded to my final email, but it's not about him anymore anyway. Or Jay. This is about them only in so much as it is about any of us. I should have realized that a long time ago. And I did. I've said what I am saying now before, I know, but I'm saying it bigger this time. All of us. We are a fact I have discovered repeatedly, but that I somehow keep forgetting. But I swear this time to remember the wonder of us. How to embrace in the dark instead of flee from the cave. How to tell stories to make sense of this world. How to find your stakes in the collective story we've already started to tell. We may feel like prisoners chained to a cave floor. Trapped in some brave new world. Watching a drama pass before us on a far wall. But we are also, always, the shadow casters, and we are also always the ones who give names to the shadows cast. Because wherever there is light, and someone to see that light, there will always be shadows. Even in the sunlight outside of the cave. Especially in the sunlight. This is how we know we exist, together, on this tiny spinning globe in this enormous unknowable universe. We cast shadows. We name the bigger light.

AFTERWORD

After this manuscript was finished, copy editors from Scribner and a fact-checker I hired separately found a handful of small mistakes that I corrected in the book's final version, the one you just read. The fact-checker, Elizabeth Barber, also reached out to those individuals whose stories I've relied on here and reviewed the facts with them. Two of those people were Jay and Dr. Whiles.

Jay told Elizabeth that he could not comment on anything regarding our lawsuit but that he was glad to help in any way that he could. Elizabeth emailed him seventy-nine questions, of which he responded to twenty-seven. He corrected small facts related to his biography and said he was only aware of two, not three, people who came forward claiming he had sexually harassed them (posts by two of those men, one of whom is a friend of mine, are no longer up online). He said he shared text messages at the time that gave more context to at least one of those men's claims, but he did not deny the allegations themselves. The only questions related to the lawsuit that Jay responded to dealt with conversations he had with Nan and that Nan then shared with me. For each of those questions, Jay wrote, "This is not my remembering of the conversation whatsoever."

When Elizabeth reached out to Dr. Whiles, he at first declined to review the facts with her, writing in an email, "I'm 76 years old and my

memories are pretty faded. I don't have anything to say about this." He
changed his mind several weeks later, but when Elizabeth sent him a
long list of questions, he responded to none of them. Instead, he explained the Socratic method to her and noted that "dialogue has to have
two sides." He also wrote this: "I would urge you to encourage Sarah to
take out statements in the areas where she obviously did not pick up the
irony, 'devil's advocate' or humor in what was going on."

I quote from their responses here because I think they are illustra-
tive. Rather than responding to specific statements of fact, both Jay and
Dr. Whiles instead attacked the credibility or intelligence of those who
witnessed their actions and decided to speak out. Public truth, that fabric of factuality that Arendt wrote about, relies on the facts we can verify
but also on the testimony of witnesses who have seen and heard what
others can't. There is room for error and manipulation in both realms.
But we should be wary of anyone who fails to engage in a discussion of
the facts and instead tries to discredit those willing to say, *This is what I
know. This is what I have witnessed.*

ACKNOWLEDGMENTS

For helping me tell the story that started this book, I'm thankful to everyone from my high school who took the time to answer my emails or pick up the phone. Talking with each of you was more than just research. It felt like a line strung between the past and the present.

The second story in this book required less historical reporting, but more support in the moment of living it. I will forever be grateful to those who came to our aid then: Lina, who sent me bags of popcorn and images of sloths; Julia, who stopped by with pasta and called all her lawyer friends; Sydney and Dan, who drank afternoon beers with us and allowed me to briefly laugh at the absurdity of it all; Kerry, who found me a Reddit expert within hours of my reaching out; my fellow writer-academics in RATAM (Rage Against the Academic Machine), who counseled me and got riled up on our behalf; our lawyer and all the other lawyers who offered us advice; my therapist, who helped me think through both violation and forgiveness; those friends and acquaintances who kept us abreast on where Jay was or what he was doing during those months in which everything felt like a threat; anyone brave enough to speak out after my story was published; and, of course, the woman I call Nan in this book, who put herself at risk in order to protect us.

For believing in the book built from these two stories, a million thanks to my agent, Matt McGowan. There was pressure to write a more traditional narrative, and I'm grateful that you trusted me to tell a weirder but I think truer story. Thanks in equal measure to my editor, Sally Howe at Scribner, who believed in that less conventional book, too, and who never tried to convince me to let go of the philosophy or interrupting narratives or talking tortoises. Your support of me and your close reading of this book have been remarkable.

To Mike Benoist, who first accepted a cold pitch from me in August of 2019 for an unbelievable story about Title IX and professional jealousy, and to Pam Colloff, a writer I've long admired but who didn't know me from Adam and nonetheless helped me get in touch with Mike when I asked. For editing that first story with *The New York Times Magazine* and all my stories since, many, many thanks to Claire Gutierrez. Your moral compass means as much to me as your smart, intuitive edits.

To everyone at Scribner, but especially Lisa Rivlin, Mark LaFlaur, Georgia Brainard, Sarah Brody, and Lauren Dooley, and to Elizabeth Barber for fact-checking this book and Riley Blanton for fact-checking the article that preceded it. To Kate Lloyd for championing my story in ways big and small.

To Laura Field for helping me see the connections between philosophy and politics more clearly, and for challenging me to see Plato as a fellow writer and human being. Your conversations, both written and in person, were a salve.

To my colleagues in the Recovering Truth project at Arizona State University. Your ideas and provocations have pushed me to think harder and write with more care. To the National Endowment for the Arts for the time to work on this book. To the producers and writers at Pineapple Street Studios, who helped me think narratively and collectively about questions of responsibility and justice that arose after I first told the story of Jay. And to Lemmy the tortoise, for making my makeshift pandemic residency magical.

To my childhood friends, Dee and Stevany, who invented that mythical world of Pompeii, but who also inspired me to start running when I was seven. I cannot imagine this book without the gift of running to help me think through its thorny problems. I cannot imagine being a writer if I were not also a runner.

To all my teachers and professors over the years, but especially to the man I call Mr. Lakatos in this book, a teacher with whom I reconnected while writing it and whose love of poetry and stories has been another salve.

To my dear friend and "writing wife," Lina Ferreira, who sees all my first drafts and always has my back. To other dear friends who read versions of this over the years: Kerry Howley, Jeremy Jones, Angela Pelster-Wiebe, Kisha Lewellyn Schlegel, and Louise Trembley. To the many, many others with whom I talked about the ideas contained herein, including Curtis Bauer, Jake Baum, Valena Beety, Matt Bell, Marta Berbes, Amelia Bird, Caro Blank, Phill Cabeen, Katie Cortese, Matt Feagan, Tara Ison, Angela Morales, Alex Niemi, Jill Patterson, Emily Skidmore, Aisha Sabatini Sloan, Jessica Smith, Emily Tipps, and Rachel Yoder.

To my uncle Robert Strozier, who has encouraged me to be a writer since middle school: by praising my stories and essays but also by example. To my mom, Anne Strozier, who reads everything I write with care (even finding typos in late copies of this manuscript) and convinces all her friends to read my work, too. To my dad, Mike Viren, who does none of that, but who is proud of me no matter what. To my two girls, who can't understand why it takes me so long to write a book and who distract me from writing said book with their own stories and questions and dreams. And finally, to Marta, who stood by me despite everything, who makes me laugh and who loves me fiercely. We're stronger at the end of all of this, and that also gives me hope.

INTERVIEW WITH SARAH VIREN
CONDUCTED BY MATT BELL

The Writer on How to Interrogate the Possibilities of a Truth

BOMB Magazine | June 13, 2023

Matt Bell

To Name the Bigger Lie is subtitled "A Memoir in Two Stories," so I thought we'd begin with the first story. It's about Dr. Whiles, a teacher you had for two years in high school, first for a class called "Inquiry Skills" and then for another titled "Theory of Knowledge." How long had you been thinking about Dr. Whiles as a subject you might write about? What were the original questions that you had as you began your investigation?

Sarah Viren

To some extent I've been thinking about Dr. Whiles ever since I graduated from high school. But it was the rise of Donald Trump, or rather the dominant interpretations of that rise, that got me thinking about Dr. Whiles in a more active and urgent way. In the lead-up to the 2016 election, I was bothered by narratives that sought to blame education alone, or rather a lack thereof, for Trump's appeal—as in, only uneducated white men are falling for Trump's shtick. As we saw from polling data after the election, that just wasn't the case. But I already knew it wasn't the case because of what had happened in my high school— namely that a bunch of students believed in or at least considered believing conspiracy theories introduced to us by Dr. Whiles.

This is not to say that Dr. Whiles was like Trump—he wasn't—but the two do share some similarities. Dr. Whiles created a cultlike following among students, and one way he did that was by being evasive, playful, and sometimes outright reckless with the truth. Starting to research and write this book, then, I was interested in thinking about how Dr. Whiles might help me better understand Trump's rise and what was happening in our country after the 2016 election. But the more I interviewed former classmates and reread books we'd read in high school and just thought about that moment in my life, the more I got interested in how Dr. Whiles was different from Trump—but also how both Dr. Whiles and Trump were different from or similar to Socrates, who was another man with a cultlike following who played with the truth, or at least pushed people to question their convictions about what is true, and good, and just.

I should add that Trump is never mentioned in the book. I don't think the questions that were driving me to write ended up being about him in the end. He was just a starting point, an inciting incident of sorts to travel back in time and address some questions and concerns I'd managed to ignore for twenty-odd years.

MB

The other story line that makes up *To Name the Bigger Lie* revolves around a person you call Jay, a fellow nonfiction writer who invented a conspiracy of false Title IX claims about your wife, Marta, including fabricated Reddit threads, emails, and other "evidence" produced to undermine a job offer you'd received, in the hopes that he'd get the job instead.

In this story line, you found yourself at the center of a conspiracy, which is a pretty different experience, I'd imagine, from evaluating their possible validity from the outside. In the viral essay version of this tale, you wrote that "while truth may be subjective, its balustrades are always the facts at hand," then went on to note that "Title IX investigations are a different genre of storytelling, so the facts the investigators want are different."

It's not so much "truth" that such an investigation is trying to get at, in your telling, but a determination between "violation of policy" and "insufficient evidence." The Title IX office isn't interested in the same core question you and Marta were: Who did this, and why?

All this makes me think of how many people spend their time "shopping" for truth now, switching news sources to get a version of events that's closer to their own desired view of the world. Assuming that we want the capital-T Truth, how do we keep ourselves from accepting some lesser Truth that feels correct or is personally pleasing to our worldviews or vanities or prejudices?

SV

It's strange, but even after writing this whole book I'm still not sure what we mean by capital-T Truth, and I waver back and forth about whether I believe it exists at all—or, if it does, if it's accessible to us, given our persnickety subjectivities. But I do think small-t truths exist. Hannah Arendt calls them factual truths, and I love the metaphor she gives in her essay "Truth and Politics" in which she talks about how lies and deceit tear at the "fabric of factuality" that comprise those smaller truths. That metaphor of fabric was helpful for me in thinking about and writing this book because it gets at an understanding we have of reality: that it is a thing with texture of its own, something we collectively experience in an embodied way.

The catch is that all of us experience reality differently, so how do we find a truthful or honest representation of that reality? That's what I think our project is: to find ways of agreeing upon what is real and what isn't, to search for a series of facts we can share even if we have different opinions about those facts. I agree with you that, in gathering facts in order to "see" reality, we each have our own biases. I know I do. But I also visit Fox News about once a week just to get a sense of what reality is playing out there. That doesn't mean that I don't also credit Fox News with a fair number of the tears in that fabric of factuality. I do. But I don't think we can ignore influences like Fox News or dismiss them in whole cloth (pun unintended but welcomed!) and I think I'm better at understanding reality when I know how it is viewed by as many people as possible.

At the risk of sounding Pollyannaish, I think the only solution is for us to communicate more, to talk more, and maybe even to debate more, but not fight. Socrates had this idea that I love. We all enter the marketplace of ideas with our own opinions, which are not true. But he thought that if we actually talk about and through our opinions, if we ask questions of them, if we approach each other's opinions in an open and thoughtful way, we have the chance of getting closer to that big-T Truth, whatever that is, even if it will always eventually escape us.

MB

You interviewed former high school classmates who were also taught by Dr. Whiles, as well as other teachers you'd had. At one point, you write that, in addition to recovering and confirming your own memories, you also occasionally learned something totally new to you. Those moments excited you most, you write, "likely because learning them felt less like the work of memoir and more like journalism, as if I were reporting on my past rather than trying to rebuild it from memories alone" (168). *To Name the Bigger Lie* is a more journalistic memoir than most, and I think that's entirely to its benefit. Could you talk about the reporting you did for the book? How was digging into your own past different from other kinds of reporting you've done, where you might have less of a personal stake in the subject?

SV

In writing the book, I was interested in thinking through the forms we have as nonfiction writers to tell a story. There's memoir, which I think of as the most novelesque mode of writing, and one that's contingent on memory, and thus time. There's also the essay, a form of writing that imitates thinking on the page, which I do a fair amount of in this book. And then there's literary journalism, which we usually think of as reporting on the external world, often with minimal use of the "I," but in this case I was interested in using my skills and instincts as a journalist to research my own past.

That felt exciting to me in part because I realized early on that many of my classmates had forgotten that Dr. Whiles encouraged us to question the Holocaust. At first, I thought, how could you forget that? But then, I realized that I'd forgotten other significant things, too, or that my memory differed wildly from the memories of others—both in the Dr. Whiles story but also in the story about Jay.

This is an issue that most memoirists face, but because this book was trying to reckon with the harm caused by lies and manipulation, it seemed especially important to address head-on—and "reporting" on myself felt like a helpful way to go about that. Though doing so was much harder than reporting on others. Mostly because I had to deal with my feelings: reading my old journals or interviewing someone from high school or reading a comment in my yearbook, there would be moments when I suddenly felt how I used to feel then, which is to say small, confused, and a little depressed.

To write the story involving Jay, I listened to the hours of recordings I'd made of our interviews with the Title IX officer, and often I ended up in tears—which felt bewildering because I'd barely cried at the time. But whenever that happened, I tried to pay attention to my response and to identify as best I could what triggered that reaction, and why. Then I wrote into that moment.

MB

One of my obsessions as a fiction writer is how we manipulate the gap between the time narrated, the time of the story being told, and the time of narration, where it's being told from. Early in your book, you write about an experience of looking at a Salvador Dalí painting as a high schooler, where a baby was depicted as having teeth "nestled into a beach scene" also seeming to "grow out of the back of a woman sitting in the wind." You write:

. . . It reminded me of reading, or dreaming, how images layer one upon the next, how a person can be your mother and then change into someone else: your teachers or your lover. But also, how the baby or child or teenager you once were stays with you as you age, digging their teeth into your back while you go about your days, deluded into thinking you have left that earlier self behind. (55)

Throughout *To Name the Bigger Lie*, you play with this layering of selves—the digging of the teeth of the younger self into the back of the older—often by explicitly pointing out that even your figurative language comes not from the past self but from the present. Many scenes in the book seem to suggest that there is no telling of a past self without the interference of the present self. How did you decide when to do this and when to let the past pretend to be less layered? Is this also a kind of self-reporting, where you're paying attention to your mind in the present as it trawls through the past?

SV

I adore this question, in part because I love thinking about writing and time and in part because this is such a difficult question to answer! But I'll start with this: I have a pet theory that another way of distinguishing between genres of writing—instead of by whether or not they use line breaks or whether or not they're "true"—would be by their treatment of time. There are those works that seek to replicate chronological time as we experience it amid the action of our daily lives, and most often we call those works novels or stories, though they can also be memoirs or poems, too.

Then there are those works that replicate time as it exists in our heads when we are thinking or feeling. In his essay, "On the Lyric Essay," Ben Marcus calls this mode of narration "timeless" or essayistic, which feels apt to me. It's also similar, I think, to time within that "moment of telling" that you mentioned, or what Virginia Woolf calls the "I now" voice in memoir. It is the writer, thinking, on the page in the ever-present now about the story being told.

So in the book, I put a lot of consideration into when to let my essayistic voice interrupt the narrated past, but also why I would let that voice interrupt at all. In the case of that scene from the Dalí museum, for instance, I let her in because that juxtaposition between what I had once known and what I now know felt vital to the meaning of the scene itself, but also because I liked the tension that the interruption allowed. It can be unsettling to be reminded of the instability of time in a story, kind of like teeth digging into your back.

Near the end of the book, I also play with what I think you're talking about when you say "time narrated." For me, that notion of "time narrated," or time as it passes while the work is being read or listened to, feels most present in poetry and drama—though obviously it exists in all reading experiences. But it's present in dialogues as well, which is one of many reasons that I began incorporating imagined dialogues into the final part of the book. I wanted to figure out how a change in form might help me untangle the concerns of the story in a more urgent or fruitful way. Because in dialogue—Socratic or otherwise—essayistic time disappears and narrated time and time narrated become one.

That conflation of two experiences of time in a book felt exciting to me as a writer. In fact, it became a new way of thinking, or essaying, which I guess is also to say that dialogues in that final part of the book allowed me to bring all three of those forms of time together, to layer them one atop the next. I liked the way that layering also brought more people into the story in a shared moment in time: Dr. Whiles was there at the same time as Jay in one dialogue, for instance, but the reader was also there alongside me.

MB

Much of *To Name the Bigger Lie* revolves around Plato's allegory of the cave and Plato's other writings in the *Republic*. Obviously, the allegory attaches to many of the questions about the nature of truth that suffuse the book, but I was also struck by a passage midway through where you invoke the *Republic*'s imagined "perfect" city as a way of thinking about the suburbs and other kinds of planned communities in the United States. You write, "What is forfeited—truth; freedom; or, in the case of our neighborhood, wilderness and diversity—in order to live in a community that is perfectly planned? . . . Who suffers when one segment of the population decides their utopia trumps everything else?" (195)

These are questions that are near and dear to my own thinking, and seem to exist in your book at both a personal and a societal level: What does it cost when a person like Jay tries to force a false narrative onto an existing system? What do we do when a demographic chooses a conspiracy theory as a preferred reality? I'm curious about your own answers to these questions you raise in the book: Do you feel like you've learned anything in writing this book about how best to resolve competing realities, competing utopias, or competing plans for the greater good?

SV

Yes! That is the question that I think is buried in Plato's *Republic*, intentionally or not. The vision that Socrates proposes is one in which only some people can know the truth of things, and others are in effect tasked with believing a lie in order to keep the peace, or, as Socrates might say, to maintain a balance in society between the various forces that are inevitably at work. But what I kept wondering, the more I reread and thought about Plato's cave allegory, but also the *Republic* as a whole, was whether there might be another way of reading the allegory, one in which perhaps all the prisoners escaped the cave en masse and together witness the light and the truth that lies outside.

Alternatively, perhaps a version in which the prisoners are released from their chains but then they're allowed to come and go as they please, to appreciate the shadows on the cave wall for what they were, stories that bring meaning to life, but also to venture into the sunlight and star-filled sky outside and experience the discomfort and exhilaration and wonder of that world too.

This is not a solution to the problem of competing utopias, I know, but I do think the stories we tell ourselves, or allegories we rely on, shape the possibilities we imagine for our future. And if the story we learn is one in which a few (mostly men) will find enlightenment and the rest of us will be left bickering over shadows in a cave, I don't have a lot of hope for what is to come.

ABOUT THE AUTHOR

Sarah Viren is a contributing writer for *The New York Times Magazine* and author of the essay collection *Mine*, which was a finalist for a Lambda Literary Award and longlisted for the PEN/Diamonstein-Spielvogel Award for the Art of the Essay. She was a National Endowment for the Arts Fellow and teaches in the creative writing program at Arizona State University.